GCSE Geography

for AQA specification B

Janet Helm • Arthur Robinson

Heinemann

Heinemann Educational Publishers
Halley Court, Jordan Hill, Oxford, OX2 8EJ

a division of Reed Educational & Professional Publishing Ltd

Heinemann is a registered trademark of Reed Educational & Professional
Publishing Ltd

OXFORD MELBOURNE AUCKLAND
JOHANNESBURG BLANTYRE GABORONE
IBADAN PORTSMOUTH NH (USA) CHICAGO

First published 2002

ISBN 0 435 35358 6

06 05 04 03 02
10 9 8 7 6 5 4 3 2

Edited by Rebecca Harmon

Designed by Paul Davis

Typeset and illustrated by Visual Image

Printed and bound in Italy by Trento s.r.l.

Acknowledgements
The authors and publishers would like to thank the following:
Mr B Lowis for information about Waterside House Farm pp. 25-27; Mr R Sears
for information about Lynford House Farm pp. 28-30; Lake District National Park
Authority for information about tourism, pp. 42-47; the National Trust for
information about Tarn Hows and Figure 3.18 pp. 48-49; Dover Harbour Board
for information about the port, aspects of pages 139-141; Nottinghamshire
County Council for information about Local Agenda 21 p. 202.

Picture research by Kay Altwegg

Websites
Links to appropriate websites are given throughout the book. Although these
were up to date at the time of writing, it is essential for teachers to preview these
sites before using them with students. This will ensure that the web address
(URL) is still accurate and the content is suitable for your needs. We suggest that
you bookmark useful sites and consider enabling students to access them
through the school intranet. We are bringing this to your attention as we are
aware of legitimate sites being appropriated illegally by people wanting to
distribute unsuitable or offensive material. We strongly advise you to purchase
suitable screening software so that students are protected from unsuitable sites
and their material. If you do find that the links given no longer work, or the
content is unsuitable, please let us know. Details of changes will be posted on our
website.

Contents

The hydrological cycle and river basin system

The **global hydrological cycle** is the continuous movement of water from the oceans to the atmosphere, to the land and finally back to the oceans (**Figure 1.1**). There is a continuous flow of water vapour, liquid water or snow and ice, and at any one time, parts of the cycle have some water held in storage.

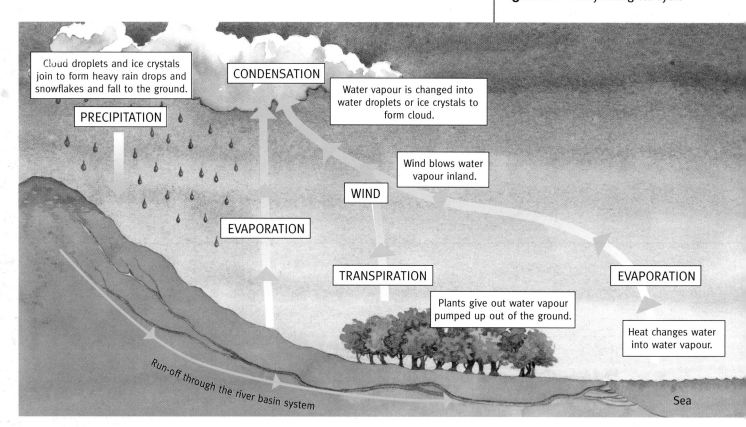

Figure 1.1 The hydrological cycle

Cloud droplets and ice crystals join to form heavy rain drops and snowflakes and fall to the ground.

CONDENSATION

Water vapour is changed into water droplets or ice crystals to form cloud.

PRECIPITATION

Wind blows water vapour inland.

WIND

EVAPORATION

TRANSPIRATION

Plants give out water vapour pumped up out of the ground.

EVAPORATION

Heat changes water into water vapour.

Run-off through the river basin system

Sea

In the hydrological cycle, the sun's heat evaporates sea water to produce water vapour in the air. Wind blows this water vapour inland where it **condenses** and turns into cloud droplets or ice crystals.

In a river basin the paths followed by water are as follows (**Figure 1.2**):

- **Precipitation**: rain, snow or hail, formed when cloud droplets or ice crystals join together and become too heavy to remain in the cloud.

- **Interception**: when precipitation is caught by vegetation before it reaches the ground.

- **Stem flow**: some precipitation flows down twigs and tree trunks on to the ground.

- **Leaf drip**: some water drips off leaves and falls to the ground.

- **Evaporation**: some of the water is evaporated from the leaves and branches back into the air.

- **Surface detention**: when precipitation reaches waterlogged ground it forms puddles on the surface. Snow and hail on the ground are also types of surface detention.

- **Surface run off/overland flow**: water flowing across the surface.

- **Infiltration**: when water reaches the ground it soaks into the soil through holes, cracks, worm tunnels etc. There is a maximum rate at which

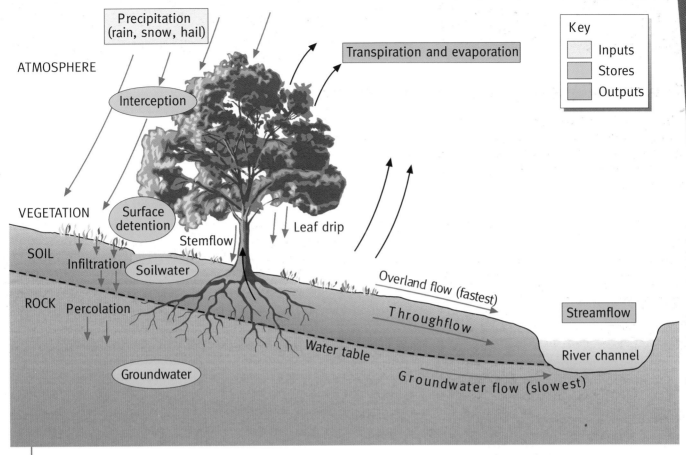

Figure 1.2 Paths of water in the river basin system

infiltration can occur, which depends on the sizes of the holes. This rate is called the **infiltration capacity** of the soil. If too much water is trying to infiltrate, the surplus will become surface storage or surface run off.

- **Throughflow**: once it is in the soil, the water flows through spaces such as natural pipes left by decayed roots.

- **Percolation**: water flows down through the pores and cracks in the rock.

- **Groundwater**: water which has percolated down and saturated the rock, i.e. all the pore spaces are filled with water.

- **Water table**: the upper surface of the groundwater.

- **Groundwater flow**: the movement of water sideways to lower levels where it reappears on the surface at springs and in the sides of river channels.

- **Transpiration**: soil moisture and groundwater are pumped by trees through their roots, stems and leaves back into the air.

Figure 1.3 Model of a system

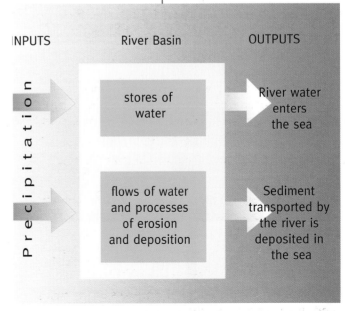

A river basin is a **system** (**Figure 1.3**). There are always inputs to a system, stores and flows within the system, and outputs from it.

In a river basin system there are:

- **Inputs**: precipitation and energy (the sun's heat).
- **Stores**: surface detention and groundwater.
- **Flows**: surface run off, throughflow, percolation etc.
- **Outputs**: the river carries the water and its load to the sea.
- **Feedback**: evaporation and transpiration return water to the atmosphere. It falls from here as precipitation back into the river basin.

The processes operating in a river

Erosion

Erosion is the wearing away of rock by the river. There are four main erosion processes:

- **Abrasion** (or corrasion) is when the load being transported by the river rubs against the river bed and banks like sandpaper and wears them away.
- **Hydraulic erosion** is when the pressure of water being forced into cracks in the river bed and banks makes the cracks wider which forces rocks out.
- **Solution** (or corrosion) is caused by acids in the river water, especially organic acids formed by rotting plants. The acids enter the water during throughflow and overland flow before it enters the river. Water is also made acidic when carbon dioxide enters it as raindrops fall through the air and as water flows through the soil. This acid is called **carbonic acid**. The acids dissolve rock such as limestone in the river bed and banks.

- **Attrition** is the erosion of the load itself. It is caused by pebbles and sand in the load rubbing against each other.

The amount of erosion increases as the **discharge** and **velocity** of a river increase. Faster rivers can pick up larger particles than slower ones. The **load** is the rock material produced by erosion which is moved downstream by the river. Individual rock particles which make up the load are called **clasts**. Load does not include the water in the river.

Transportation

Transportation is the movement of the river's load downstream. There are four main transportation processes (**Figure 1.4**):

- **Traction** is the rolling and *dragging* of the load along the river bed. It ranges from sand if the river is flowing slowly, up to boulders if the river is fast-flowing.
- **Saltation** is a hopping or *bouncing* motion of the load. The particles are smaller than clasts moved by traction. When particles are transported by saltation they hit the river bed and knock others up into the water. The parts of the load transported by traction and saltation are together called the **bed load**.
- **Suspension** moves the smallest particles in the load (usually clay and silt). They are carried in the water without touching the river bed.
- **Solution** is dissolved material in the river water. It cannot be seen.

Before a storm, when the river is at a low level and is slow with clear water, solution is the only type of

Figure 1.4 Processes of transportation

River flow

TRACTION	SALTATION	SUSPENSION	SOLUTION
Rolling and dragging clasts along the river bed.	Sand-sized particles bounce along the bed in a hopping movement.	Silt and clay-sized particles are carried within the water flow.	Some minerals are dissolved in the water. (This needs the least energy.)

Bedload is the load transported by traction and saltation

transportation which occurs. As the river level rises during a storm, it flows faster, and small clasts are moved by traction. At a higher velocity the small clasts are moved by saltation and larger ones by traction. At even higher velocities the smallest clasts are transported by suspension, the larger ones by saltation, and the largest ones by traction. The size of the largest clast transported by a river depends on its velocity. This is called the river's **competence**. If the velocity is doubled, competence increases 64 times. The total weight of the load which can be transported is called the **capacity** of the river. It depends on the river's velocity. If it is doubled, the capacity increases 512 times.

Deposition

Deposition is the putting down of the load on to the river bed or sides and occurs when the river reduces speed and loses energy. Deposition also occurs when the river level decreases after a storm.

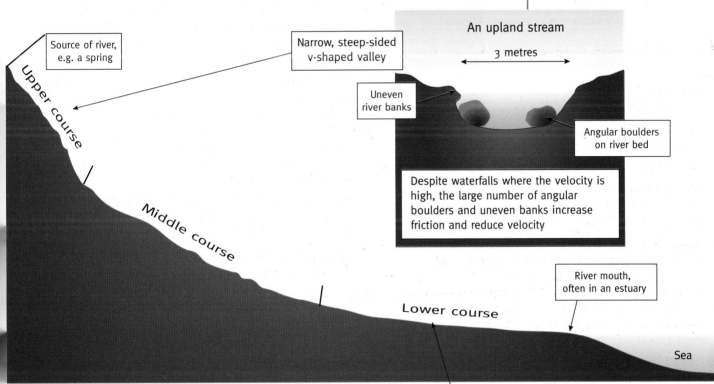

Figure 1.5 The long profile of a river

Source of river, e.g. a spring

Upper course

Narrow, steep-sided v-shaped valley

Middle course

Lower course

An upland stream

3 metres

Uneven river banks

Angular boulders on river bed

Despite waterfalls where the velocity is high, the large number of angular boulders and uneven banks increase friction and reduce velocity

River mouth, often in an estuary

Sea

Wide valley and flood plain

How do these processes vary along a river?

The **long profile** of a river is shown in **Figure 1.5**.

The **source** of a river is where it starts, usually at a spring, bog or lake.

In its **upper course** the channel is small with large boulders in it. These slow the water down. The channel is bigger in the **lower course** because more **tributaries** have joined the river. The channel is smoother with small, rounded clasts in it. These differences mean that when the river is at a low level, it flows faster in the lower course. However, after a storm, the river has a higher velocity in the upper course because it has a steeper gradient. The river does most erosion and transportation at these times, and deposition occurs as the river level falls.

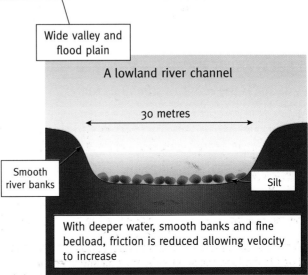

A lowland river channel

30 metres

Smooth river banks

Silt

With deeper water, smooth banks and fine bedload, friction is reduced allowing velocity to increase

The high velocity in the upper course means erosion is the dominant process. Large clasts are deposited in the channel in the upper course as the river level falls after a storm. The lower velocity can then transport only small clasts to the lower course. Clasts are eroded further by attrition during their journey to the lower course. Deposition is the main process in the lower course, especially at the river **mouth** where the river enters the sea. The mouth is usually at an **estuary** which is a V-shaped arm of the sea extending into the land.

Figure 1.6 A valley in the upper course of a river

Landforms created by rivers

Upland landforms

V-shaped valleys
Figure 1.6 shows a typical valley in an upland area. In cross-section it has very steep sides, is narrow, and the river channel fills the valley floor. It is often described as a deep and narrow **V-shaped valley**.

The V-shape is the result of several factors (**Figure 1.7**):

- **Vertical erosion**: erosion processes in the river channel rapidly lower its bed.

- **Weathering**: rock forming the valley sides is broken up to form soil.

- **Frost shattering**: a type of weathering common in upland valleys. Water enters cracks in the rocks. As the temperature drops at night, the water freezes and expands, widening the crack and breaking the rock.

Figure 1.7 Cross-profile of an upland valley

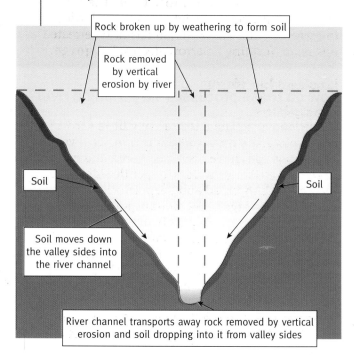

Rock broken up by weathering to form soil

Rock removed by vertical erosion by river

Soil

Soil

Soil moves down the valley sides into the river channel

River channel transports away rock removed by vertical erosion and soil dropping into it from valley sides

- Some rocks *expand* when they are wet and *contract* when they dry out. This continual movement breaks them up.

- *Roots* of plants enter cracks, and as they grow they widen the cracks.

The soil on the steep valley sides moves quickly down to the river channel because:

- It is pulled down by *gravity*.

- *Raindrops* hit soil particles and knock them downhill.

- *Landslips* occur.

- *Animals walking* along slopes push soil down the slope.

The soil drops from the channel sides into the river and then is transported away during the next storm flow.

Interlocking spurs

Upland valleys are not straight. **Figure 1.6** shows that fingers of higher land jut out from one side of the valley into the other. They do this alternately and so are called **interlocking spurs**. They may be caused by the fact that water which flows in a river does not flow in a straight line as it erodes vertically downwards.

Waterfalls

Waterfalls are another way in which rivers lower their river channel. In **Figure 1.8** the resistant cap rock is eroded slowly. The river is able to erode the less resistant rocks underneath faster. It does this in several ways:

- After dropping from the waterfall, the river is moving fast and is able to erode a deep and wide **plunge pool** by abrasion and hydraulic action.

- Spray from the waterfall keeps the rock wet behind the fall and this increases the rate of weathering.

The erosion of the weaker rock leaves the resistant rock overhanging. Its weight makes it fall off into the plunge pool. The waterfall has now retreated upstream, forming a narrow steep-sided **gorge**.

Lowland landforms

Floodplains

In lowland areas there is relatively little vertical erosion by the river because it is near sea level. The valley sides have been weathered and eroded so the valley is now wide with gentle sides. The river channel is broad and deep. During a storm its capacity is large so it can transport a large load. However, it may overtop its banks and flow out on to the valley floor. The water is shallow and has a lot of friction on it, which slows the water. It deposits its load of clay and silt, called **alluvium**. This builds up to form a wide, flat **floodplain**. The greatest deposition is on the floodplain next to the river where the water is first slowed down and drops the coarsest silt in its

> **EXAM TIP**
> The bends in the upper course of a river are not meanders.

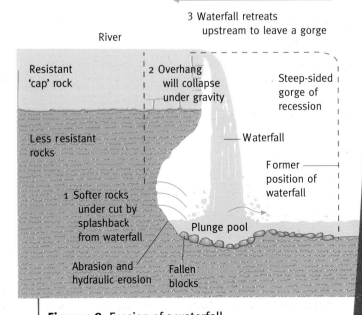

Figure 1.8 Erosion of a waterfall

load. The floodplain is higher here than further from the channel and the raised embankments are called **levées**. They are often only a metre or so high and 10 to 20 m wide. They are not obvious like man-made flood embankments, which have steep sides and may be 2 or 3 m high.

Meanders

Meanders are large bends in a river where it flows across its floodplain. In the upper course, the river uses its energy for vertical erosion; in the lower course the river is near sea level and the energy is used instead for sideways or **lateral erosion**.

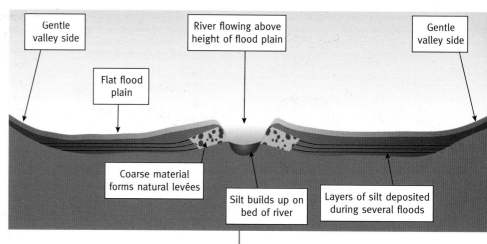

Figure 1.9 Cross-section of a floodplain

In a meander the fastest water is next to the outer bank of the meander (**Figure 1.10**). The fast water erodes the outer bank and makes it into a steep **river cliff** which can collapse. The debris is eroded away and the channel moves sideways.

Meanwhile, there is shallow water near the inner bank of a meander, and the increased friction slows the water, causing deposition of a **point bar** with a gentle slope called the **slip-off slope**.

Figure 1.10 A cross-section of a meander

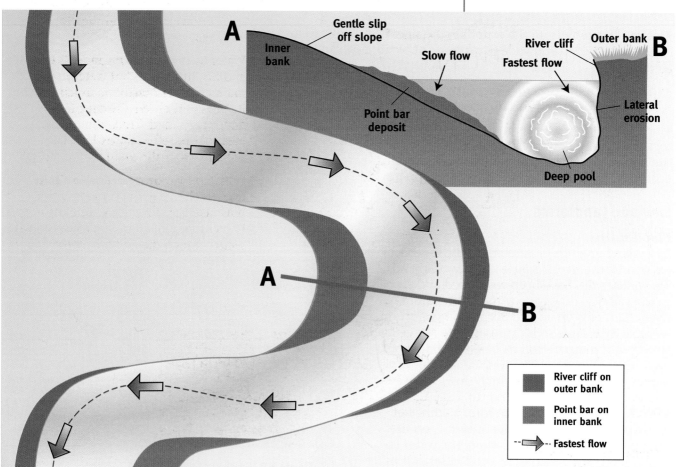

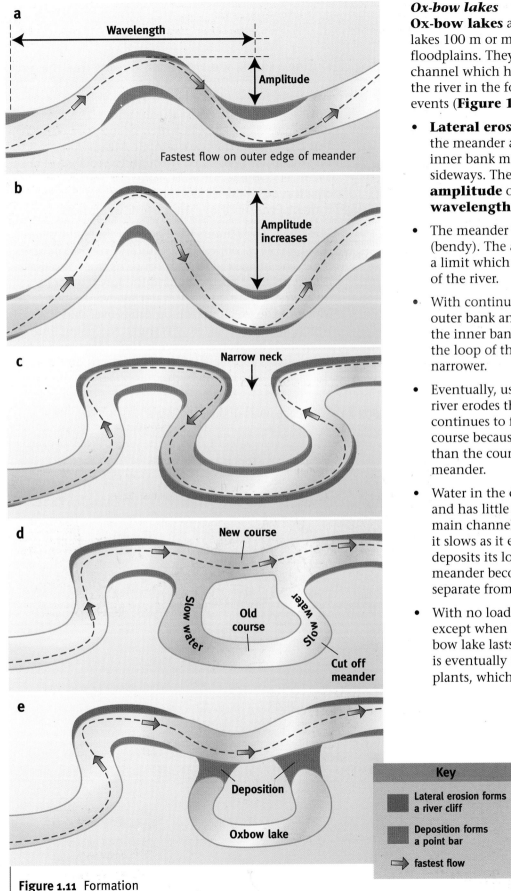

a
Wavelength
Amplitude
Fastest flow on outer edge of meander

b
Amplitude increases

c
Narrow neck

d
New course
Slow water
Old course
Slow water
Cut off meander

e
Deposition
Oxbow lake

Key

Lateral erosion forms a river cliff

Deposition forms a point bar

fastest flow

Figure 1.11 Formation of an ox-bow lake

Ox-bow lakes

Ox-bow lakes are crescent-shaped lakes 100 m or more long formed on floodplains. They are parts of the river channel which have been abandoned by the river in the following sequence of events (**Figure 1.11**):

- **Lateral erosion** of the outer bank of the meander and deposition at the inner bank move the channel sideways. They increase the **amplitude** of the meander, but the **wavelength** is not increased.

- The meander becomes more **sinuous** (bendy). The amplitude can increase to a limit which depends on the discharge of the river.

- With continued lateral erosion on the outer bank and point bar deposition on the inner bank, the neck of land within the loop of the meander becomes narrower.

- Eventually, usually during a flood, the river erodes through the neck. It continues to flow along the new shorter course because the gradient is steeper than the course around the old meander.

- Water in the cut-off meander is calm and has little load, but water in the main channel transports much. Where it slows as it enters the cut-off it deposits its load. Thus, the cut-off meander becomes an ox-bow lake separate from the main river channel.

- With no load being deposited in it, except when the river floods, an ox-bow lake lasts for a long time before it is eventually filled in, mainly by marsh plants, which die and form peat.

The drainage basin and flood hydrograph

A **drainage basin** (river basin) is the area of land from which precipitation flows into a stream. The basin usually includes many tributary streams which take water into the main river (**Figure 1.12**). The junction where one of these tributaries joins the main stream is called a **confluence**.

The edge of a drainage basin is called the **watershed** and goes along the tops of the ridges. A raindrop falling on one side of the watershed drains into one river system. Another raindrop falling on the other side of the watershed flows into another drainage basin.

The **discharge** of a river is the volume of water passing a point on its river bank each second. It is measured in cubic metres per second or cumecs.

A **flood** or **storm hydrograph** is a graph which shows how the discharge of a river within a drainage basin changes during and after heavy rainfall (**Figure 1.13**). It has a steep rising limb and a gentler falling limb.

During a storm, some rain falls directly into the river channel (channel input), but the main reason for the rising discharge shown by the hydrograph is overland flow, together with some throughflow. The river's discharge reaches a peak which occurs some time (the **lag time**) after the peak rainfall. Meanwhile, rainwater has percolated through the rocks and raised the level of the water table. After the **peak discharge**, water enters the river by the slower routes of throughflow and groundwater flow.

The River Wyre drains the Forest of Bowland where there are steep slopes, thin soils and **impermeable** rock. The moorland vegetation of heather and grass intercepts little rainwater, and the low temperatures mean there is little loss of water by evaporation. Much of the precipitation becomes overland flow, which means the lag time is short, the rising limb is steep and the peak discharge is high (**Figure 1.13**). Soon after the peak, the river level drops quickly and the falling limb of the hydrograph is therefore steep.

Figure 1.12 Drainage basin of the River Wyre

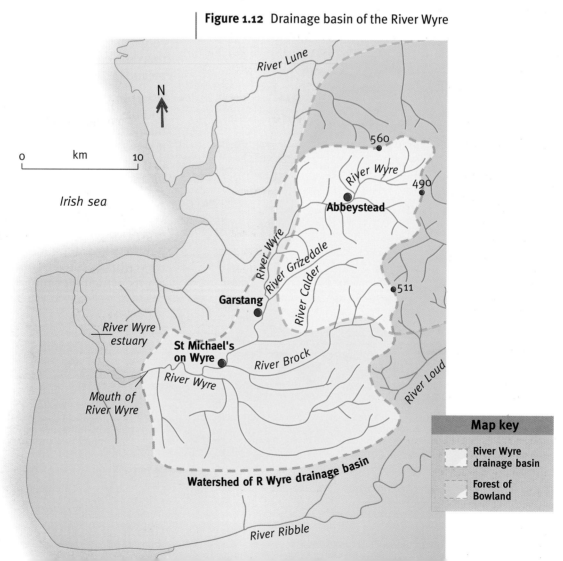

Why do rivers flood?

A flood occurs when the river level rises higher than the river banks and it spills on to its floodplain. This occurs when the peak discharge is greater than the **bankfull discharge**.

The main causes of the River Wyre floods are:

- When there is a heavy rainstorm, most of the rain cannot infiltrate the soil. It becomes overland flow and quickly enters the river. The same happens after a long period of rain when the water table is at the surface.

- In winter, temperatures are low so there is little evaporation and plants are not transpiring. Little rainfall is returned to the atmosphere, so almost all of it reaches the river.

- After heavy snowfall there is much surface storage in the form of snow on the ground. If melting is faster than infiltration, the meltwater becomes overland flow.

- Over time, the forests have been removed. Drains and ditches have been dug to remove water faster from farmland. All these have reduced the lag time and increased peak discharges and the frequency of floods.

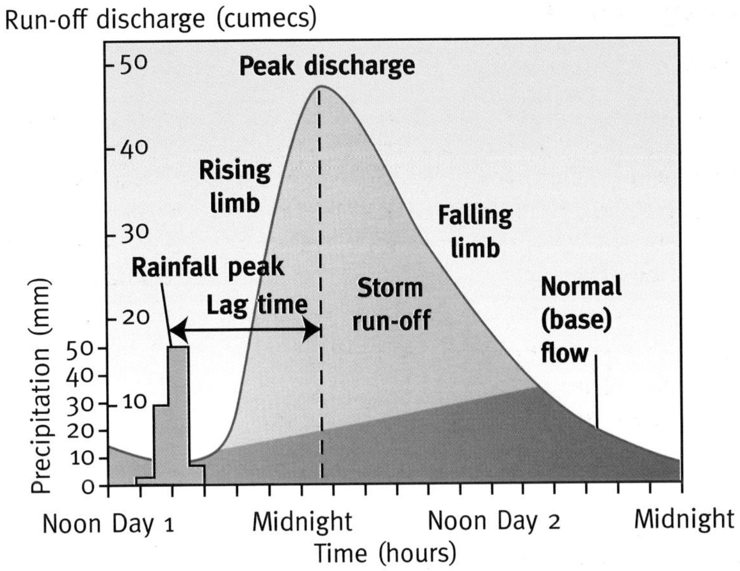

Figure 1.13 Storm hydrograph of the River Wyre

How are floods controlled on the River Wyre?

St Michael's on Wyre is a village at the confluence of the River Wyre and its main tributary, the River Brock. Floods are frequent. 400 houses were affected by flooding in 1980. In Britain it is the responsibility of the Environment Agency to control flooding, which it does in several ways (**Figure 1.14**):

- A meander on the River Brock has been cut off to speed up the flow of the river.

- Flood embankments over 3 m high have been built. Most are some distance from the river to allow it to spread out over the floodplain.

- The river level is continuously measured at the village and the information is sent by

Figure 1.14 The flood control system

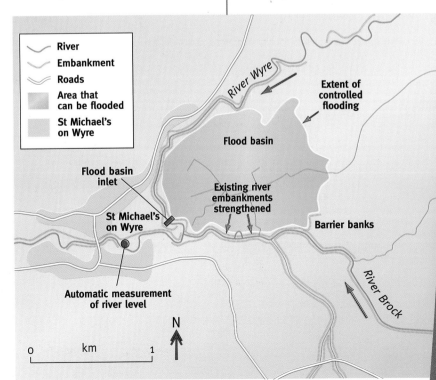

radio to a central computer so that warnings can be given when necessary.

- An area of floodplain has been kept free of buildings east of the village. When the river level is very high part of the flood embankment can be lowered (**Figure 1.15**) and the land is flooded. This stops the river rising further. The flooded farmland is drained when the river level falls.

- A similar flood defence scheme has been constructed 6 km upstream on the River Wyre at Garstang and this also reduces the water flow at St Michael's.

Management of water quality and amenities

River water can be polluted in many ways, including:

- Excess nitrate fertiliser from farmland can be washed into rivers where it causes rapid plant growth, which de-oxygenates the water and kills other life in the river, causing eutrophication.

- Water taken from the river for cooling in power stations is returned much warmer, and this also de-oxygenates the water.

- Poisonous and sometimes smelly waste is put into rivers from industrial sites.

- Most domestic sewage is treated so that only clean water enters the river, but even this contains dissolved chemicals such as phosphorus from washing powder.

Pollution control officers from the Environment Agency continually take water samples to monitor its quality. It is their job to trace offenders when regulations are broken.

Water which is extracted from rivers for drinking has to be treated in various ways by water companies. Sediment such as the suspended load is filtered out, and chlorine is added to kill bacteria. In some areas fluoride is added to strengthen teeth against decay.

Fishing rights on rivers are owned by individuals, companies and angling clubs. The Environment Agency monitors the number and quality of fish and controls the amount of fishing by issuing licences.

The Agency also promotes wildlife conservation in rivers. This means that wild animals and plants are protected from the effects of people. One of the Agency's schemes is to provide suitable habitats for otters, such as clean water, good fish stocks and places where they can rear young.

How is drinking water supplied?

Figure 1.16b shows that the heaviest rainfall (over 1500 mm per year) is in highland areas on the west side of Britain. These areas are also cloudy and have low summer temperatures, which lead to little loss of water by evaporation or transpiration. **Figure 1.16a** shows that they are also areas with low population densities (less than 20 people per km²), so little water is used by local people. These are the areas of **surplus** where water supply is greater than demand.

Figure 1.15 The flood basin inlet

The eastern part of Britain is an area of **deficit** where demand exceeds supply. Rainfall is lower, evaporation and transpiration are high. One-third of Britain's population lives in south-east England. Water is therefore stored in the surplus areas and is transferred to the deficit areas.

Demand for water is increasing for the following reasons:

- Increased domestic use, e.g. more dishwashers are being bought and they use ten times more water than washing up by hand.

- Increased use in farming, e.g. with hotter and drier summers, arable farmers are irrigating more crops, especially those which need a lot of water such as potatoes and sugar beet.

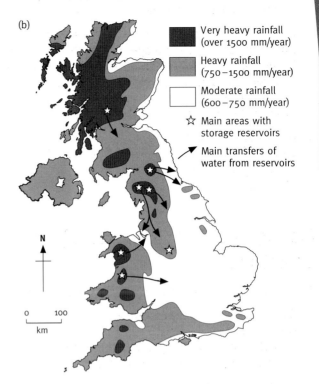

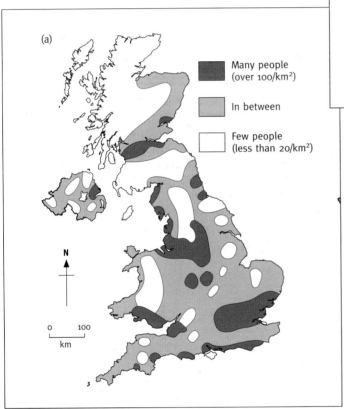

Fig. 1.16 (a) Population density, (b) Rainfall and water supply in the UK

Water storage

Drinking water is most easily obtained from rivers, but the greatest demand for water is in summer when rivers are at their lowest level. Therefore, water has to be pumped from natural underground stores or from reservoirs. The type of store depends on the rock types of the area:

- A **porous** rock is one with tiny holes between the particles which make up the rock.

- A **non-porous** rock has no such tiny holes.

- A **permeable** (pervious) rock is one through which water can pass along cracks in the rock and from pore to pore.

- An **impermeable** (impervious) rock is one through which water cannot pass because it has no cracks, or because the pores are not connected.

Groundwater supplies occur in areas of permeable rock. Reservoirs are built where the rock below is impermeable.

Greater London – groundwater supplies

The rock types found in the Greater London area are sandstone, chalk and limestone which are porous and permeable, and clay which is porous but impermeable because the pores are not connected.

Although the clay on which London is built is impermeable, there is a thick layer of chalk underneath it (**Figure 1.17**). Rain falling on the Chiltern Hills and the North Downs percolates through the chalk and adds to the ground water. The chalk layer is called an **aquifer** because ground water supplies can be taken from it. The water table reaches the surface in places where the water comes out as springs. Some towns which are now part of Greater London, e.g. Reigate and Hemel Hempstead, were built at these springs in order to have a good water supply.

Where the water table is always below the surface, a well has to be dug to reach the ground water. The water table rises in winter when there is much precipitation and little evaporation or transpiration, and falls in summer. To ensure there is water in the well all year round, the bottom of the well must be below the lowest summer level of the water table. The water is pumped out of the well.

Most of London's wells go through the London clay into the chalk aquifer below it. When they were first dug, the water table was so high above the bottom of the wells that there was great pressure on the well water, and it flowed out of the top without being pumped. These are called **artesian wells**.

Greater London needs more water than the ground water can yield, so extra supplies come from:

- Pumping (**abstraction**) from the River Thames.

- Waste water from factories and homes is purified in sewage works and reused. It is said that the same water can pass through 12 people before reaching the sea!

Kielder Water – an upland reservoir

Kielder Water in Northumberland is a **reservoir**. In the late 1960s and early 1970s there was rapid industrial growth in North East England. New chemical works, oil refineries and steel works were built on Teesside and new engineering industries grew on Tyneside and Wearside. It was expected that the demand for water would soon outstrip the supply. A dam 1.2 km long and 50 m high was built in the River North Tyne valley near Falstone (**Figure 1.18**). The valley is relatively narrow here so the costs of building the dam were minimised. The rock is impermeable shale. The reservoir is 10 km long and took two years to fill.

There are many uses of Kielder Water:

- The water from Kielder Water flows down the River Tyne and is abstracted at Riding Mill (**Figure 1.19**). It is pumped uphill to Airy Holm Headpond, a small reservoir which helps to balance supply and demand. The water flows through tunnels and pipes and can be released into the Rivers Wear and Tees to supply the urban areas at their mouths where the water is pumped from the rivers again. It is used in industries such as the Nissan car plant at Sunderland (Wearside) and oil refineries at Middlesbrough (Teesside). However, industry declined in the 1980s and the remaining industry recycles water and uses it more efficiently to cut costs. The demand for water has therefore not increased as much as was predicted. There are now proposed schemes to transfer the water from the reservoir further south to deficit areas in Yorkshire and even the south of England.

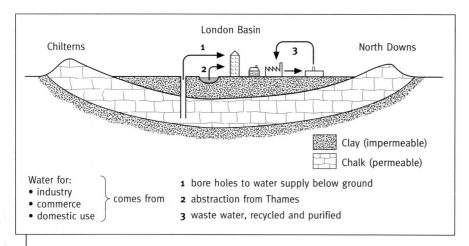

Figure 1.17 The sources of London's water

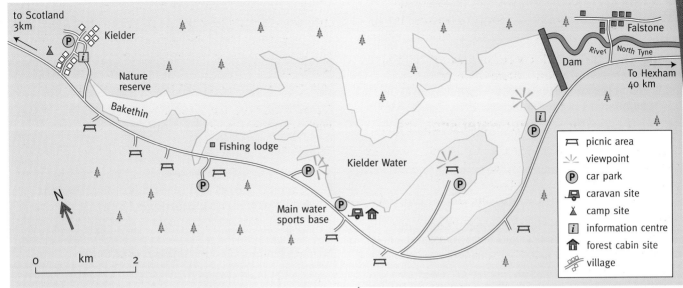

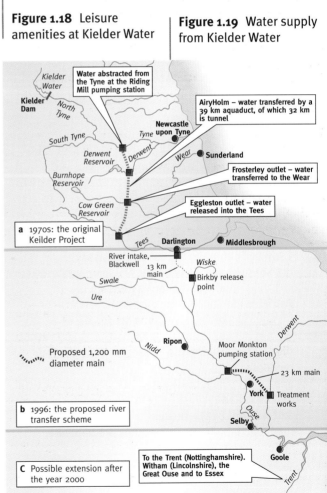

Figure 1.18 Leisure amenities at Kielder Water

Figure 1.19 Water supply from Kielder Water

- Kielder Water is used to manage the flow of the River Tyne. It stores water during storms to reduce the flood risk downstream, and water is released during periods of low discharge in summer.

- Hydro-electric power is generated at the dam where water can fall up to 50 m on to a turbine. The power is fed into the National Grid and is enough for a small town of 10 000 people.

- Wildlife conservation is an important purpose of the reservoir. The Bakethin Arm (**Figure 1.18**) is managed to conserve wildlife. Boating and other noisy activities are not allowed, as they would disturb nesting birds. The variety of marshland plants encourages a wide variety of insects as well as birds and mammals.

- Kielder Water has a number of leisure amenities, some of which are free, such as picnic areas, nature trails and information centres. Many of the leisure amenities employ local people in amenities such as serving behind the counter in the information centre, or teaching waterskiing at the ski school. This is an important aspect as the only other employment opportunities in the area are in the timber industry in Kielder Forest and in farming, both of which employ few people.

EXAM TIP

When writing about employment, you should say what people do, not just where they work.

1 *Pages 4 – 6*

a Name the six processes of the hydrological cycle numbered 1 to 6 in Figure 1.20.

b List two places shown on the diagram where there are stores of water.

c What are the meanings of the terms:
   • Transpiration
   • Water table.

d Make a copy of the table below and extend it to include all the labels shown in Figure 1.20; the first two have been done for you. Complete the table by writing 'more' or 'less' or 'higher' or 'lower' as appropriate. Use the information to explain why rivers have more water in them in winter than in summer.

Path/store	Winter	Summer
precipitation		
interception		

2 *Pages 6 – 8*

a Copy and complete the following passage:
In the upper course of a river, the main process is _____ and in the lower course it is _____.
Particles of rock become part of the river's _____ by the three erosion processes of _____, _____ and _____. They are then transported to the lower course by the four processes of _____, _____, _____ and _____. During transportation the particles of rock called _____ are often made smaller and rounder by the process of _____. When they reach the lower course they are deposited mainly at the _____ _____.

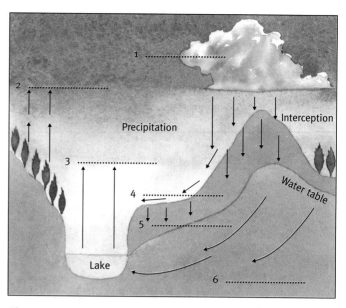

Figure 1.20 Some features of the hydrological cycle

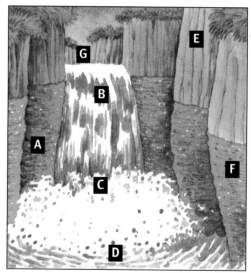

Figure 1.21
A sketch of High Force waterfall

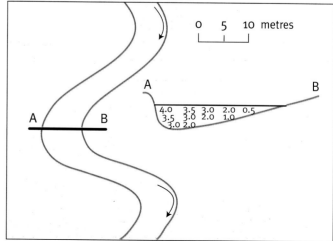

Figure 1.22
A meander

Questions

3 *Page 9*

Figure 1.21 is a sketch of High Force waterfall.

a   Match the letters A B C D E F and G with the following:
- Plunge pool
- Resistant volcanic rock
- Undercutting
- Steep-sided gorge
- Unresistant limestone and shale
- Rock collapse
- Waterfall.

b   With the help of your completed diagram explain how the waterfall and gorge at High Force have been formed.

4 *Pages 10 – 11*

a   Describe the shape of the meander in Figure 1.22 (remember to use the scale).

b   On a copy of Figure 1.22, colour the areas of erosion and deposition.

c   Describe the variations in river velocity in the cross-section from A to B.

d   Explain why erosion and deposition are occurring at the places you have coloured.

e   Describe how the meander will change over time to form an ox-bow lake.

5 *Pages 12 – 13*

a   What is a storm hydrograph?

b   What are the meanings of the following terms:
- Peak rainfall
- Peak discharge
- Lag time
- Rising limb
- Falling limb.

c   Copy Figure 1.23 and label it with the terms listed in b.

d   Use Figure 1.23 to complete the following:
Peak rainfall occurred at _____ hours in a rainstorm which lasted for _____ hours. Discharge in the river increased to a maximum at _____ hours. This is called the _____ discharge. The lag time was _____ hours.

e   Explain the steep rising limb on Figure 1.23.

f   Why is the falling limb less steep?

6 *Pages 14 – 16*

a   In the 1990s there were water shortages in parts of Britain. Give three reasons that help to explain this.

b   In some parts of Britain, groundwater supplies are more important than surface reservoirs. Explain why.

c   On a copy of Figure 1.24 label each of the following terms:
- Impermeable rock
- Aquifer.

d   Explain the different ways in which settlements X and Y could obtain supplies of water from underground sources.

7 *Pages 16 – 17*

Kielder Water is a multipurpose scheme. Describe how this scheme benefits people:
- Living near the reservoir
- Living in the rest of the North East of England.

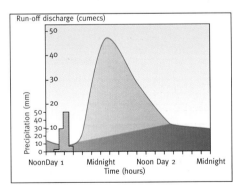

Figure 1.23 A storm hydrograph

Figure 1.24 An area of underground sources of water

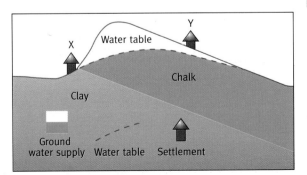

2 Farming, food and the environment

The farming system

Farming is a system with **inputs** going into the farm, **processes** taking place on the farm, and **outputs** from the farm (**Figure 2.1**). Outputs are products that the farmer sells.

There are of several types of inputs:

- *Physical* (or natural) inputs, such as climate (e.g. summer and winter temperatures, sunshine and rainfall) and land inputs (e.g. soil, altitude and steepness of slopes).

- *Economic* inputs for which the farmer has to pay money. These include labour (wages), capital inputs (e.g. the costs of a new building, tractor, or drainage system) and the cost of inputs which are used up (e.g. fertiliser, pesticides, transport).

- *Subsidies and grants* are money which the farmer receives. Subsidies depend on government policies, such as those to encourage the conservation of wildlife.

Processes include shearing sheep, making silage, ploughing, harvesting wheat and spreading manure.

Outputs depend on the type of farming, and include wool, lamb meat, wheat and potatoes. Waste such as manure is not an output; it is used in farm processes e.g. spreading manure.

Pastoral farms rear only animals, while *arable* farms grow only crops. The government imposes **constraints**, restrictions on, for example, the number of sheep kept on a farm or the amount of sugar beet grown. These constraints limit the choice of what can be done on each farm.

Farmers farm to earn money. Some of the money from the sale of outputs becomes their personal income. The rest is used to buy economic inputs; this money is called **feedback**.

EXAM TIP

Figure 2.1 is a model to help you organise your learning and thinking. Exam answers are often based on it. A similar systems diagram is used in Chapter 5 (manufacturing industry).

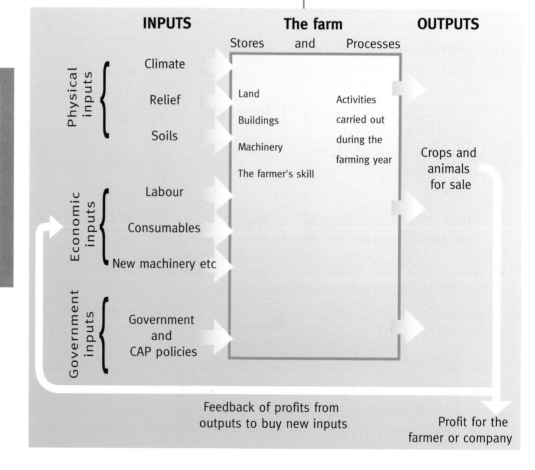

Figure 2.1 The farm system

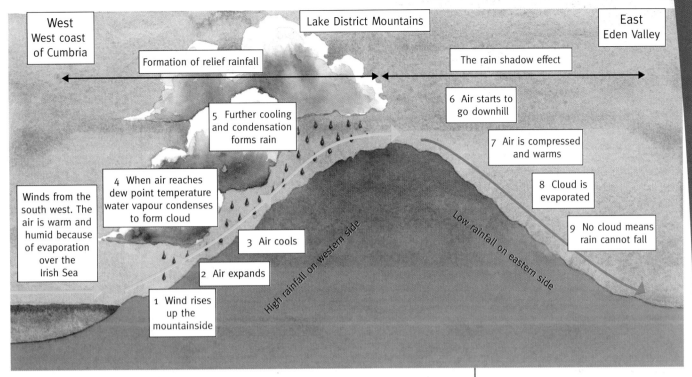

West
West coast
of Cumbria

Lake District Mountains

East
Eden Valley

Formation of relief rainfall

The rain shadow effect

5 Further cooling and condensation forms rain

6 Air starts to go downhill

7 Air is compressed and warms

4 When air reaches dew point temperature water vapour condenses to form cloud

8 Cloud is evaporated

Winds from the south west. The air is warm and humid because of evaporation over the Irish Sea

3 Air cools

9 No cloud means rain cannot fall

2 Air expands

High rainfall on western side

Low rainfall on eastern side

1 Wind rises up the mountainside

Figure 2.2 Relief rainfall and the rain shadow effect

How does climate affect farming?

Rainfall

Rain is formed when air rises, cools and water vapour in the air condenses to form cloud and rain. There are three different types of rainfall, named according to how the air is made to rise:

1 **Relief rainfall**

- Winds from the west of Britain are humid, which means they contain much water vapour.

- They are forced to rise over highlands in the west such as the Lake District (**Figure 2.2**).

- As the air rises, it expands and cools because air pressure is lower.

- This cooling means that it can hold less water vapour, so its relative humidity rises until the air is saturated.

- Further rising and cooling means it can hold even less water vapour, so the surplus condenses to form cloud (tiny droplets of water or ice crystals).

- Thousands of these droplets or crystals collide to form one raindrop, which is then heavy and falls to the ground.

Once the air passes over the mountains, it sinks on the eastern side and is compressed in what is known as the **rain shadow effect**:

- Compression warms the air so it can hold more and more water vapour.

- The formation of raindrops and cloud stops. Cloud is evaporated.

- The eastern sides of the mountains (e.g. eastern Britain) therefore have lower rainfall, less cloud and more sunshine than the western side. This is the rain shadow effect.

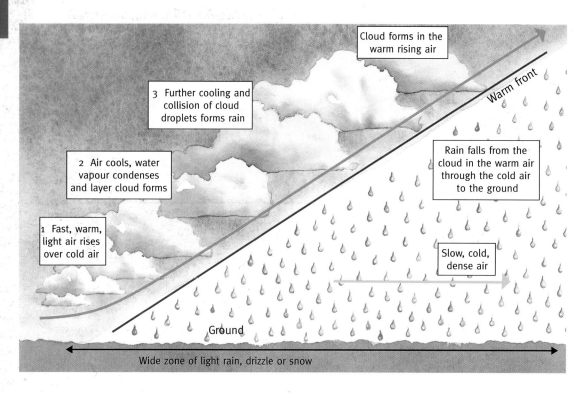

Figure 2.3
Frontal rainfall

Cloud forms in the warm rising air

Warm front

3 Further cooling and collision of cloud droplets forms rain

Rain falls from the cloud in the warm air through the cold air to the ground

2 Air cools, water vapour condenses and layer cloud forms

1 Fast, warm, light air rises over cold air

Slow, cold, dense air

Ground

Wide zone of light rain, drizzle or snow

2 Frontal rainfall

- Warm **air masses** and cold air masses do not mix. The sharp boundary between them is called a **front** (**Figure 2.3**)

- Warm air masses travel to Britain from tropical areas to the south west, and cold air masses come from polar latitudes to the north west. They occur together in low pressure areas called **depressions**.

- Warm air is less dense than cold air, so the warm air rises over the cold air.

- As the warm air rises, it expands, cools, and water vapour condenses to form cloud from which raindrops fall.

- The angle of the warm front is gentle, so there is a large area of continuous rain or drizzle.

- Depressions and the fronts in them move from west to east across Britain, so frontal rain can fall anywhere.

3 Convectional rainfall

- In areas with darker or drier land, the Sun heats the ground, which then warms the air next to it more than nearby land (**Figure 2.4**).

- This warm air expands more than colder air next to it. It becomes lighter and rises like a hot air balloon. This is **convection** and the rising air is called a **thermal**.

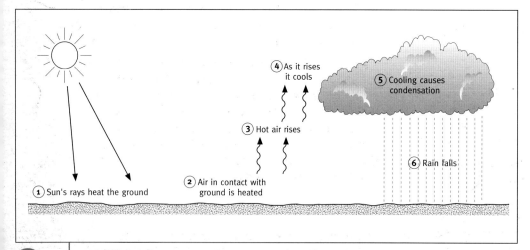

4 As it rises it cools

5 Cooling causes condensation

3 Hot air rises

6 Rain falls

1 Sun's rays heat the ground

2 Air in contact with ground is heated

Figure 2.4 Convectional rainfall

- As the thermal rises, it expands, cools, becomes saturated, and water vapour condenses to form cloud from which rain falls.

- When many thermals rise, a **convection current** is formed. Small clouds grow into thunder clouds, producing heavy rain.

- These clouds are soon blown away. This means that the rain falls in showers and the Sun shines between the clouds.

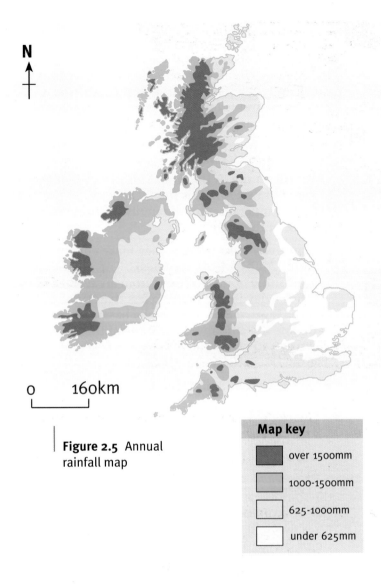

Figure 2.5 Annual rainfall map

Map key	
■	over 1500mm
▨	1000-1500mm
□	625-1000mm
□	under 625mm

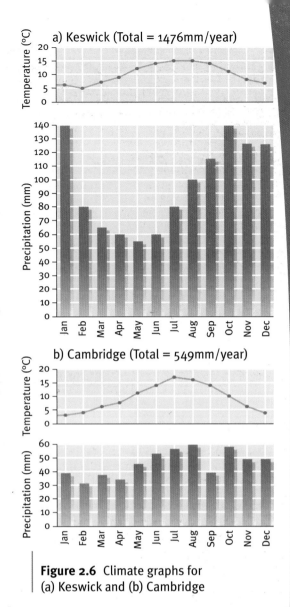

a) Keswick (Total = 1476mm/year)

b) Cambridge (Total = 549mm/year)

Figure 2.6 Climate graphs for (a) Keswick and (b) Cambridge

Why does rainfall vary in Britain?

Mean annual rainfall (**Figure 2.5**) decreases from over 2500 mm on mountains over 500 m high in the west to less than 625 mm on lowland under 200 m above sea level in the east.

The pattern shown in Figure 2.5 is due to many factors:

* Winds blow mainly from the west and south west, so the air contains more water vapour in the west and more rain falls there. The air travelling eastwards contains less water vapour so less cloud and rain are formed when it reaches East Anglia.

* High land, such as the Lake District, is found along most of the west coast of Britain. This creates a lot of relief rainfall.

* On the eastern side of the highlands, there is a rain shadow effect, e.g. in north east England. East Anglia is too far from highlands for the rain shadow effect to be important.

At Keswick in the Lake District, there is high rainfall throughout the year, with the wettest seasons being autumn and winter (**Figure 2.6**). These are the parts of the year when depressions are most active, so there is much frontal rain which is increased further by relief rain. The cool summers create little convectional rainfall.

Cambridge has a different rainfall pattern. Winter is still wetter than spring because depressions are more frequent in winter, but the wettest season is summer because the high temperatures create much convectional rainfall. Nevertheless, the summer rainfall is less than in Keswick because Cambridge is in the east, where the air has lost much of its water vapour.

Temperature

In Britain, average July temperatures (**Figure 2.7**) decrease northwards from 17°C in the south east to 13°C in the north.

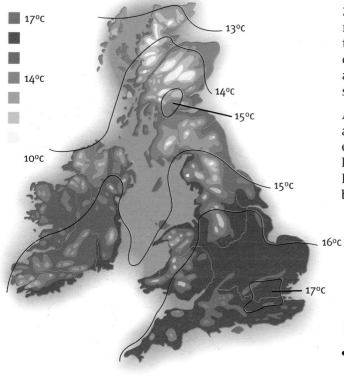

■	17°C
■	
■	14°C
■	
■	

13°C

14°C

15°C

10°C

15°C

16°C

17°C

Figure 2.7 July temperatures

East Anglia (16°C) is warmer than the Lake District (15°C). Temperature decreases with latitude for two reasons:

- Further north, heat from the sun has a longer path through the atmosphere (**Figure 2.8**). More of it is reflected back into space by clouds and dust, so less reaches the ground than in the south.

- The sun is at a higher angle in the sky in the south of the UK. Its heat is concentrated on a smaller area, which therefore warms up quickly.

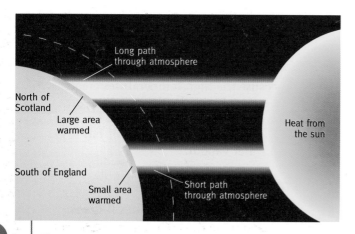

Long path through atmosphere

North of Scotland

Large area warmed

South of England

Small area warmed

Heat from the sun

Short path through atmosphere

Figure 2.8 The effect of latitude on temperatures

Average July temperatures increase inland (**Figure 2.7**). This is because the winds in Britain blow mainly from the west and south west. As they cross the Atlantic Ocean and Irish Sea they are cooled down and they then cool the west coast. This is another reason for the Lake District having lower summer temperatures than East Anglia.

As well as latitude, relief also affects temperature. On average, temperatures decrease by about 1°C for every 100 m rise in the land. This means that the lowland of East Anglia is hardly affected. In the Lake District temperatures drop rapidly in short distances because of the high land.

Plants can grow because they make energy from sunlight by **photosynthesis**. The number of sunshine hours decreases from an average of over five a day in the south to less than three in the north (**Figure 2.8**). East Anglia has more than double the amount of sunshine of the Lake District, so plants can grow much faster and much bigger. The pattern is the result of:

- in the west and highland areas there are more clouds whose tops reflect the sun's rays back into space.

- sunshine is more concentrated in the south because of the effect of latitude (**Figure 2.8**).

In January temperatures decrease from over 7°C in the south west of Cornwall to below 4°C in the north east of Scotland and parts of East Anglia. The sea takes much longer to heat up than the land in summer but, once warmed, it cools much more slowly than land during winter. This means that the sea is warmer than the land in January. The most common winds are from the west and south west, and they are warmed as they pass over the Atlantic Ocean and Irish Sea. They are especially warmed because of the **North Atlantic Drift**, a large current of warm water which flows northwards from the Gulf of Mexico and passes to the west of Ireland. The warm winds affect the temperature of the west coast of Britain in winter. The result is that lowland parts of the Lake District have temperatures of just below 5°C in January, while parts of East Anglia are colder than 4°C. Farm crops such as sugar beet and potatoes are not planted in winter so the cold does not harm the farming in East Anglia. Animals, however, need to keep warm, so the higher winter temperatures in the west help farming there. The growing season is also longer, which means that the grass on which the animals feed grows for longer.

Hill sheep farming in the Lake District

Waterside House farm is on the eastern shore of Lake Ullswater (**Figure 2.9**). It covers 113 ha. Mr Lowis is one of 12 farmers with grazing rights on Barton Fell where his share is equivalent to 69 ha.

The purpose of hill sheep farming is to rear sheep in highland areas. It is a type of **pastoral farming** because only animals are kept on the farm and no arable crops are grown. It is also a type of **extensive farming** because it requires low inputs to each hectare of land and low outputs are obtained from each hectare.

The farm extends from the floor of the U-shaped glacial trough (see Chapter 3) up the valley side to the mountain tops. It can be divided into three parts (**Figure 2.9**):

1 **Inbye land** is the flat land on the edge of Lake Ullswater, which covers most of the valley floor. The 32 ha of inbye is mainly improved grassland and is used for growing grass to make into silage in summer and to graze sheep and lambs for the rest of the year. It is the best land on the farm, but there are problems with it which mean it cannot be used for other types of farming:

- It is gently sloping so tractors can be used, but 4 ha are flat. They are at lake level and are boggy.

- Some of the soil is gravelly and silty, so it is well drained, but higher parts are a sticky clay which is impermeable and acidic.

- Rainfall is high (1476 mm per year). Water also drains down the valley side (throughflow) so the water table is near the surface for much of the year. The soil is too wet for growing arable crops.

- The average summer temperature is 15°C, which is cool but warm enough for grass to grow.

- The average winter temperature is 5°C, which is mild and snow does not lie for long on the inbye land but there is too little space for crops.

2 **Intake land** (81 ha) rises from 160 m up to 330 m and is rough pasture land with many scattered trees and bushes. It is the second best land on the farm, but can only be used for grazing sheep.

- Much of it is too steep to use farm machinery on.

- The soil is thin and stony in the higher areas, and composed of sticky acidic clay in the lower parts.

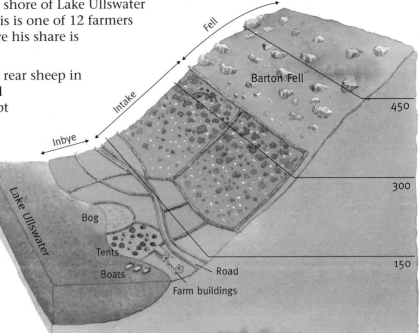

Figure 2.9 A block diagram of Waterside House farm

- Rainfall in the higher parts is over 2000 mm per year, but the steepness means it runs off quickly.

- Temperatures are lower than on the inbye land.

3 **Fell land** Barton Fell rises to 520 m. Sheep can be kept on this land, but it supports many fewer than the intake land because:

- Parts of it are cliffs, and all of it is too steep to use machinery to improve the vegetation.

- Bare rock is common, and the soil is thin, stony and acidic with few plant nutrients.

- Annual rainfall is very high (over 2000 mm) and leaches any plant nutrients from the soil.

- Low cloud is common; it blocks sunlight which plants need for photosynthesis.

- Temperatures are 5°C lower than in the valley, which makes the growing season very short (only three months).

- Winter temperatures are often below freezing, and snow lies for a long time making it difficult for sheep to feed.

- The vegetation is cotton grass, heather and moss. Bracken has spread widely in recent years due to overgrazing, but it is poisonous to sheep. Most of the 880 ewes are Swaledales which can survive the cold, wet climate and poor nutrition.

The hill sheep farmer's year

January to March

- Sheep graze mainly on the inbye and intake land, as the weather on the fell is too severe.

- The sheep are fed silage made in the previous summer.

- Some sheep are over-wintered on lowland dairy farms elsewhere in Cumbria where the weather is milder and there is more nourishing grass.

April to May

- All ewes are given ultrasound scans two or three weeks before lambing, and those with twins or triplets, or weak ewes, are kept in a building for extra care until they lamb.

- All ewes are on the inbye and intake land to be near the farmhouse so that they can be observed continually. There were 950 lambs born in 2000.

May to June

- Sheep and lambs are moved to the intake land and fell to allow grass to grow on the inbye land.

July

- Grass is cut and made into round bale silage; no hay is made now because the weather is too wet in summer and silage making is more mechanised so labour costs are saved. The workers are Mr Lowis, his son (Mark) and a casual labourer who is employed at busy times.

- The first-born lambs are sold to local butchers.

August

- 880 ewes were sheared in 2000 and the wool sold to merchants in Bradford for making carpets.

September to October

- The main sheep sales are held; 475 fattened lambs were sold, many for export to Europe after being slaughtered.

- 325 female lambs were sold to other farmers for breeding.

- 150 lambs are kept on the farm for breeding.

- The sheep are dipped to kill parasites.

November to December

- The ewes are mated.

- The sheep graze the sheltered, warmer inbye and intake land.

What factors affect the hill sheep farmer's income?

The part of the European Union (EU) which deals with farming is called the **Common Agricultural Policy (CAP)**. The CAP was set up to:

- Increase productivity and increase the self-sufficiency of the EU.

- Give all farm workers a fair standard of living.

- Keep prices of agricultural products stable.

- Maintain food supplies.

- Ensure reasonable prices for customers.

The CAP works by guaranteeing prices for each commodity. However, the prices have often been fixed too high. This has encouraged farmers to produce too much, leading to surpluses. The surplus is the extra which cannot be sold. It is known as a beef, wheat or butter mountain, or a milk, wine or olive oil lake. The cost of storing the surplus is very high.

The EU is trying to reduce the lamb meat, mutton and wool mountains by:

- Lowering the guaranteed prices. However, this led to farmers keeping more sheep to stop their income decreasing. This led to over-grazing of the fells.

- Imposing sheep quotas. A quota is the maximum number of sheep for which a farmer can receive a subsidy. The subsidy is the difference between the selling price of the sheep and the guaranteed price, and without it the farmer would make a loss. At Waterside House, the quota is 880 sheep.

- The CAP has classified land according to how easy it is to farm. Waterside House farm has 'severely disadvantaged status' so Mr Lowis gets extra payments to offset the higher costs.

EXAM TIP

To gain the highest marks, do not merely learn what the CAP is. Learn also the details of how it affects the hill sheep farm.

World markets affect hill sheep farming. The income which Waterside House farm receives has dropped sharply in recent years because the prices paid at markets depend on the demand for the products. Lambs in 2000 were half the price of three years ago for several reasons:

- The higher value of Sterling against the Euro has meant that British lamb is more expensive to buy in Europe.

- Swaledale wool is of low quality and there is an oversupply of high quality Australian wool on the world markets.

- Fewer people have been eating mutton and lamb because of the BSE health scare in cattle. More prefer to eat white meat and fish for health reasons.

- Russians wear hats made from lamb skins, but the collapse of the Russian economy means few can afford the hats.

How can a hill sheep farmer diversify?

Because the income from hill sheep farming has dropped, farmers have diversified. **Diversification** means making money in ways which are not to do with farming. Generally, they are connected with conservation and tourism.

Conservation
The intensification of farming in the last 50 years has caused a big reduction in wildlife. EU and government policy is now to pay farmers to maintain and increase wildlife habitats. Mr Lowis has signed a

Figure 2.10 Bracken on fell land

ten year contract to take part in the **ESA (Environmentally Sensitive Areas) Scheme** to:

- Limit the spreading of fertiliser on meadows to reduce the effects of nitrogen pollution in water.

- Restore and maintain dry stone walls and hedges.

- Lower the number of his sheep on Barton Fell by two thirds. Over-grazing has reduced the cover of heather and caused the spread of bracken, which is tall and its shade kills other plants.

- Spray bracken to kill it.

Tourism
At Waterside House farm tourist facilities have been developed by Mrs Lowis in two ways:

1 Part of the inbye land is a large campsite for 120 tents from 1st March to 31st October. There were big costs in setting it up:

- Conversion of an old hay barn into a laundry, reception/shop and the building of a toilet block.

- Construction of hard roads across the field.

- Planting of trees along the edge of the lake, along the road and in the field to screen the site. These were necessary to get planning permission.

- Employment of a full-time worker in summer in the shop.

The campsite is a 6 ha field which is about 20 per cent of the total inbye land. Not enough silage can now be grown to feed the sheep in winter, so land elsewhere has to be rented to replace it.

2 Being on the edge of Lake Ullswater, canoes and boats are available for tourists to hire.

Diversification began as a way of increasing farm income, but with the recent falls in revenue, the expansion of the tourism related activities means that they make up half the income at Waterside House. Planning controls prevent new ventures such as a caravan site.

EXAM TIP
An answer about diversification should include conservation as well as tourism.

Arable farming in East Anglia

Lynford House farm is at Manea near March in the Cambridgeshire fens (**Figure 2.11**). It is an **arable farm** covering 570 ha of land and is run by Mr Sears.

Figure 2.11 Aerial view of Lynford House farm

Arable farming is the growing of crops; animals are not kept. It is an example of **intensive farming**. This means that there are large inputs to each hectare in order to produce large outputs of crops. The inputs include fertiliser, pesticide, fuel for machinery, and the cost of buying machinery. Activities carried out during the year at Lynford House farm are shown in **Table 2.1**.

Table 2.1 The farming year at Lynford House Farm

	Jan.	Feb.	March	April	May	June	July	Aug.	Sept.	Oct.	Nov.	Dec.
Wheat			fertilise	fertilise spray	spray		harvest	plough	sow	→	→	
Potatoes	plough	→	fertilise	plant	spray	irrigate	→ spray		harvest	→	plough	→
Sugar beet	plough	→	sow	spray	spray					harvest	fertilise	plough
Peas			plough	sow	spray		harvest		subsoil-ing*		plough	→
General farm maintenance	→	→										

* subsoiling is deep ploughing to improve water percolation through the soil   crop growing

THE UNITED KINGDOM

The physical environment of the area has many advantages for arable farming:

Landforms

- All the land is flat and just above sea level. Large machinery such as the combine harvester can easily travel over it.

- Up to 200 years ago the area was marshland. It is now kept dry by drainage ditches along the sides of the fields and pipe drains under them. The farm has a JCB digger which is used to clean the ditches and re-lay drains when there are no crops in the fields. Poor drainage does not now influence the land use.

Soil

When the area was marshland, the rivers Nene and Ouse used to flood their floodplains and alluvium was deposited. The remains of plants accumulated in the marshland and formed peat. These two types of soil which are many metres deep are very fertile. They are a rich supply of nutrients for crop growth, although fertiliser is also added.

Climate

- The warm summer temperatures (16°C) and high sunshine totals (over 1500 hours per year) increase the rate of photosynthesis so crops grow faster than in the Lake District. The sunshine is very important to create a high sugar content in beet.

- Although there is a peak of rainfall in summer caused by convection, it falls in short sharp showers with long periods of sunshine in between. These are ideal conditions for plants to grow and ripen.

- The sunshine dries cereal crops quickly so harvesting can go ahead in August.

- The low annual rainfall of 559 mm at Lynford House farm means there is little cloud cover, so much sunshine can reach the crops.

- In winter, temperatures are lower than in the west, with an average of 4°C in January, and there are many frosts during the night. These are an advantage to arable farming because they break up the alluvial soils which helps the crops sown in spring to germinate. Frosts also kill pests such as greenfly which could harm crops when they are germinating and growing.

Although most of the physical factors favour arable farming at Lynford House farm, the climate does have a few disadvantages:

- Winter wheat which is sown in September and October is hardy and is not affected by frosts, but if hard frosts occur in spring after sugar beet, potatoes and peas have been sown, young shoots can be killed.

- If the showers in summer are very heavy or contain hail, they can flatten cereal crops. The grain might then go mouldy if it lies on the ground.

- Dry periods in summer reduce plant growth and yields, especially for crops such as potatoes and peas which have a high water content.

Mr Sears has built a 55 000 m³ reservoir for irrigation water.

How do national and international policies affect arable farming at Lynford House farm?

The British government's farming policy is the CAP. It works in the following ways:

- A target price is set for farm produce each year.

- A subsidy is money given to a farmer when the market price for his crop is lower than the target price; it is the difference between the two prices.

- A threshold price is also set. The threshold price is always higher than the target price. It is the lowest price at which imports can be sold. EU producers are therefore protected from cheaper imports from outside the EU.

- An intervention price is set which is lower than the target price. If prices paid to farmers in the EU fall to the intervention price, the EU buys up part of the product and tries to push prices back up to the target price.

These three guaranteed prices take some of the risks out of arable farming, such as droughts and changes in market prices. Farmers know they will get good prices for their crops so they are strongly influenced by the target prices set by the EU. There have been two major effects from this:

1 The CAP aims to be self-sufficient in the main types of food. Vegetable oils, used in making products such as low-fat margarine, have had to be imported because the EU did not grow enough. High target prices were set for oil-seed rape in 1973. As a result, many farmers were encouraged to grow it. The EU is now self-sufficient and imports are not needed.

2 High subsidies for crops such as cereals have encouraged farmers to grow more. Mr Sears has increased his wheat yield by one third in the last five years. There is now a surplus and this has to be stored unsold in order to keep the market prices above the intervention price. It is often called the grain mountain. Surpluses are expensive to store, and consumers do not like them because they help to keep food prices higher in the EU than in the rest of the world.

Figure 2.12 Set-aside land

In order to reduce the surpluses, the EU adopted two policies in the 1990s:

- To reduce subsidies so that farmers would not be encouraged to grow so much.

- To introduce the system of set-aside.

Set-aside land

Set-aside is the policy whereby some farm land is taken out of production (**Figure 2.12**). Farmers receive compensation for their loss of income. It affects only farms that grow crops such as cereals, oil-seed rape, linseed and peas. Farmers have to set land aside if they want to claim certain EU subsidies. The amount of set-aside land is decided each year and depends on the level of production and on stocks in the rest of the world. Since 1995, the proportion of land set aside on each farm has dropped from 12 per cent to 5 per cent. This is because the guaranteed prices have also been decreased, so some farmers are producing less because they are finding more profitable crops.

Farmers can either keep the same fields as set-aside land from year to year or they can change them. The land cannot be used to bring in cash which is not to

do with farming. For instance, it cannot be used for quad bike racing or a golf course, nor can it be used for grazing animals, except for a pony for riding by the farmer's family. Most farmers leave the land fallow. They are encouraged to set aside land next to hedges, woods and rivers because it is more likely to be colonised by wild plants, and birds can eat the seeds of the weeds which grow on it. At Lynford House Farm, 5 per cent (27.1 ha) of the land was set aside in 2000. Many farmers use their least productive land for set-aside.

Diversification

As the EU tries to reduce surpluses by lowering target prices, farmers are less sure of the income they will receive. They are trying to find other ways of making money by diversifying. Set-aside is a form of diversification because money is gained for leaving some land fallow.

Early in the twentieth century, farm work was still done by horses, and many labourers were employed. They usually lived in houses owned by the farmer. Mechanisation has now reduced the number of workers. At Lynford House farm, 10 of the 12 bungalows are being sold or are let out.

Wind power turbines are being built on the farm and Mr Sears will receive rent for the small area of land they use. The current rate is up to £3000 per year for each turbine.

How do supermarket chains and food processing firms affect arable farming?

Major supermarket chains such as Tesco, Sainsbury, Asda and Safeway sell a large proportion of the food eaten in Britain. There is strong competition between them so they do all they can to provide what the customer wants, such as high quality and low prices. The supermarkets pass on these demands to the food processors which supply them, and they in turn pass them on to the farmer.

Changes in the crops grown

Customers in the supermarket are not only interested in low prices. They want crops to be as fresh as possible and to be of high quality. Farm produce must have a good appearance and not be damaged. The supermarket chains and food processors influence the farmer to do these in many ways:

- **Perishable crops**, such as garden peas, have to be grown within 45 minutes travelling time of the factory where they will be frozen or canned. The skins become tougher if transport takes longer. Crops such as these are grown near the factories and near motorways and good roads. The farmer agrees a contract with the firm and uses scientific advice to grow the crop to the highest quality. There were 400 tonnes of peas grown at Lynford House Farm in 1995 and 1996 for the Hillsdown Canning Company and the Albert Fisher Group, who froze the peas.

- **Packaging**. Supermarkets usually want crops such as potatoes to be the same size and to be in bags of particular weights. Many arable farmers have sheds which are mini-factories. They do jobs such as washing, sorting into sizes, and packaging. The farmers make sure they will earn a profit by having contracts with the supermarkets. These arrangements favour large, well organized arable farms. Lynford House farm does not have such a shed, but the potato crop of over 3000 tonnes is kept in a cool ventilated store to keep it fresh.

- **Organic farming**. Recent concern about chemicals in food has caused a huge increase in the demand for organically grown crops. In order to be recognized by the Soil Association as an organic farm, farmers have to stop using all chemicals. It takes three years to change, during which time there are some grants available from the government. Yields per hectare are much lower on organic farms, but the prices that supermarket chains and food processors will pay are much higher. Lynford House Farm is not an organic farm

- **Bulky crops**. Sugar beet is a bulky crop. This means that it is heavy, takes up a lot of space in a lorry and is of low value because only about 15 per cent of it is actually sugar. The costs of transporting it are high compared with its value. For this reason it is grown fairly close (within about 60 km) to a sugar beet refining factory. The sugar beet from Lynford House farm is taken only 10 km to the factory at Ely.

Changes in farming practices

Crop rotation: 50 years ago farmers used crop rotation to keep the soil fertile. This involved growing a different crop in a field each year in a four-year cycle. Each crop needed different nutrients so the soil was not exhausted. Now that farmers want to increase yields and grow fewer types of crop, many have stopped using crop rotation and rely on fertiliser to increase their yields. This is the case at Lynford House farm.

Agribusiness: Supermarket chains and food processors want to buy crops in bulk. They can then be confident of enough supplies and good quality. This has encouraged the growth of agribusiness in which large farms specialize in just a few crops. They work closely with scientific advisers to produce the maximum yields and quality, and often have contracts with supermarkets and processors to buy the crops even before they are planted. The farms are often owned by a company such as an insurance company and are controlled by a farm manager.

Co-operatives: The buyers of farmers' crops want to pay as low a price as possible to maximize their own profits. In turn, farmers have to cut their own costs to make a profit. A co-operative or buying group is a system in which farmers join together to buy inputs. Because the co-operative can order inputs in bulk from manufacturers, it can buy at a lower price per tonne than a farmer could alone. The group then passes on the saving. Mr Sears saved 20 per cent of the costs of chemicals in his first year as a member of a co-operative.

Increased mechanisation: Powerful machines such as John Deere tractors and combine harvesters get farm work done faster with fewer people. This saves money on wages. In the last year, the number of workers has been cut from six to five at Lynford House Farm.

Figure 2.13 Mechanisation on an arable farm

Economics of scale: As the costs of machinery and other inputs rise, it becomes more important to use them as much as possible. For example, a combine harvester was bought in 1991 for £82,000. If it had been used for ten years to cut only 1 ha of wheat per year, the cost of harvesting would have been £8,200 per ha/per year. However, it cuts about 280 ha per year, so the cost is much lower, at about £30 per ha. Farmers gain economies of scale by farming on a big scale. Over recent years, the increased importance of economies of scale has led to there being fewer but bigger arable farms. It has also caused farmers to grow a smaller number of crops, but each is grown in larger amounts. In the last five years, the number of crops grown at Lynford House Farm has decreased from five to just two, wheat and sugar beet.

Figure 2.14 Eutrophication

What is the impact of intensive farming on the environment?

The high inputs to arable farming have damaged the environment, but steps are now being taken to reduce the impact.

Use of fertiliser

Fertiliser adds nitrogen, phosphorus and potassium to the soil to increase crop yields. Plants cannot absorb all of it. It is dissolved and carried by soil water into streams and drainage ditches. There it causes the rapid growth of algae and floating plants such as duckweed. They cover the surface so sunlight cannot reach the river bed. Most of the oxygen in the water is used up so life under the water surface dies. This process is called **eutrophication**.

Farmers are now being advised how to avoid spreading too much fertiliser. Machines can apply it nearer to the plant rather than spreading it over the ground. Guidelines suggest that it should not be spread within 2 m of streams so that there is more chance of it being dissolved and going into the soil rather than being washed off into the streams.

Use of pesticides

Pesticides are chemicals which kill weeds (herbicides), insects (insecticides), and fungus (fungicides). In the past, they were sprayed on to crops but often also killed insects which eat the pests. This left crops vulnerable to stronger attacks by pests a few weeks later. More pesticide was needed and costs rose further. Because pesticides kill weeds there are very few weeds and also very few insects which live on them. This loss of **biodiversity** has caused a large decrease in other wildlife such as skylarks, thrushes, butterflies and voles.

Farmers now know the best times to spray their crops and better pesticides have been developed which kill only the pests desired such as greenfly. Farmers can be fined heavily if they pollute streams. At Lynford House farm, 23 per cent less pesticide is now used than ten years ago.

EXAM TIP

Do not confuse fertilisers and pesticides. Fertilisers help plants to grow, but pesticides kill species which harm crops.

Removal of hedgerows and other habitats

A hundred years ago, most arable farms also reared animals, and hedges were needed to keep the animals in the fields. As farms have increasingly specialised in growing crops, hedges are no longer necessary. Farmers are under pressure to use all their land to increase their profits. This has led them to drain ponds and marshes and to remove woodlands. Since 1950, the length of hedgerows in Cambridgeshire has declined by 80 per cent (**Figure 2.15**).

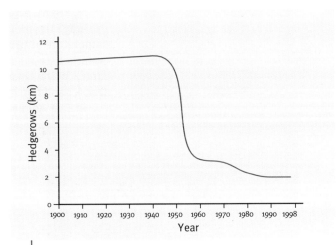

Figure 2.15 Hedgerow decline in Cambridgeshire

Farmers have removed hedges for several reasons:

- The cost of maintaining hedges is eliminated.
- Land formerly occupied by hedges, ponds, marshes and woods can now grow more crops.
- Hedgerows were refuges for pests such as rabbits which in the 1950s ate a considerable amount of the crops growing near them.
- Machines such as tractors now have to turn less frequently in the larger fields. This speeds up the work.

However, the destruction of hedgerows has harmed the environment in several ways:

- **Habitats**, such as hedgerows, are where wildlife species can find food, breeding sites, protection from predators and routes from one woodland to the next.
- With no hedgerows to slow the wind down, soil erosion by the wind is a problem, especially in winter when the soil is often bare and winds are strong. It is a particular problem on the fens, which are flat, and the peat soil dries out.

- On slopes with no hedgerows surface run off is not slowed down, and rainwater can erode channels on the upper slopes, remove seedlings, and cover crops on the lower slopes with soil (**Figure 2.16**).

The EU is now trying to reduce the harm to the environment and to encourage biodiversity (more varied wildlife):

- Grants which were available to farmers until the 1980s to help meet the costs of removing hedgerows have now been replaced by grants to plant new hedgerows and repair old ones. This is part of the **Countryside Stewardship Scheme**. About 1500 km of new hedges are being planted each year and 2000 km of derelict hedgerows are being restored.
- The **Farm Woodland Premium Scheme** gives grants to plant new woodlands, mainly traditional broadleaf trees. About 6000 ha per year are being created, often in unused corners of fields. A tree planting programme is now in progress at Lynford House farm.
- Land which has rare species is protected from agricultural change by law. These areas are called **Sites of Special Scientific Interest (SSSIs)**.

Figure 2.16 Soil erosion by rainwater

1 *Page 20*

Figure 2.17 shows some of the influences on farming. On a copy of the diagram, write factors to fill in the blanks.

2 *Pages 21–23*

Study Figure 2.18

a   Describe the pattern of precipitation along the line V to Z.

b   Give reasons for the differences in annual precipitation across the Lake District.

3 *Pages 23–24*

Look at Figure 2.19.

a   Which station is in the Lake District?

b   Describe the differences in temperature between the two stations.

c   Give reasons for the differences in temperature.

4 *Pages 23–24*

Study Figure 2.20.

a   Describe the following patterns of farming in Britain:
   • Pastoral farming
   • Arable farming.

b   Give reasons for the patterns you have described.

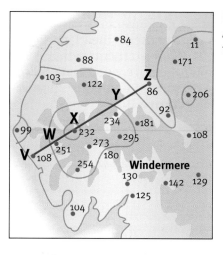

Figure 2.18
Average rainfall in the Lake District

Figure 2.19
Average monthly temperature at two weather stations. One is in the Lake District and one is in East Anglia.

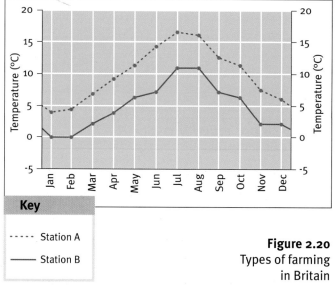

Key

---- Station A

—— Station B

Figure 2.20
Types of farming in Britain

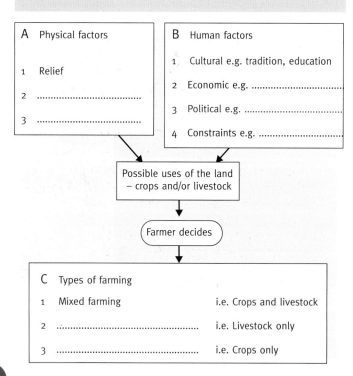

A	Physical factors
1	Relief
2	....
3	....

B	Human factors
1	Cultural e.g. tradition, education
2	Economic e.g. ....
3	Political e.g. ....
4	Constraints e.g. ....

Possible uses of the land – crops and/or livestock

Farmer decides

C	Types of farming	
1	Mixed farming	i.e. Crops and livestock
2	....	i.e. Livestock only
3	....	i.e. Crops only

Figure 2.17 Some influences on farming

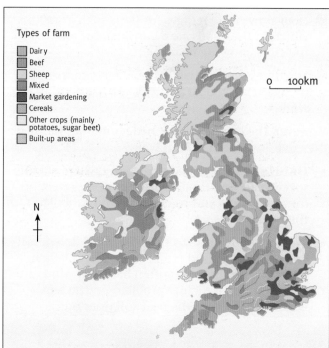

Types of farm
- Dairy
- Beef
- Sheep
- Mixed
- Market gardening
- Cereals
- Other crops (mainly potatoes, sugar beet)
- Built-up areas

0   100km

N

Questions

5 *Pages 25–26*

a Using Figure 2.21, match areas A, B and C with the labels:
  * Inbye land
  * Open fell (high fell)
  * Intake.

b The farmer uses the open fell (high fell) and the inbye in different agricultural ways. State the differences and explain why the farmer uses the areas differently.

6 *Pages 26–27*

a What do the letters CAP stand for?

b What is the correct term for grain 'mountains' and milk 'lakes'?

d Explain what 'diversification' means.

e Describe one way in which a hill sheep farmer can diversify.

7 *Pages 25–29*

Look at Figure 2.6b on page 23.

  a Give the temperature of the warmest month.

  b Give the temperature of the coldest month.

  c Calculate the annual range of temperature.

  d Name the season with most precipitation.

  e State two ways in which farming in East Anglia is different from farming in the Lake District.

  f Explain the differences you have stated in e.

8 *Pages 30–32*

a Explain how set-aside operates.

b How can an arable farmer diversify?

c Explain why each of the following changes is happening on arable farms:
  * Farmers are packaging some crops.
  * More farmers are growing organic crops.
  * More farmers are joining co-operatives.
  * Farming is becoming increasingly mechanized.
  * Arable farms are growing in size.
  * More fertiliser is being used.

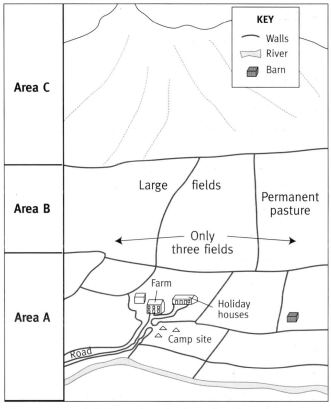

Figure 2.21 A hill sheep farm in the Lake District

9 *Pages 30–33*

a Describe three ways in which the landscape has been changed by modern farming methods.

b Describe three problems for wildlife which have resulted from these changes.

c Describe two schemes which are helping to protect wildlife in arable farming areas.

d There are many different opinions about the changes in arable farming. Describe the attitudes of the following people:
  * A farm labourer
  * An official in the Department of the Environment, Food and Rural Affairs
  * A conservationist
  * An agribusiness farmer.

3 Tourism in the Lake District National Park

What are the aims of National Parks?

The aims set out in the 1949 Act of Parliament are:

1 To preserve and enhance the natural beauty of the area.

2 To promote people's enjoyment of the countryside.

A national park is, therefore, an area where:

• The landscape is preserved.

• Wildlife, buildings and places of historical interest are protected.

• Existing farming practices are maintained.

• Access and facilities for public open-air enjoyment are provided.

The Lake District National Park Authority (LDNPA) has the task of putting these policies into practice. This involves getting a balance between two sorts of conflicts:

• Providing facilities for tourists encourages more tourists to come, which causes more damage to the natural beauty of the area.

• The needs of tourists often conflict with the needs of local people.

Tourists are attracted to the Lake District by the spectacular landscape, which has been formed mainly by glacial erosion.

A glacially eroded landscape

The world's climate is continuously changing. Between 14 and 20 **glacial** periods have occurred in the last 1 million years. The most recent **Ice Age** started 100 000 years ago and ended only 10 000 years ago. During it, ice sheets covered most of Britain north of the Midlands and changed the landscape by glacial erosion and deposition.

A **glacier** is a mass of moving ice. It erodes by two main processes:

• **Plucking**: water enters cracks in the rock and freezes so that it is attached to both the rock and the glacier. When the glacier moves, the block of rock is pulled out of the ground.

• **Abrasion**: blocks of rock (or load) in the base and sides of the glacier are scraped over the rock surface. They scratch it, making parallel grooves called **striations**. Abrasion has a sandpaper effect so the rock surface looks smooth.

Frost shattering also occurs in glacial environments. This is a weathering process, not an erosion process. When water enters a crack in the rock it expands by 10 per cent. The ice pushing on the sides of the crack widens it. Blocks of rock can then fall on to the glacier from the valley side above. Frost-shattered rock surfaces are easier for glaciers to erode by plucking.

[
EXAM TIP
Notice that it is the blocks of rock held in the ice, not the ice itself, which do the abrasion.
]

Landforms of glaciated mountains

Corries

Red Tarn **corrie** (grid reference 3415 in **Figure 3.1** and **Figure 3.2**) is an armchair-shaped hollow on the eastern side of Helvellyn mountain in the Lake District. It is 0.5 km wide and 1 km from front to back. The steep back and side walls are up to 220 m high. A small round lake called Red Tarn lies in the hollow in the base of the corrie. The water is kept in by a rock ridge on the floor of the corrie called a **rock lip**. The quickest way to identify a corrie on a map is to find a round lake less than 0.5 km in diameter with a U-shaped pattern of contours. However, many do not have lakes in them.

Figure 3.2 Red Tarn corrie

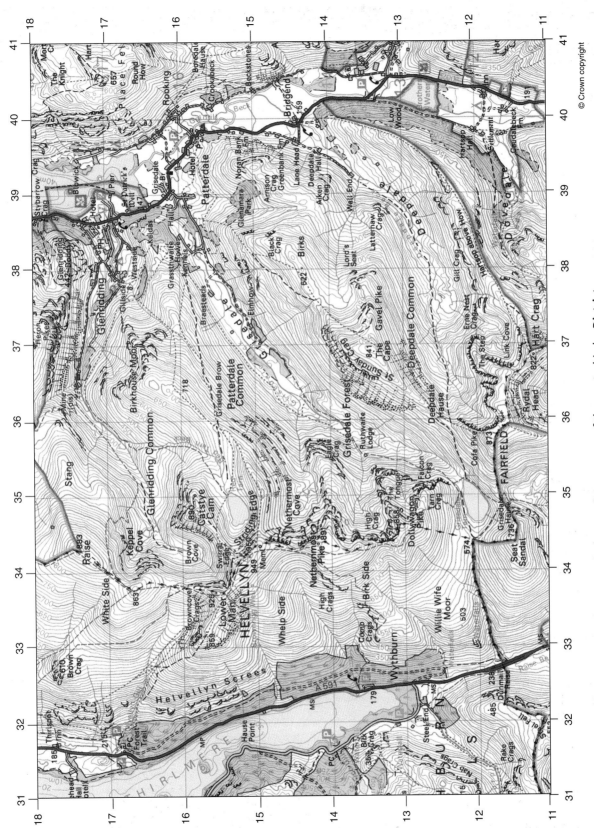

Figure 3.1 Ordnance Survey map of the central Lake District 1:50 000

Corries are formed by the following processes (**Figure 3.3**):

- Snow accumulates in a gully on the cold northern or eastern sides of a mountain. The weight of the snow compacts the base of the snow patch to form **glacier ice**.

- As gravity moves the corrie glacier downhill it moves away from the back wall. Blocks of rock are removed by plucking.

- Rock is removed from the corrie floor by abrasion.

- Frost shattering on the cliffs around the glacier loosens rocks, which fall on to the glacier.

- The glacier becomes thicker away from the back wall. Thicker ice can erode faster than thinner ice, so the floor of the corrie is rapidly deepened.

- At the same time the glacier is rotating, so the erosion of the corrie floor makes a hollow which is later filled by a tarn.

- The rotational movement also means that the ice is moving upwards near the mouth of the corrie, so the rock lip is left where there has been less erosion.

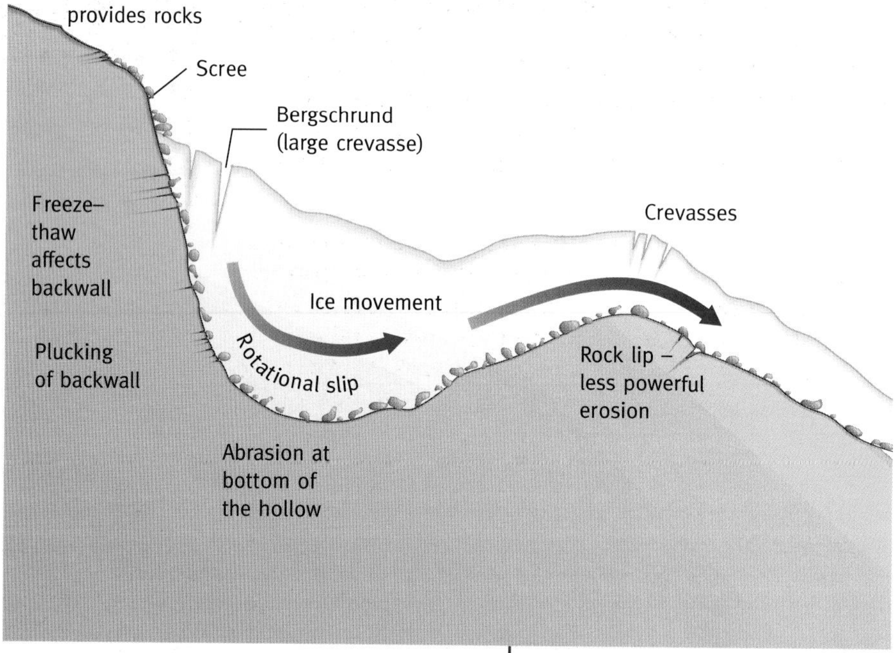

Figure 3.3 Formation of a corrie

Frost shattering on the cliffs provides rocks

Scree

Bergschrund (large crevasse)

Crevasses

Freeze–thaw affects backwall

Ice movement

Rotational slip

Plucking of backwall

Rock lip – less powerful erosion

Abrasion at bottom of the hollow

EXAM TIP

For each landform:

- Know how to describe it, including a named example and sizes.

- Know how to explain its formation by applying glacial erosion processes.

Figure 3.4 Striding Edge

Arêtes

Striding Edge (**Figure 3.4**) is the **arête** (knife-edged ridge) on the southern side of the Red Tarn corrie. An arête usually lies on each side of a corrie. Striding Edge is only 1 m wide in places along its top. It rises 200 metres above the floor of Red Tarn corrie. Its sides are very steep and the lower slopes are covered with **scree**.

The glacier which formed Red Tarn corrie eroded its back wall and side walls by plucking and abrasion. As the corrie grew in size, the ridge between it and the adjacent corrie became narrower and eventually formed the Striding Edge arête (**Figure 3.5**). After the glacier melted, frost shattering loosened blocks of rock, which fell to the foot of the slopes, forming scree.

Pyramidal peaks

A **pyramidal peak** is a mountain in the shape of a pyramid. It is formed when three or more corries erode into a mountain from different sides. There are no good examples in the Lake District, but the Matterhorn in Switzerland is a pyramidal peak (**Figure 3.6**).

Figure 3.6 The Matterhorn near Zermatt in Switzerland

Figure 3.5 Formation of an arête

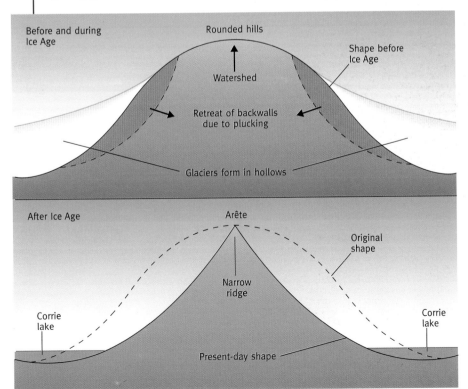

Before and during Ice Age

Rounded hills

Shape before Ice Age

Watershed

Retreat of backwalls due to plucking

Glaciers form in hollows

After Ice Age

Arête

Original shape

Narrow ridge

Corrie lake

Corrie lake

Present-day shape

Landforms of glaciated valleys

Glacial troughs

Glacial troughs are the main glaciated valleys. Patterdale in the Lake District (northwards and southwards from grid reference 3916 in **Figure 3.1**) is more than 9 km long. It has a flat floor up to 1 km wide and its very steep sides rise to 300 m. Glacial troughs are often described as U-shaped in cross-section (**Figure 3.7**). They are also fairly straight when seen on a map.

Glacial troughs are eroded by valley glaciers. The V-shaped cross-section of a river valley is turned into the U-shape as the glacier erodes downwards by plucking and abrasion. River valleys have interlocking spurs. Unlike a river, a valley glacier is solid, so it does not bend easily. It flows over the ends of the interlocking spurs and erodes them away by plucking and abrasion. The spurs are then called **truncated spurs**. Truncated spurs are often difficult features to identify on maps. They are found between tributary valleys to the glacial trough, and the sharp corners and straight lines of the contours form a triangle.

If the glacier deposits its load of rock debris over the floor of the glacial trough, the layer is called **ground moraine**. Deposition also occurs at the sides of the glacier and is then called **lateral moraine**.

After the glacier which formed them melts, glacial troughs are changed in three ways:

- A river flows in the trough and deposits alluvium on the floor. The river is usually very small compared to the wide valley and is called a **misfit river**.

- Tributary rivers flowing on to the flat valley floor have been slowed down and deposit **alluvial fans**. An example is near Hartsop at grid reference 405132 on **Figure 3.1**.

- Frost shattering on the valley sides forms scree (**Figure 3.7**).

Hanging valleys

Tributary valleys such as Grisedale (grid reference 3715 on **Figure 3.1**) are smaller than the glacial trough. They often join it high on the valley side. This means that their floors are above the floor of the glacial trough so they are called **hanging valleys**. The floor of Grisedale is at about 200 m and it joins Patterdale, whose floor is at 150 m. The difference in height results in the tributary stream forming a waterfall as it drops to the floor of the glacial trough. There is no waterfall at the mouth of Grisedale, but there are rapids. The reason for the difference in height is that the thicker valley glacier in the glacial trough is able to erode downwards faster than the smaller glacier in the hanging valley.

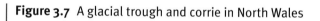

Figure 3.7 A glacial trough and corrie in North Wales

Ribbon lakes

Long, thin, deep lakes called **ribbon lakes** are common on the floors of glacial troughs. Ullswater, whose southern end is shown in **Figure 3.1**, is 12 km long, up to 1 km wide, and is 60 m deep (**Figure 3.7**). Ribbon lakes are formed in three different ways:

- Where weaker rock is at the surface, the main valley glacier can erode faster and make a hollow in the valley floor.

- Where the main valley glacier is joined by one or more hanging valley glaciers within a short distance, its thickness is quickly increased and it can erode faster.

- A glacier transports a load of rock debris. At its **snout** the glacier melts and deposits the load. If the rate of melting is the same as the rate at which the glacier is moving forward, the snout stays in the same place and the deposited load builds up to form a ridge across the valley called a **terminal moraine**. After the glacier has melted, the terminal moraine acts as a dam which holds back water behind it, forming a ribbon lake.

Ullswater is a ribbon lake which fills a hollow in the floor of the Patterdale glacial trough, where the rock was less resistant to glacial erosion. At the southern end of the lake, two large glaciers in the Grisedale and Glenridding valleys joined the Patterdale glacier, so it was able to erode faster as it flowed further north. Ullswater does not have a terminal moraine at its northern end. After its formation, rivers flowing into the lake have deposited **deltas** and made it slightly smaller. An example can be seen at the mouth of Goldrill Beck (grid reference 393166 on **Figure 3.1**).

A typical glacial landscape showing all these features is shown in **Figure 3.8**.

Figure 3.8 A typical glacial landscape

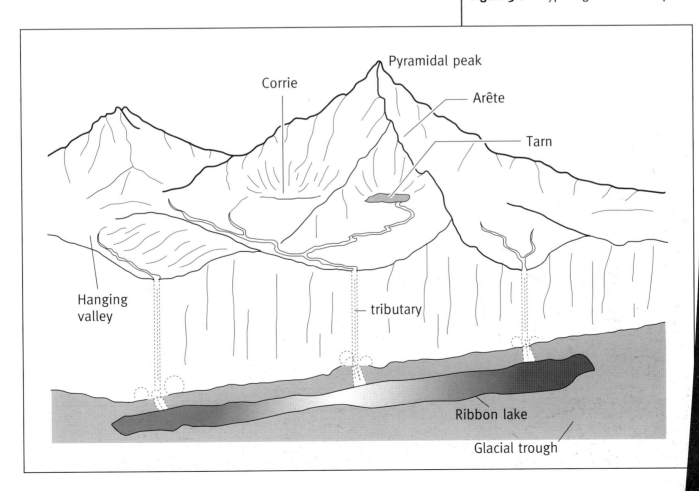

What are the impacts of tourism on the Lake District?

In 1995 it was estimated that the Lake District had:

- 10 million day visitors.

- 12 million staying visitor-days (one person who stayed for two days and a night was counted as two visitor-days).

The aspects tourists enjoy most are shown in **Figure 3.9**. The quality of the landscape is the reason most visitors go to the Lake District. 80 per cent have been more than once. However, one in four also say that overcrowding spoils their visit.

Most visitors travel by car. The M6 motorway passes the eastern edge of the National Park. 10 million people live within a three-hour drive. Visitors travel from all parts of Britain, with more coming from northern England and the South East than from the Midlands, East Anglia and the South West. These patterns are related to the length of time people are willing to travel if they are making a day visit, the size of the population and the nearness of other National Parks to where they live.

More than one-third of those who stay in the Lake District use serviced accommodation (**Table 3.1**). They have a big impact on employment in the area. Just under two-thirds use self-catering premises, such as camping and caravan sites and holiday homes.

The number of visitors to National Parks has increased since 1950 for many reasons:

- Paid holidays for most working people have increased from two to three or four weeks per year.

- Most workers have a shorter working week; for many it has decreased from 45 hours to 37.5 hours per week.

- Household equipment such as automatic washing machines, vacuum cleaners and dishwashers have reduced the time spent on housework and created more time for leisure.

- Average salaries have increased so most people have more money to spend on leisure.

- Far more families own a car, which gives them the freedom to choose when to go on day trips.

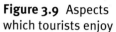

Key
- Very important
- Important
- Not important

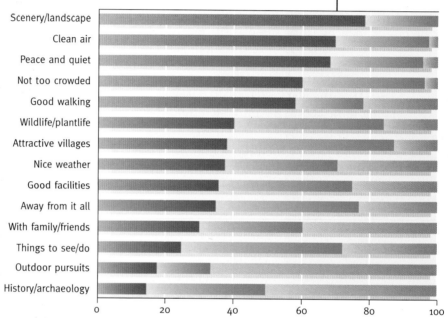

Figure 3.9 Aspects which tourists enjoy

Scenery/landscape, Clean air, Peace and quiet, Not too crowded, Good walking, Wildlife/plantlife, Attractive villages, Nice weather, Good facilities, Away from it all, With family/friends, Things to see/do, Outdoor pursuits, History/archaeology

Table 3.1 Types of accommodation

SERVICED	
Hotel/Motel	23
Bed & Breakfast	13
Farmhouse (B&B)	2
Outdoor activity/Training centre	1
Total	**39**
SELF CATERING	
Caravan	20
Camping	12
Self-catering accommodation	19
Timeshare	1
Youth hostel	2
Second home	2
Wooden chalet/Log cabin	1
Total	**57**
Homes of friends/relatives	**4**

- The accessibility of an area is how quick and easy it is to travel to. The accessibility of the Lake District increased in the 1960s and 1970s with the building of the M6 motorway. It also allowed people to travel from further away.

- Inter-city coaches and tour coaches are now common, and competition has kept fares low.

What is the impact of tourism on farming?

A National Park is not a park in the same sense as a town park. The public do not have the right to walk wherever they want. A National Park is not owned by the nation; most land belongs to farmers. **Figure 3.10** shows the figures for the Lake District where, unusually, a large percentage is owned by the charity The National Trust, which has 91 farms worked by tenants.

Tourism can be both a benefit and a problem to farmers:

Benefits

Chapter 2 explained the difficulties of making a living from hill sheep farming. Through the CAP and schemes such as ESA (Environmentally Sensitive Areas), more than 80 per cent of the income of many farmers comes from government subsidies. To gain more income many farmers diversify into tourist-related activities such as farmhouse teas, self-catering accommodation, campsites, etc.

Problems

There are many ways in which the actions and intentions of tourists conflict with the interests of farmers.

The farmer wants the following:

- No disturbance of pregnant ewes during the lambing season.
- No damage to the grass which is growing for hay.
- To drive a flock of sheep along the narrow road.
- To take a wide hay baler to the field along the narrow lane.

On the other hand, the tourist wants the following:

- To let the dog run off its lead.
- To walk on the public footpath across the hay meadow.
- To drive past the sheep as quickly as possible.
- To park on the roadside and go for a walk.

What is the impact of tourism on traffic?

In Langdale, traffic more than doubles in summer compared with winter (**Figure 3.11**) and the roads are busiest on Sundays.

- Traffic congestion is worst at peak periods such as late mornings and afternoons on Sundays in August. It is made worse by the narrow twisty roads and steep hills. Many of the roads have only one lane.

EXAM TIP

If you are asked about a conflict of interest, you should describe the attitudes of at least two groups of people to a particular issue. See **Figure 3.21** for an example.

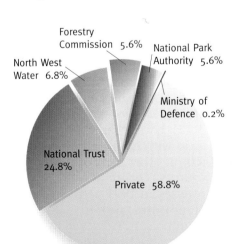

Figure 3.10 Land ownership

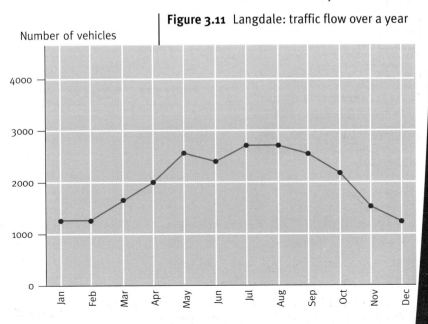

Figure 3.11 Langdale: traffic flow over a year

- 25 per cent of tourists report that overcrowding, especially on the roads, spoiled their visit. This can harm the number of tourists wanting to return and spend money in the Park.

- Congestion due to tourist traffic increases transport costs for local farmers and businesses because of increased delays.

- Noise from traffic disturbs nesting birds and other wildlife in the many woods next to the roads.

To combat these problems in other areas, traffic policy has been to widen roads or build new ones to reduce traffic congestion. In National Parks, where the landscape must be preserved, this policy is not appropriate. The solution is to adopt negative planning; no improvements are made as these would just encourage extra traffic. Drivers must adjust their travel times or routes to avoid possible congestion.

In towns such as Windermere the narrow twisty streets add to the congestion, and there is also danger to pedestrians on the narrow pavements. Some solutions include:

- Double yellow lines to prevent parking on the streets.

- Big lorries heavier than 7.5 tonnes are not allowed through the Lake District.

- Park and ride schemes are being planned for Windermere.

What is the impact of tourism on house prices?

The National Park has 23 000 homes. Three-quarters of the dwellings in the Lake District and the rest of Cumbria are privately owned, but in the National Park there are more **second homes** (Figure 3.12). These are owned by people who live somewhere else, usually outside Cumbria. They use their second homes only for holidays and weekends, so they are empty for most of the year.

The private rented sector is also much larger in the Lake District than in Cumbria as a whole. It consists mainly of holiday homes, which are houses that holiday-makers can rent as self-catering accommodation for one or two weeks. They make money for the owner but are often empty during winter.

Nearly 20 per cent of all dwellings in the National Park are now second homes and holiday homes. There are several reasons why people want to buy them:

- They are attracted to the beautiful scenery and have the money to buy a property there.

- They want to invest their money in a house in an area where the prices are rising. It is a relatively safe investment, and a profit can be expected when it is sold. Until 2001, second home owners had to pay only half the Council Tax paid by residents of the National Park.

- Holiday home owners buy properties to make money. Houses in the central Lake District are in most demand by holiday-makers and owners can charge very high rates, especially during the period of school summer holidays.

The National Park status of the Lake District means that the landscape has to be preserved so there are strict planning controls on building new homes. The great demand for second homes, holiday homes and homes to retire to, as well as the usual demand from local people for homes to live in, create much competition for houses when they are sold. The highest bidder gains ownership. The result is that house prices rise. There are several knock-on effects of the high house prices:

- **Falling population**. The total number of people living in the National Park fell continuously until 1981 as more houses became holiday and second homes (**Figure 3.13**). Local people moved to areas with more permanent jobs in other parts of the country. The trend was reversed in 1991 partly because of measures taken to counteract it. However, in parishes such as Langdale, in the very heart of the Lake District, the decline has continued.

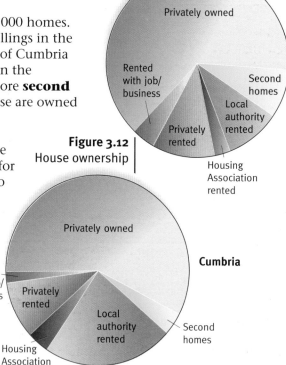

Lake District

Privately owned

Rented with job/ business

Second homes

Local authority rented

Privately rented

Housing Association rented

Figure 3.12 House ownership

Cumbria

Privately owned

Rented with job/ business

Privately rented

Local authority rented

Second homes

Housing Association rented

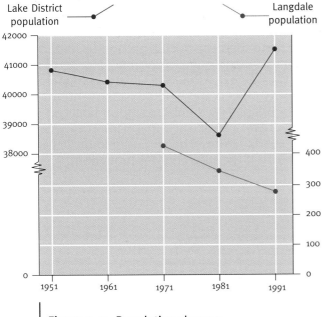

Figure 3.13 Population changes

- **Changes in population structure**. There are few people under 45 years old and more over 45 in the Lake District than in the rest of Cumbria (**Figure 3.14**). Younger families cannot afford to buy or keep the houses and they move away. Because of this there are fewer children under 15. Older people, often about to retire, can use money saved during their lives to buy properties in the Lake District.

- **Changes in rural communities**. Chapel Stile is a village in Langdale. Half the houses in the village are now second homes and holiday homes. In 1970, 27 cheap modern houses were built on a former quarry site for young local families, but only one is now permanently occupied.

These changes in population and communities affect the services provided in rural areas:

- Public bus services are removed as demand decreases. In Langdale, there are more services in summer for tourists.

- With few children in the area, primary schools are closed or are amalgamated. Chapel Stile now has the only school in the Langdale valley. Primary schools are often the centre of much community activity such as fêtes and sports and when they close, the community spirit is damaged.

- Second home owners and holiday-makers often buy food cheaply in a large supermarket near their homes and bring it to the Lake District. The result is that village shops close. This has happened in Chapel Stile, but the Co-op remains open.

- Some employment has been created by the growth of holiday homes, but jobs such as cleaning are low-paid and seasonal.

- Second home owners have ways of living and thinking typical of townspeople, and these are often not in tune with those of local people. They often do not speak the Westmorland (southern Lake District) dialect and do not support local leisure activities such as Cumberland wrestling, sheepdog trials and fox hunting. They are usually absent so they know few people. The community spirit of the village changes.

High house prices are such a problem that it is estimated that one quarter of the families in the Lake District will never to be able to buy their own home. Solutions which are being tried are:

- In Windermere, Staveley and Rosthwaite housing associations have been allowed to build terraced houses which can be rented only by local people who work in the area or who have lived there for three years.

- Elsewhere, starter homes have been built but can be bought only by local people.

The effects of high house prices lead to several possible conflicts. Examples include those between:

- holiday home owners and a young couple wanting to buy a house

- second home owners and a couple who have lived in the village for 70 years.

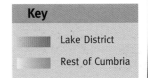

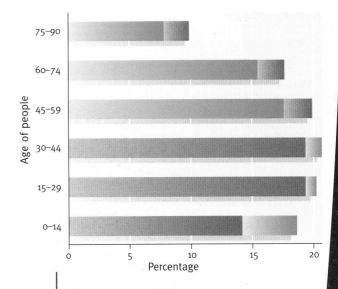

Figure 3.14 Population structure

What is the impact of tourism on employment?

In the Lake District approximately 50 per cent of the workforce is employed in hotels, catering and retail jobs (the national figure is 6 per cent). The aims of the National Park do not allow large industrial sites to be developed. Employment in farming has decreased because of mechanisation and the current depression in farming. Tourism, therefore, has become the main source of employment. In turn, people employed in tourism create demands for other services and employment such as schools and health care. However, as **Figure 3.15** shows, work in the tourist industry can be seasonal, with unemployment doubling or tripling in winter compared with summer.

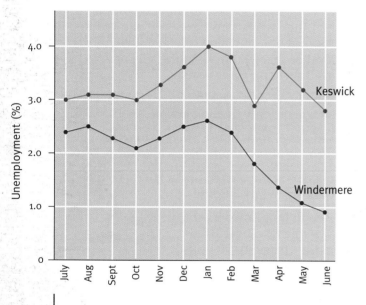

Figure 3.15 Unemployment rates

Characteristics of employment in the Lake District are:

- The work tends to be low paid. Waiters, maids, car park attendants, etc. do not need high levels of education and skill for their jobs.

- The nature of work has been changed by tourism. Shops in towns such as Ambleside which used to sell food, shoes or clothes for local people have now been replaced by gift shops and outdoor clothing shops, which cater for the needs of the tourists and are more profitable.

- The National Park is dominated by small businesses. 48 per cent are in the tourism sector and 80 per cent employ fewer than five people. There are many types of tourist activity and small businesses have sprung up to meet these needs.

There are many examples of conflicts between people concerned on the one hand about the environment and tourism which does not harm it, and on the other hand tourism which is seen to be harmful but which also employs many local people. An example is on the one hand the Lake District National Park Authority officers and wildlife conservationists who want a 10 kph speed limit for motor boats on Lake Windermere, and on the other hand the owners of water sports centres who will have to make people redundant if the speed limit is brought in.

Good vegetation cover, with roots binding soil particles together.

During trampling the soil compacts, reducing the infiltration rate of the rainfall and forming a shallow gully. Water will tend to run overland rather than soak into the soil, so washing away soil particles. Continued trampling and soil loss causes some vegetation to die away. There are now fewer roots to hold soil particles together, so that even more soil is washed away or blown by wind.

With further trampling all vegetation on the path dies. As soil particles are removed, a gully forms which acts as a channel for water running off the fell. This causes more soil to be washed away. Underlying rocks are now exposed.

The gully becomes deeper as water erodes yet more soil. As it becomes less pleasant to walk in the gully, people will trample the grass at the sides and so cause a further widening of the path.

Figure 3.16 Stages in footpath erosion

What is the impact of tourism on the landscape?

A National Park is an area where the public can enjoy the natural environment and yet, if there are too many tourists, they destroy what they have come to experience.

Footpath erosion is the most obvious result of too many tourists. The process is not simply too many feet wearing away the soil. It involves the interaction of walkers, plants, soil and rainwater and is summarised in **Figure 3.16**.

Footpath erosion is greatest:

- Where the slope is steeper than 10 degrees.

- At high altitudes, where there is a short growing season so plants cannot repair the damage done to them.

- Where the soil can be easily compacted and is relatively impermeable.

- Where there is a popular route to, for instance, a mountain top such as Helvellyn.

- At pedestrian exits from car parks.

- On popular routes for mountain bikers.

Solutions to try to keep the footpath as natural as possible are as follows:

- Reducing visitor numbers by limiting car parking or by using publicity to encourage people to use other paths which are less likely to suffer damage.

- Educating walkers and mountain bikers through leaflets and notices explaining how path erosion happens and asking them to keep to hard wearing routes.

- Resting routes by changing the line of the paths and fertilising and re-seeding the damaged ones. However, in the cold wet climate of the Lake District this can take a long time and simply moves the problem to the new path.

- Constructing hard wearing paths. On slopes of less than 15 degrees, loose gravel is used. It is cheap and looks fairly natural, but is eventually washed away. On steeper paths the surface is made from local stones and grass can grow between them to make it look more natural. Channels direct water off the path. Regular steps are avoided if possible as they do not look natural. However, these paths are slow and very expensive to build, and walkers do not always like the rough surface; they walk along the side, thus widening the path.

Many conflicts can be identified between tourists who want to use the environment in some way and people such as National Park wardens or **conservationists** who want to protect the environment. Some examples include:

- The rambler who wants to use the public footpath to the top of Helvellyn and the National Park officer whose duty is to reduce damage to the environment by footpath erosion.

- The motor boat owner who wants to drive fast on Lake Windermere and the National Park warden who wants to reduce the waves from boats which are damaging duck nests on the edge of the lake.

> ## EXAM TIP
>
> Students often find conflicts of interest difficult. Try to use the following guidelines:
>
> a   name two groups of people, e.g. farmers and ramblers; do not write simply 'people'
>
> b   write about the views or attitudes specific to each group, e.g. 'the farmer does not like ramblers because they drop litter which can kill his animals if they eat it' is a poor answer because only one attitude is given (the farmer's), and it is not specific to the group (it should be 'sheep' not animals')
>
> c   the attitudes of the two groups must be linked by 'but', 'whereas' or a similar word so that a proper comparison is made. Consider the answer 'The farmer does not like the ramblers because they drop litter which can kill his sheep. The rambler wants to drop litter because he does not want sticky toffee wrappers to make a mess in his pocket.' It is a statement of two attitudes, but it could be improved by comparing them. This could be done by joining the two sentences with 'but' or 'whereas', or by starting the second sentence with 'However, . . .' or 'On the other hand, . . .'

What are the problems of the 'honeypot' site at Tarn Hows?

A **honeypot site** is one where there is attractive scenery or historical interest, and tourists visit in large numbers. Tarn Hows is a beautiful place owned by the National Trust (**Figure 3.17**). It is 4 km from Coniston and 7 km from Ambleside in the central Lake District.

In the 1970s Tarn Hows had over half a million visitors each year. The tourists were attracted by the famous landscape, easy road access, car parking, and the opportunities to walk, picnic and play. Surveys show that they stay for over three hours on average. Many day trippers come from as far as Liverpool and Manchester, 150 km away, and some from the Midlands. Day trippers form 90 per cent of visitors early and late in the year. During summer 65 per cent of visitors are holiday-makers staying for several days in the National Park.

Tarn Hows shows not just the types of problems at honeypot sites, but also how they can change over time as solutions for one problem create other problems. As we change our attitudes to the environment, damage which was previously acceptable is later seen as a problem.

Access

By 1949 there was so much traffic congestion on the narrow twisty road to the tarn that the following steps were taken:

- Heavy traffic such as coaches were banned.

- Passing places were built on the road.

- The road was made one-way.

Figure 3.17 Tarn Hows

Figure 3.18 An eroded
path in the 1970s

Car parks
- In 1960 it was decided that two car parks were spoiling the view of the landscape so much that they were closed and three new ones were built in more hidden places.

- The paths from the car parks to the lake were down a steep slope. Severe erosion occurred (**Figure 3.18**).

- By 1986 the costs of maintaining the site were so great that the National Trust introduced car park charges. This is one reason for the reduction in visitors to 250 000 per year. It has reduced some of the pressure on the environment.

Footpaths
- In 1984 some severely eroded footpaths on steep slopes were covered with soil and re-seeded. They could not be maintained cheaply and were harming the landscape.

- The main badly eroded path around the lake has been improved by covering it with gravel to match the rocks of the area. It has also been widened to 2 or 3 metres because ramblers like to walk side by side, so a wider path prevents erosion of the edges. The wide paths and gentle slopes have also been designed to allow wheelchair use, which was previously impossible.

Other improvements
- In 1993 wooden benches were placed along the path. They were a departure from the policy of making the area look natural.

- A place has been made for an ice cream van so that it is not in the general view of the landscape.

- Litter bins have been removed from around the lake to encourage people to take their rubbish away. Some have been built next to the car park entrance and lids stop the wind blowing the rubbish away.

Figure 3.19 A Tarn Hows
path in November 2001

1 *Pages 36–39*

a Name the landforms labelled A, B and C in Figure 3.20.

b Name a Lake District example for each of these.

c On a copy of Figure 3.20 shade (colour) in and label:
   • The steep headwall
   • The rock lip
   • An area of scree/loose rocks

d The three processes which helped to form these features are listed below. Explain how each one works:
   • Frost shattering or freeze-thaw weathering.
   • Abrasion by the moving glacier.
   • Plucking by the moving ice.

e What is likely to be the main land use or human activity in the area covered by the sketch? Explain your answer.

2 *Pages 36–41*

a Name the different types of lake labelled A and B in Figure 3.21.

b With the help of a labelled diagram, explain the formation of one of the following landscape features:
   • Arête
   • Corrie (cirque/cwm)
   • Ribbon lake
   • Terminal moraine.

c Suggest two reasons why lake B is likely to receive more tourist visitors than lake A.

d Explain where and why glaciers deposit their load to form valley features, such as landform C in Figure 3.21.

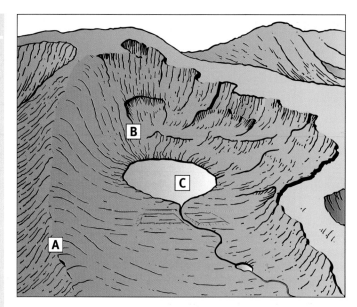

Figure 3.20 A field sketch of part of the Lake District

Figure 3.21 Some landforms produced by glaciation in the Lake District

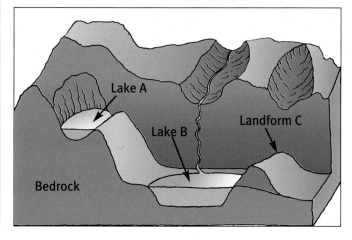

Figure 3.22 Conflicts of interest

Questions

3 *Pages 36–41*

Look at the Ordnance Survey map extract in Figure 3.1 on page 37.

a   What would you see at the following grid references (there might be several answers at one place):
  • 397168
  • 315170
  • 386170
  • 405132
  • 343139

b   What is the six figure grid reference of:
  • The public house in Glenridding (in the north east corner of the map)?
  • The telephone box near Hartsop (in the south east corner of the map)?
  • The hotel in Patterdale (north east corner)?
  • The summit of Helvellyn?
  • The summit of Fairfield (south centre of the map)?

c   What is the compass direction from:
  • Fairfield to Helvellyn?
  • Patterdale hotel to Helvellyn?

d   What is the compass direction of:
  • Glenridding from Helvellyn?
  • Glenridding from the telephone box at Hartsop?

e   What is the bearing from the summit of Fairfield to the Patterdale hotel?

f   What is the distance in a straight line between:
  • The summits of Fairfield and Helvellyn?
  • The public house in Glenridding and the Patterdale hotel?
  • What is the distance along footpaths or the main road between these points?

g   Draw a sketch of the Patterdale valley and on it:
  • Mark the route of the A592.
  • Add labels to describe the relief of the valley sides.

h   Draw a sketch of the area whose corners are 340150, 370150, 340130 and 370130, and on it:
  • Draw Grisedale Beck.
  • Add labels to describe the landforms created by glacial erosion.

4 *Pages 43–44*

Read the exam tip on page 47. Describe conflicts of interest between farmers and tourists over the issues of:
  • Traffic on the narrow roads in the Lake District.
  • The rights of tourists to walk across fields when sheep are giving birth to lambs.

5 *Pages 43–46*

a   State whom the conflicts of interest are between in Figure 3.22

b   Describe the conflicts of interest.

6 *Pages 47–49*

Study the data in Table 3.2.

Table 3.2 Changes in a footpath in the Lake District		
Date of Study	Measurements	Observations
September 1993	Greatest width 1.3m Average depth 0.1m	Mainly vegetation but with some bare soil.
September 1994	Greatest width 2.8m Average depth 0.25m	Mainly bare soil but some loose stones and rock showing through.
September 1995	Greatest width 3.9m Average depth 0.35m	Mainly stones and bare rock.

a   Describe one of the changes to this footpath between 1993 and 1995.

b   Explain where and why the change you have described is likely to have happened.

c   Study Figure 3.18
  • Describe the evidence on the photograph which suggests that this path at Tarn Hows suffered from visitor pressure in the 1970s.
  • Give reasons why the path was so heavily eroded at this point.

7 *Pages 42–49*

Explain how tourism affects each of the issues shown in Figure 3.23.

Figure 3.23 Issues in the National Parks

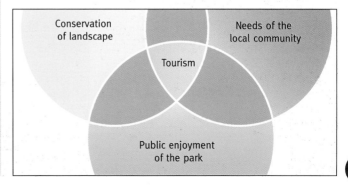

(4) Electricity generation for the future

Gas fired power stations in Britain

In 1999 gas fired power stations supplied 38 per cent of Britain's electricity.

- The majority are on the eastern side of the country, e.g. around the Humber estuary (**Figure 4.1**).

- In the west of the country there are a number of stations close to the Irish Sea and Morecambe Bay.

- There are four stations in the south east close to the London area.

- There is only one station in Scotland and very few in the industrial areas of northern and central England.

This locational pattern can be explained in the following ways:

- The gas power stations are found where there is easy access to the 90 gas fields found in the North Sea and Irish Sea.

- The south east stations supply the London area where there is a high demand from a large urban population and the extensive number of factories, shops and offices in the area.

- There are very few gas power stations in areas such as Scotland, as this is mainly supplied by coal and hydro-electric power stations. Similarly the Midlands is supplied by a large number of coal fired power stations.

Figure 4.2 Killingholme power station

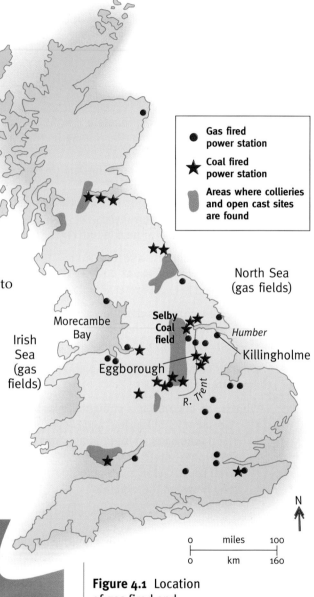

Gas fired power station

Coal fired power station

Areas where collieries and open cast sites are found

North Sea (gas fields)

Morecambe Bay

Selby Coal field

Humber

Killingholme

Irish Sea (gas fields)

Eggborough

R. Trent

N

| 0 | miles | 100 |
| 0 | km | 160 |

Figure 4.1 Location of gas fired and coal fired power stations in Britain

Killingholme gas fired power station, Humberside

The location of Killingholme is shown in **Figure 4.1**. It is situated 5 km from the town of Immingham close to the Humber estuary (**Figure 4.2**).

This location is suitable because:

- It is on the east coast close to the North Sea gas fields. The gas brought ashore at a number of terminals is fed by an underground pipeline to Killingholme.

- Cooling water and water needed to make the steam is removed from the nearby Humber estuary.

- The water used for cooling is released back to the nearby Humber estuary.

- The large, flat site provides sufficient space for the necessary buildings.

- It is an area of low population density and limited agricultural value. This meant the land was relatively cheap, and local opposition to the building and emissions of carbon dioxide, nitrogen oxides and steam was small.

At the power station potential environmental damage is reduced by:

- Thermal efficiency is constantly being improved so that less carbon dioxide (which contributes to **global warming**) is released (see Chapter 20). At present the power station converts fuel to electricity at an efficiency of 50 per cent and the amount of carbon dioxide produced is half the level emitted by a conventional coal fired power station.

- Special appliances are fitted to the gas turbines to reduce the release of the oxides of nitrogen which contribute to **acid rain** formation (see page 60).

- At present the cooling water is returned to the Humber at a slightly higher temperature than when it was extracted. This encourages eutrophication (see Chapter 2). However, a cooling water plant is being installed which will reduce this problem

- The power station has a 'good neighbour' policy, e.g. it recently helped to finance the restoration of a stone trough and village pump at the nearby village of East Halton.

Coal fired power stations in Britain

In 1999 coal fired power stations supplied 28 per cent of Britain's electricity.

- The majority are close to collieries and existing open cast coal mining sites, e.g. the large number close to the Selby coalfield (**Figure 4.1**).

- Many are close to a water supply, e.g. the large number along the River Trent.

- Many are near to major urban areas, e.g. around the West Midlands conurbation.

This locational pattern can be explained in the following ways:

- Coal is a bulky raw material so it is expensive to transport. By locating close to the mining areas the cost of moving the coal is reduced.

- By locating close to a river or the coast the water needed for cooling and steam production can easily be obtained.

- There is a high demand for electricity in urban areas for domestic and industrial use. Many of the large conurbations developed on the coalfields, encouraging the development of nearby coal fired electricity generating stations (see **Figure 6.19**, page 89).

Eggborough coal fired power station, Humberside

The location of Eggborough is shown on **Figures 4.1** and **4.3**. This location is suitable because:

- The power station (5724) is only 5 km from Kellingley coal mine (5223). There is a direct rail link from the mine to the generating station which reduces transport costs. Additional coal is available from other nearby mines on the Selby coalfield.

- Water for cooling is obtained from the River Aire which flows close to the power station.

- There is a high demand for electricity in the nearby urban and industrial areas of Yorkshire. Eggborough power station produces the equivalent of half the annual sales of the Yorkshire Electricity Board.

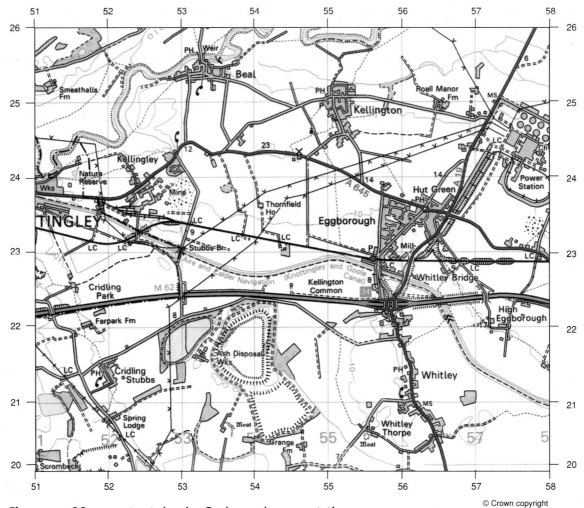

© Crown copyright

Figure 4.3 OS map extract showing Eggborough power station 1:50 000

- The power is moved by the **National Transmission Grid** (5625). The National Grid is the system of cables through which electricity is carried around the country on pylons or underground.

- The absence of contours (**Figure 4.3**) indicates that this is a large flat site of 154 ha which is suitable land for the power station to be built on.

- Waste can be disposed of locally. 8 km from the power station is the Gale Common ash disposal site (5321). Any remaining ash dust can be sent by pipeline to the lagoons where it is allowed to settle and is then used to create an artificial hill which has been restored, grassed, and is used for grazing livestock by a local farmer.

Eggborough power station attempts to reduce environmental damage by:

- Recycling the steam used to drive the turbines.

- Special appliances have been installed to reduce the amount of oxides of nitrogen emitted.

- Most of the ash produced by burning the coal is used to make building blocks and material used in concrete manufacture, or it is landscaped.

- The land around the power station has been landscaped and planted with trees.

Nuclear power stations in Britain

In 1999 nuclear power stations generated 24 per cent of Britain's electricity. As **Figure 4.5** shows, they are mainly located:

- In coastal locations.
- Where the geology provides firm foundations.
- Where the land is easily reclaimed.
- Away from major centres of population.

How can the locational pattern be explained?

- The coastal location means cooling water can be extracted from the sea and returned when it has been used.
- The firm foundations reduce the risk of earth movements damaging the reactor.
- Land can often easily be reclaimed which reduces costs.
- By locating away from major centres of population, the public perceives the risk of radioactive leaks or accidents to be less and so there is less opposition to the building of the power station.

Heysham nuclear power station, Lancashire

The location of Heysham is shown in **Figure 4.5**. This location is suitable because:

- The power station is on Morecambe Bay which means cooling water can easily be extracted and returned to the sea.
- The underlying rock is firm sandstone.
- The site was undeveloped and so was cheap.
- The only large settlement in the area is Morecambe so opposition was not very strong.
- The west coast rail route is close to the power station so uranium can be transported easily to Heysham and spent fuel rods transported to Sellafield (**Figure 4.5**) for storage or reprocessing.

At Heysham risks of radioactive material polluting the environment are reduced by:

- Monitoring discharges to ensure that they remain within authorised limits.
- Transporting used nuclear fuels in specially designed containers known as 'flasks' which are made of tough forged steel.

In a public demonstration organised in 1984, a 140 tonne locomotive travelling at 100 miles per hour was deliberately crashed into a full flask placed across a railway line (**Figure 4.4**). The locomotive was destroyed, but the flask received only minor damage.

Figure 4.4 1984 crash test of a 'flask'

Hydro-electric power stations in Britain

In 1999 **Hydro-electric power** (HEP) produced 0.01 per cent of Britain's electricity.

- HEP stations are mainly located in the north and west of the country (**Figure 4.5**). There are two in Wales and five in Scotland. There are none in England.

- They are in upland areas.

This locational pattern is explained by the fact that:

- The north and west upland areas where HEP stations are found nearly all receive over 1500 mm of rain per annum which provides sufficient water to generate electricity all year round.

- The upland areas provide the ideal physical conditions for water storage and power generation.

Cruachan hydro-electric power station

Cruachan is situated on the western side of Scotland in the Grampian mountains (**Figure 4.5**). The rainfall is over 2500 mm per annum and is evenly distributed throughout the year. This provides sufficient water to keep the reservoir at a high level throughout the year so there is always enough water to turn the turbines (**Figure 4.6**). At off-peak periods water can be pumped back up to the reservoir to guarantee a constant fuel source. With high cloud cover there is little water loss by evaporation.

- The **impermeable** slate rock in the area gives a high surface run off to fill the reservoir with water and means the water does not soak away through the rocks.

- A corrie on the side of Ben Cruachan provides a basin shaped hollow to act as the reservoir.

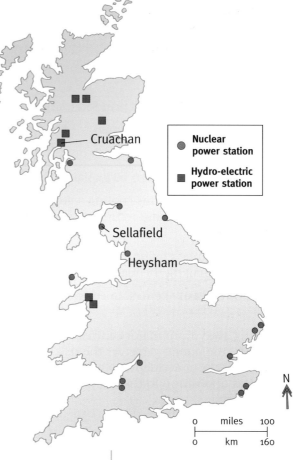

Figure 4.5 Location of nuclear power and HEP stations in Britain

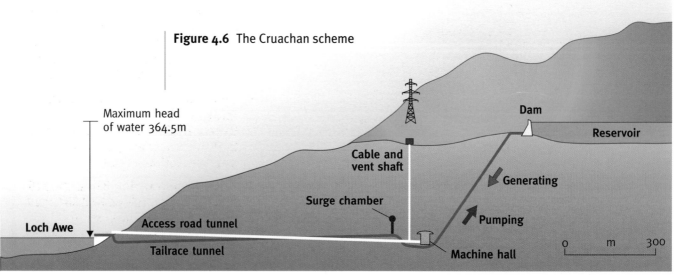

Figure 4.6 The Cruachan scheme

- The narrow exit to the corrie is dammed by a concrete barrage 316 metres long and 46 metres high.

- The steep sided U-shaped valley provides a height of 364.5 m to the machine hall (**Figure 4.6**). This supplies the energy to generate the electricity.

- The reservoir is built on an area of low cost moorland.

- The rock was excavated to house the turbines thus reducing the possible harmful visual effects on the area.

- Only 75 km away there is a high demand for electricity in Glasgow and a surface transmission line takes the electricity produced to this urban area.

Wind farms in Britain

In 1999 wind generation supplied approximately 0.02 per cent of Britain's electricity. Wind farms are located in the following areas:

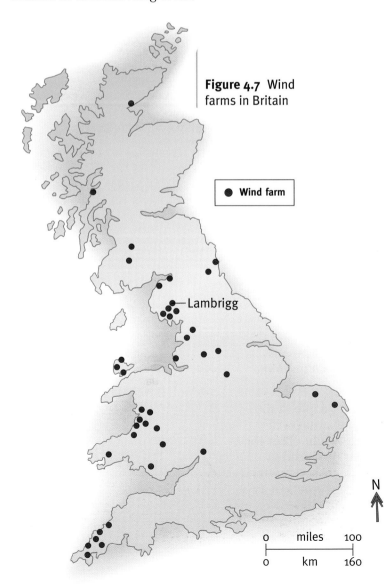

Figure 4.7 Wind farms in Britain

● **Wind farm**

Lambrigg

- The majority are in the west of the country (**Figure 4.7**).

- Most are in upland areas.

- There are no wind farms in the National Parks.

This locational pattern can be explained by the fact that:

- The wind speeds are higher in the west of the country because they have not been slowed down by blowing over the sea.

- In Britain there are more days when winds blow from the west than from any other direction, so there are more days in the west when the wind turbines can be operated.

- Higher up, wind speeds are faster and there are fewer obstacles to block the wind.

- They are not built where they would spoil the natural beauty of the National Parks.

Lambrigg wind farm in Cumbria

Lambrigg wind farm was built in 2000. It is in southern Cumbria on Lambrigg Fell (**Figure 4.8**). There are five turbines which generate 6.5 megawatts of electricity. This is enough power for 4000 homes.

The location of this wind farm has many advantages:

- It is on high land, 260 m above sea level, and near the top of a ridge so there are high wind speeds for much of the year.

- It is on the western side of Britain so it is directly in the path of the prevailing westerly winds.

- The land is moorland so the farmer can continue to graze his sheep on the moorland between the turbines whilst also receiving an annual rent from National Wind Power Limited.

- An existing electricity transmission line runs along the side of the site so there were few extra costs needed to feed the power generated at the site into the National Grid.

- It is next to junction 37 on the M6 motorway and the main A684 road. This meant that the costs of building access roads were very low. The roads were needed for the large lorries which transported the long turbine towers and blades.

Figure 4.8 Lambrigg wind farm

Often, gaining planning permission to build wind turbines is a major problem, but there were few objections to this particular site because:

- Although close to both the Lake District and Yorkshire Dales National Parks, Lambrigg is in a narrow strip between them so the ban on wind farms which exists in the National Parks to preserve the landscape did not apply here.

- The turbines are positioned just below the top of the ridge so that only some of the blades can be seen on the skyline.

- The turbines are on the eastern side of the ridge and so are hidden from almost all tourists and residents in southern Cumbria.

- The local population did not object on noise grounds because the nearest house is over 1 km away and any noise is drowned by traffic on the M6 motorway.

- National Wind Power Ltd. gained the support of most people in the local area through its publicity campaign about the advantages of wind power. It was emphasised that the five turbines would offset the release of 14 000 tonnes of carbon dioxide every year produced by burning fossil fuels. Also it developed a Good Neighbour Policy which will last for 20 years. The turbines are named after the winners in an art competition held in the local primary schools. Grants have been given locally; for example, the village hall received money towards new kitchen equipment.

Table 4.1 A comparison between different forms of electricity generation

ECONOMIC IMPACT				
FACTOR	GAS FIRED	COAL FIRED	NUCLEAR	HYDRO-ELECTRIC
Capital costs in relation to eventual production level	Moderate	Fairly high	High	Very high
Fuel costs	Moderate	Fairly high and rising as easily accessed coal resources are exhausted	Low because only small amounts are used	None
Total cost per unit of electricity produced	Cheapest	Moderate	Most expensive	Fairly expensive
Employment	Very few are employed at the power station but people are needed to extract the gas	High, if those mining coal are included	Fairly large number employed, often in areas where there are few other jobs	Once built, employment numbers are low

ENVIRONMENTAL IMPACT				
FACTOR	GAS FIRED	COAL FIRED	NUCLEAR	HYDRO-ELECTRIC
Renewable/non-renewable	Non-renewable	Non-renewable	Non-renewable but can be recycled	Renewable
Air pollution	1. Releases carbon dioxide which contributes to global warming but the amount is far less than coal 2. Releases nitrous oxides which contribute to acid rain	1. Releases carbon dioxide which contributes to global warming 2. Releases sulphur and nitrous oxides which contribute to acid rain	No carbon dioxide, sulphur or nitrous oxides are released	No air pollution
Water pollution	Warmed cooling water is returned to rivers which can increase eutrophication	Warmed cooling water is returned to rivers which can increase eutrophication	Some people would claim that the cooling water released back to the sea may be radioactive. Radioactivity can cause cancers and genetic deformities	No water pollution
Solid waste	No solid waste	Ash is produced which has to be disposed of	Nuclear waste is radioactive. At present it remains toxic for a long time so it has to be stored safely. People are concerned about potential leaks and accidents. Some fuel rods are reprocessed	No solid waste

Pollution from electricity generation

In a **thermal power station**, the fuel (gas, coal or oil) is burned to produce heat. The heat converts water to steam, which turns the turbines to make electricity. This is known as **electricity generation**. Burning these fossil fuels causes air pollution.

The main pollutants which cause acid rain are:

- **Sulphur dioxide** which is released from coal fired power stations.

- **Nitrous oxides** which are released from gas fired and coal fired power stations.

Some pollutants fall close to the power station as **dry deposition** but they combine with any moisture on the surface of buildings, trees, etc. to form an acid. Other particles combine with moisture in the air to form acid rain. This **wet deposition** can travel a long way from the power station (**Figure 4.9**).

The effects of acid rain are as follows:

- Acid rain in the soil destroys the roots of trees so they cannot absorb nutrients. They lose their leaves and die.

- Acid rain in rivers releases poisonous metals from the surrounding rocks so that plant life and fish are poisoned.

- Buildings are eroded by acid rain.

Figure 4.9 Acid rain

Oxidation in clouds (turns gases into acids)

Sulphuric acid and nitric acid

Prevailing wind

Sulphur dioxide and nitrogen oxide from power stations

Dry deposition (usually within a day and within 250 km of source)

Wet deposition (as acid rain, usually after several days and over 800 km from source)

Affects vegetation – kills trees

Affects water life – poisons fish and plants in rivers and lakes

Affects buildings, corrodes bricks and stones

Affects groundwater – may cause illness

Run off – acid water leaches aluminium from the soil into rivers

Why should alternative sources of power be developed?

1 **Non-renewable energy**, e.g. gas, coal and nuclear power, will become exhausted, but **renewable energy** can be used again and again.

2 Non-renewable resources are expensive to extract, whereas renewable resources are free.

3 Non-renewable resources, i.e. gas, coal and oil, release carbon dioxide which causes global warming. This is because they are **fossil fuels**, formed from decayed plant and animal matter millions of years ago. They also release sulphur dioxide, which creates acid rain.

4 The generation of nuclear power produces radioactive waste which is dangerous and difficult to dispose of.

5 The movement of non-renewable fuels from the point of extraction to the power station can cause damage, e.g. leakages from gas pipes. Renewable resources are not moved because the generating plant is at the source.

6 Many renewable resources are suitable for small scale developments to serve isolated communities which are not connected to the National Grid.

7 If Britain generates electricity from a variety of sources there are fewer problems if one fuel becomes exhausted or expensive.

EXAM TIP

For any type of electricity generating station you should be able to name groups who would be for or against its construction and to give reasons for their attitudes. See page 47 for help on how to write answers on conflicts of interest.

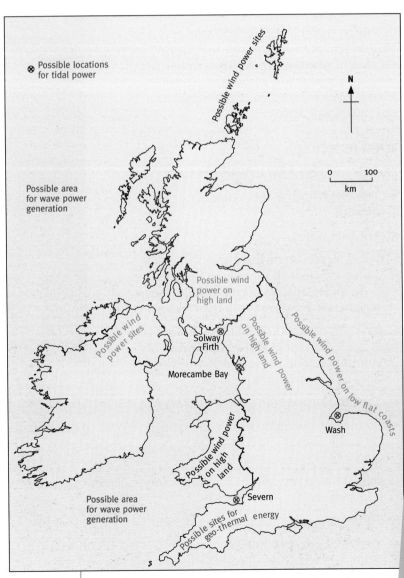

Figure 4.10 Sites of possible development of alternative power sources

Solar power

The advantages of solar power include:

- The fuel (the Sun) is renewable, i.e. it will not run out.

- The fuel is free.

- With no carbon dioxide released solar power does not cause global warming.

- With no sulphur dioxide released acid rain is not formed.

- Small systems to serve a local community or large systems to feed a national grid can be built.

The disadvantages of solar power include:

- The amount of radiation received varies according to the time of year and amount of cloud cover.

In winter, under cloudy conditions, it is low. This means that in a country such as Britain, the number of **photovoltaic devices** needed to produce a significant amount of electricity would cover a large area and it would be extremely expensive.

Wind power

The advantages of wind power include:

- The fuel (wind) is renewable, i.e. it will not run out.

- The fuel is free.

- Wind farms can be built on a variety of scales, e.g. a small number of turbines can serve an isolated local community, larger installations can feed into the National Grid.

- No carbon dioxide is released so wind power is not a cause of global warming and no sulphur dioxide is released so wind power does not contribute to acid rain.

- The land surrounding wind turbines can still be farmed.

- Producing electricity from wind costs 4p/kWh (1p more than gas, the same as coal and half the price of nuclear power).

- Britain has many suitable sites for wind farms and it is estimated that 10 to 20 per cent of British electricity demands could be met relatively easily.

The disadvantages of wind power include:

- The wind does not blow constantly so it is difficult to predict when and where wind power will be available.

- If the wind speed is too low the blades will not turn and electricity will not be generated.

Figure 4.11 Solar panels

- If the wind speed is too high the blades cannot turn or they will be damaged.

- The most suitable sites tend to be remote areas such as on hill tops or along exposed coasts. These areas are often unsuitable because:

  - They may be areas of outstanding beauty so people object on aesthetic grounds.

  - They are frequently far from centres of electricity demand.

  - Access roads may need to be built. These can be unsightly and add to the cost.

- A low frequency noise is emitted by the turbines which can be irritating for nearby residents.

- There is some evidence that birds can collide with the turbines.

- The turbines can interfere with telecommunications, particularly television reception.

- The cost of building the turbines (**capital cost**) is high per unit of electricity produced. 2400 turbines would be needed to produce 1 per cent of Britain's electricity. The largest wind farm in Britain produces in one year the amount of electricity produced in one day by a coal fired power station. 7000 turbines would be needed to replace one nuclear power station.

Figure 4.12 Opponents of wind power

Opponents of wind power

Welsh environmental campaigners yesterday branded wind farms a waste of money, with the millions of pounds in subsidies to wind power developers better spent on energy saving and cutting consumers' bills.

The Campaign for the Protection of Rural Wales has decided to oppose all new plans for wind power stations – after 17 of them have either been built already or are awaiting development.

In a change of policy, the organisation's general council urged the government to impose a moratorium on payments to wind power developers 'until substantial results have been achieved through conservation and energy saving matters'.

Speaking on the campaign's behalf, Dr Neil Caldwell, director of the Council for the Protection of Rural England, said: 'All people using electricity have to pay a surcharge on their bills which the government collects and hands over to multinational companies so that they can cover our beautiful Welsh hills with turbines that only produce a trickle of energy.

'If we really want to tackle global environmental problems in the British countryside, this money must be used instead to help cut energy consumption and everyone's electricity bills.'

Owners of wind power stations sell electricity into the National Grid for up to 11p per unit, of which about 8p is a government subsidy.

Wales, with its exposed hills and ridges, has been one of the most popular areas for wind farm schemes.

1

a   In 1999 Britain's electricity was generated in the following ways:
Gas 38%
Coal 28%
Nuclear 24%
Wind 0.02%
HEP 0.01%
Other 9.97%
Copy Figure 4.13, colour each section differently and complete a key, title and axes.

b   Name a source of electricity generation which could be in the 'other' section.

2

a   Study Figure 4.14. The areas marked with A have many electricity lines. Name areas A1, A2 and A3.

b   The areas marked with B have few electricity lines. Name areas B1, B2 and B3.

c   Choose one area marked A and one area marked B. Give reasons why the A area you have chosen has many electricity lines whilst the B area you have chosen has very few.

3 *Pages 52–53*

a   Figure 4.15 shows the location of Killingholme power station. Copy the map and complete the labels about its location using the information on page 52 to help you.

b   Copy and complete Table 4.2.

c   Suggest reasons for the pattern you found in b.

d   In 1990 very little electricity was produced from natural gas. It is the most important fuel source for electricity in 1999. Suggest three reasons why natural gas has grown in importance.

e   Killingholme power station is described as having a 'good neighbour policy'. What is meant by this and why does the power station see it as necessary?

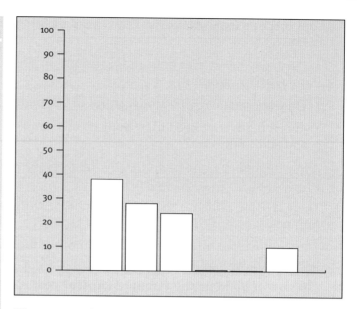

Figure 4.13 Electricity generation in 1999

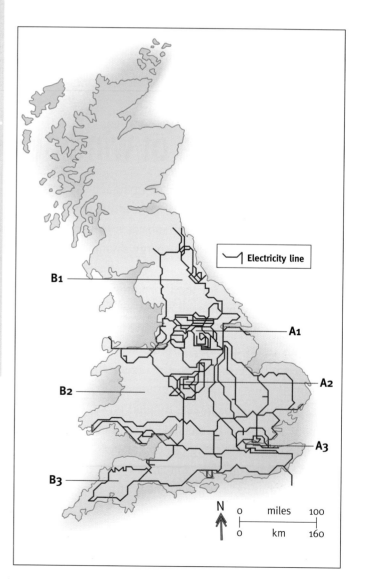

Figure 4.14
The National Electricity
Grid in England and Wales

Questions

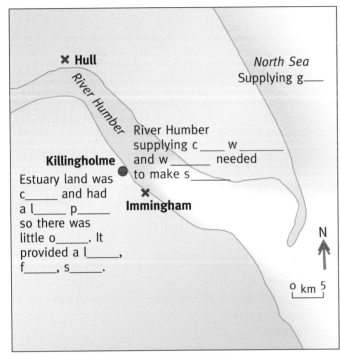

Figure 4.15 Location of Killingholme power station

Labels on map:
- ✕ Hull
- River Humber
- North Sea — Supplying g____
- River Humber supplying c____ w_____ and w_____ needed to make s____
- Killingholme — Estuary land was c_____ and had a l_____ p____ so there was little o_____. It provided a l_____, f_____, s_____.
- ✕ Immingham
- N
- 0 km 5

	Number of gas fired power stations
Eastern England	
Western England	
London area	
Scotland	
Other areas	
Total	

Table 4.2 Number of gas fired power stations in Britain

4 *Pages 52–54*

a Figure 4.3 shows the location of Eggborough coal fired power station. Draw a sketch map of the area and label in the correct place:
- Power station
- National grid transmission lines
- Coal mine
- Ash disposal site
- Railway line
- Ash lagoons
- River Aire
- Flat land.

b Using the labels from your map to help you, write a paragraph describing why Eggborough is a suitable location for a coal fired power station.

c Give three reasons why the local residents might be concerned at living so close to Eggborough power station and explain how the operator has tried to reduce their fears.

d Figure 4.1 shows the location of coal fired power stations along the River Trent. Give three reasons why there are so many coal fired stations in this area.

5 *Pages 57–59*

a Draw a sketch of Figure 4.8. Label it to show the main features and give reasons why Lambrigg was a suitable site for a wind farm.

b Give reasons why National Wind Power Ltd. may not have had the full support of the local population when the scheme was first proposed.

c Lambrigg and Sellafield Nuclear Power Station are both next to the Lake District. Why might people in the Lake District prefer the building of wind farms to the building of more nuclear power stations?

6 *Pages 59–63*

a   What is meant by a renewable energy source?

b   What is meant by a non-renewable energy source?

c   Divide the following fuel sources into renewable and non-renewable forms:
  • Gas
  • Coal
  • Nuclear
  • Hydro-electric
  • Solar
  • Wind.

d   At present wind power contributes 0.02 per cent of Britain's electricity generation, whereas gas and coal contribute 66 per cent. Why is wind power not developed more?

e   Copy and complete Table 4.3 comparing gas fired and solar power stations.

f   Draw a star diagram to show the reasons why Britain should develop alternative fuel sources.

7

Look at Figure 4.20.

a   Locate the power station at 763590.

b   How is electricity being generated here?

c   What is the evidence that this is an area of impermeable rock?

d   Why is it important that there is a natural lake in 7158?

e   What is the name of the feature running from 724591 to 763588?

f   Why is this feature needed?

g   Name some groups of people who might have objected to the building of the power station. Give reasons for their opposition.

Table 4.3
A comparison of gas fired and solar power stations

Factor	Gas fired	Solar
1. Non-renewable/ renewable		
2. Fuel cost		
3. Effect on global warming		
4. Effect on acid rain		
5. Cost		

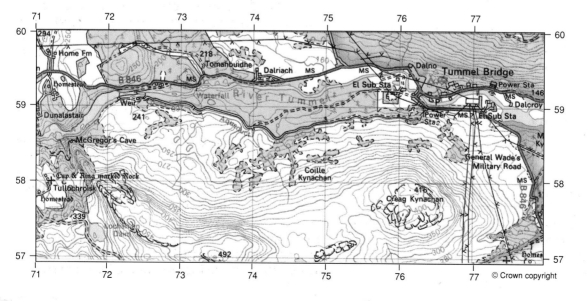

Figure 4.20
The location of a power station
1:50 000

© Crown copyright

5 The changing location of manufacturing industry

How can manufacturing industry be seen as a system?

Manufacturing is the making of a product. Manufacturing industry is also known as **secondary industry** and is shown as a system in **Figure 5.1**.

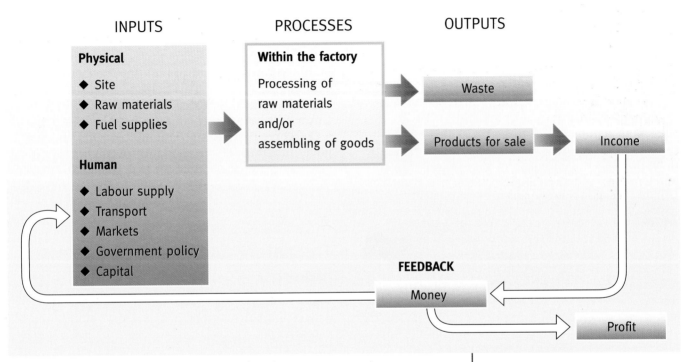

Figure 5.1 Manufacturing industry as a system

The inputs can affect the **location** of manufacturing industry in the following ways:

Site
Most factories require flat land since this is easier to build on. Depending on the type of transport used, the site should have access to road, rail or water links.

Raw materials
Raw materials are the items needed to make a product. If bulky and heavy raw materials are being used they are expensive to transport so the factory will be located near to them.

For example, if the cost of transporting raw materials to the factory is greater than the cost of transporting the product to the market, the factory will be located nearer the raw materials. This was especially important when transport was less developed and more expensive.

If a factory needs many different raw materials (e.g. during the assembly of a car) the location of the source of the raw materials (or **components**) is not very significant, but the factory has to be located at a point to which the components can be transported cheaply (e.g. a motorway junction).

Fuel supplies
Fuel is needed to power the processes in a factory, i.e. to work the machines. Early industry used fast-flowing streams and so had to be sited next to rivers. Later, coal was used. This is bulky and expensive to transport, so factories were built near the coal mines. Nowadays most factories are powered by electricity or gas. The National Grid (Chapter 4) means electrical power is widely available throughout Britain, and gas is distributed easily through pipelines. This means fuel sources have a much weaker effect on the location of modern industry,

particularly **footloose industries** such as electronics. (Footloose industries are those which have a relatively free choice of location since they are not tied to raw materials or fuel supplies).

Labour supply

Older industries tended to be **labour intensive**, i.e. they employed a large number of workers in relation to the volume of goods produced. Factories requiring a large labour force tend to be attracted to areas where there are potentially plenty of low-cost employees. Recently this has encouraged some firms to open new factories overseas. If a factory in Britain needs to employ large numbers of relatively unskilled labourers today, there is not a strong pull to any particular location since this type of worker is available throughout the country.

Newer industries are more likely to be **capital intensive**, i.e. they employ few people in relation to the number of products made. A large part of the investment expenditure is in machinery. However, the labour required is often highly skilled and therefore the factory needs to locate where this type of employee can be found, e.g. close to universities and in pleasant parts of Britain where these workers will want to live.

Transport

Bulky, non-perishable raw materials such as iron ore are cheaper to move by rail or water, so factories processing this type of raw material are located near railways or ports. A port location is particularly important where the raw material is imported in bulk and then broken down into smaller units, e.g. when crude oil is refined into different components. The port is known as a **break-of-bulk point**.

Road transport is used for industries needing smaller amounts of raw materials and components to make lighter finished goods. Motorway junctions become attractive locations for industries such as electronics, as lorries can easily supply the raw materials and distribute the product to the market, whilst highly skilled workers can be drawn from a wide area.

Markets

This is where the products are sold. For many modern industries, it is a very important pull and so they choose to locate close to urban areas where there are many people who can afford to buy their goods.

Government policy

The government tries to attract industries to particular areas by offering financial incentives, e.g. grants towards the cost of building the factories and training the workers. This helps to supply the **capital** – the money needed to start up a firm. In this way it hopes to encourage manufacturing in areas where there is high unemployment. Also the government invests in road improvements which can attract new development (e.g. the building of the M65 in Blackburn).

The nature and location of heavy industry

A **heavy industry** is one which uses bulky raw materials and usually manufactures a substantial volume of finished product. There could also be large amounts of waste.

Figure 5.2 The Merseyside chemical industry

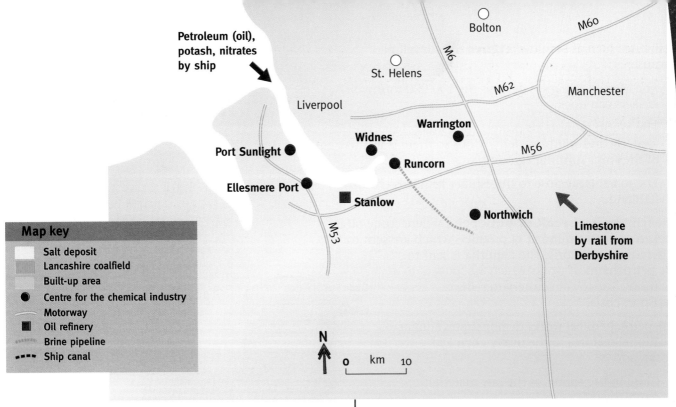

Figure 5.3 Location of the Merseyside chemical industry

The Merseyside chemical industry

This is a heavy industry because:

- Large quantities of a bulky raw material (salt) are used as an input.

- Large quantities of a bulky waste material are produced as an output (**Figure 5.2**).

The location of the Merseyside chemical industry (**Figure 5.3**) is affected by the fact that it is a heavy industry in the following ways:

- The raw materials, particularly salt, are bulky and heavy so transport costs are high. The finished product weighs less, so the transport costs for this are not so high. This means the industry is 'pulled' towards the raw materials so it is located within 25 km of the salt deposits of Cheshire. Originally the salt was moved by barge along the Weaver Canal, but it is now sent to towns like Runcorn via a pipeline. Limestone is moved by rail from Derbyshire, a distance of 50 km (**Figure 5.3**). By locating next to the Mersey estuary the large quantities of water required can be extracted easily. Ships from abroad can dock in the estuary bringing the other products needed, e.g. potash and nitrates.

- The large volumes of waste water can be returned to the River Mersey.

- Much inert bulky solid waste is used as landfill locally.

- Heavy industry requires a large, flat site because of the storage of the raw materials and the size of the factory. The estuary is bordered by former marshland which was relatively cheap and easy to reclaim because it was undeveloped.

- Heavy industry is not attractive to people living in the area because factories are large and unsightly. The chemical industry also gives off unpleasant fumes and presents a fire risk. This area was suitable because there are few houses close to the river. Local towns such as Runcorn and Widnes can supply a labour force.

By developing along the Mersey estuary the market for the products is close, and major motorways, e.g. the M56 (**Figure 5.3**), mean the goods can be transported by road from the chemical works. Destinations include:

- The textile industries of Lancashire which use soaps and detergents to wash the cloth.

- Soda ash is used in the glass industry at St. Helen's.

- Bleach is used in the paper industry at Bolton.

The Merseyside petrochemical industry

Although not as 'heavy' as the production of materials such as soda ash, the petrochemical industry shows similar locational factors. The system involved in oil refining is shown in **Figure 5.4**.

Refineries such as Stanlow (**Figure 5.5**) developed because:

- The Mersey estuary is deep so the 100 000 tonne oil tankers can dock.

- The Welsh mountains protect the estuary from the westerly and south-westerly winds so there is less risk of the ships running aground.

- The marshland close to the estuary provides cheap, flat land.

The refinery is a **break-of-bulk** point where crude oil is broken up into a number of products which are sent to different destinations. The naphtha is sent to the petrochemical works which are 'pulled' to a location close to the refinery to reduce transport costs.

The petrochemical works demonstrates similar locational features to the heavy chemical works, and is:

- Close to the source of the raw material, naphtha.

- Close to the river for cooling water and to dispose of waste water.

- On a large, flat site on cheap, reclaimed marshland.

- Away from residential areas because of its unsightly appearance and the potential risk of air pollution and fire.

- Close to motorways such as the M6 so that products such as plastics, dyes and paints can be distributed easily.

- Easily accessible by motorway for employees to travel from a wide area.

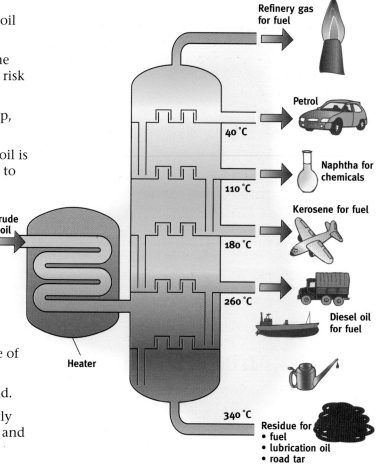

Figure 5.4 Oil refining

Figure 5.5 Stanlow refinery

The nature and location of footloose industry

Footloose industries are industries which use a large number of different components to produce a low weight, high value product. They are footloose because they can choose where to locate – neither the raw materials nor the power source exert a strong 'pull' as they are not bulky.

The sites chosen by footloose industries are usually **greenfield sites** since these are cheaper to develop, although some footloose firms locate on **brownfield sites**. A brownfield site is one which was previously built on, i.e. another factory or housing had been on the land and has since been demolished. A greenfield site is one which was previously fields or similar and has not been built on before.

> ## EXAM TIP
> 'Footloose' does NOT mean that the factory moves around.

Aztec West Business Park

Aztec West is a science/technology park located at the M4/M5 junction on the outskirts of Bristol (**Figure 5.6**).

It is typical of the sites chosen by high-tech, footloose industry. The characteristics are:

- A greenfield site on the edge of the city which reduces the cost of the land and its development.

- A variety of science and high-tech firms, some of which work together on products.

- Modern buildings with surrounding landscaped areas and plenty of car parking, which attracts highly skilled employees.

- Proximity to the M4 and M5 making access easy for lorries supplying components, for the markets and for employees.

- Local expertise from firms such as Rolls Royce and British Aerospace existed already, whilst nearby universities such as Bristol and Bath can supply research support and highly trained graduates.

- The proximity of the attractive Cotswold countryside and cultural facilities such as the Bristol Old Vic theatre are an added attraction for highly qualified employees.

Figure 5.6 Aztec West

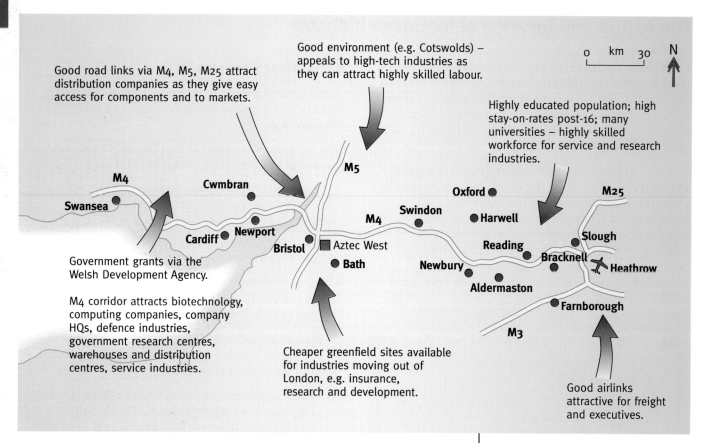

Good road links via M4, M5, M25 attract distribution companies as they give easy access for components and to markets.

Good environment (e.g. Cotswolds) – appeals to high-tech industries as they can attract highly skilled labour.

Highly educated population; high stay-on-rates post-16; many universities – highly skilled workforce for service and research industries.

Government grants via the Welsh Development Agency.

M4 corridor attracts biotechnology, computing companies, company HQs, defence industries, government research centres, warehouses and distribution centres, service industries.

Cheaper greenfield sites available for industries moving out of London, e.g. insurance, research and development.

Good airlinks attractive for freight and executives.

Figure 5.7 Map of M4 corridor

Sunrise Valley – the M4 corridor

The M4 corridor is the area of land on either side of the M4 motorway (**Figure 5.7**), particularly the section from London to Bristol. Sunrise Valley is an alternative name which is sometimes given to this region.

The following factors have attracted footloose industry to the M4 corridor:

- The M4 motorway is a fast, reliable road route by which components can be delivered to the factories and finished goods delivered to the market. Many firms use **just-in-time methods** to keep costs down. This means the factories order the components they require only a few days before they are needed. In this way they do not need large warehouses and capital is not 'tied up' in stockpiling. However, it is important to be located where road transport can access the firm quickly or production will be held up.

- Heathrow Airport is close to the motorway, so expensive high-tech products can be transported by air to anywhere in the world. Also, many of the footloose firms are **transnational corporations (TNCs)** who have their headquarters abroad but whose employees need to fly regularly between branches of the organisation.

In particular, Japanese and American firms (e.g. IBM, Hewlett Packard and Intel) have established plants along the M4 corridor so that they are within the EU. This means they do not need to pay tariffs (taxes) to bring products into the EU. Also, being located in Britain gives easy access to the large EU market of 300 million people.

- Other motorway links from the M4, e.g. M5, M40, M25, M3, provide fast road links to other manufacturing and urban areas (e.g. the Midlands) for easy access to components and to a large market for selling the products.

- Cheaper land sites are found along the M4 corridor compared to costs in London, but access to the large market of the capital city is easy and fast. The section west of Bristol into South Wales has been most attractive to TNCs since the Welsh Development Agency has provided government grants to assist new firms opening in the area. This is because the decline of coal mining and steel making in South Wales has created high unemployment and there is a need to attract new jobs.

- Many large government research laboratories e.g. Harwell and Aldermaston, are situated west of London to be near government ministries (**Figure 5.8**). They create new ideas for equipment so high tech firms locate near them so that they can design and make what the laboratories need.

Figure 5.8 Harwell/Aldermaston research laboratories

- Nearby universities e.g. Oxford, Bristol, Reading and London train very skilled people. Firms set up nearby to attract them. In addition, university researchers often set up their own firms.

- The attractive environment, e.g. Cotswolds and Chilterns (**Figure 5.9**), and the easy access to cultural centres e.g. Oxford, London and Bristol make this a pleasant area to live, so a highly skilled work force can be recruited.

- A labour force to assemble the products is available from the expanding towns and villages along the M4 corridor. People have moved out of London and they provide reliable employees who are flexible and willing to learn new skills.

Figure 5.9 The Cotswolds

EXAM TIP

For questions on the location of the manufacturing industry, you must learn detailed case studies. This should include names of towns, components, products, markets and transport links.

1 *Pages 67–69*

Copy Figure 5.10 and complete the missing words to show the factors affecting the location of manufacturing industry.

2 *Pages 67–69*

Write a short paragraph under each of the following headings giving reasons how these factors encouraged the development of the heavy chemical industry along the Mersey estuary.

- Site
- Raw materials
- Fuel
- Labour
- Transport
- Markets.

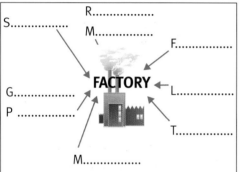

Figure 5.10
Inputs affecting the location of manufacturing industry

R.................
S.................
M.................
F.................
G.................
L.................
P ....
T.................
M.................

FACTORY

3 *Pages 68–71*

a Classify the following terms into those associated with traditional heavy industry and those associated with modern footloose industry:
  - Bulky/heavy raw materials
  - Often rail/water transport
  - Electricity power source
  - Light/small raw materials
  - Road transport
  - Often coal/oil power source
  - Small number medium/high skill workers
  - Large number medium/low skill workers
  - High weight product
  - Low weight, high value product
  - Large site for factory
  - Small site for factory.

b Look at Figure 5.11 and suggest reasons why firms such as IBM Computers are attracted to this location.

4 *Pages 72–73*

a Copy Figure 5.12 and label the following:
  - M4
  - M5
  - M25
  - London
  - Heathrow
  - Swindon
  - Harwell
  - Oxford
  - Cotswolds.

b Give five reasons why footloose firms might be attracted to Swindon rather than central London.

Figure 5.11
Footloose industry in Scotland

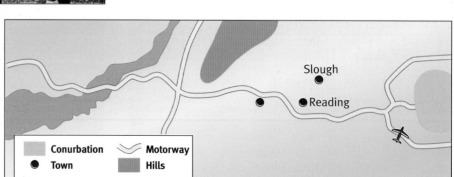

Figure 5.12
The M4 corridor

Slough
Reading

Conurbation
Town
Motorway
Hills

6 Understanding the modern urban environment

What are the characteristics and morphology of Blackburn?

Blackburn is a northern industrial town in Lancashire (**Figure 6.1**) which illustrates many of the features of the modern **urban** environment.

Its main development took place between 1800 and 1914 when the town rapidly expanded as textile mills were built. During this period many of the **characteristics** (present day features) and the **morphology** (shape) of the town were established.

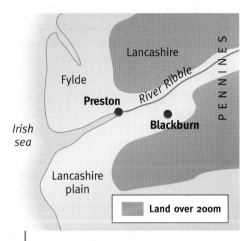

Figure 6.1 Location of Blackburn

Nineteenth century Blackburn

By the end of the nineteenth century Blackburn had very little open space. The railway and canal both followed the Blakewater valley running in a north east to south west direction through the town (**Figure 6.2**). Blackburn's industrial base was textile and engineering factories. They were located alongside the canal and railway so that coal, which was used as the power base, could be brought by rail from the mines between Blackburn and Burnley. Raw cotton for the textile industry came by canal barge from Liverpool, and steel was brought from steel works in Yorkshire. Industrial areas like Lower Audley developed with large, multi-storey brick and stone factories backing on to the Leeds and Liverpool Canal and leading out on to narrow streets.

Map key

- CBD
- Inner city 19th century low cost housing
- Higher cost 19th century housing
- 19th century industry
- .... Railway
- Canal

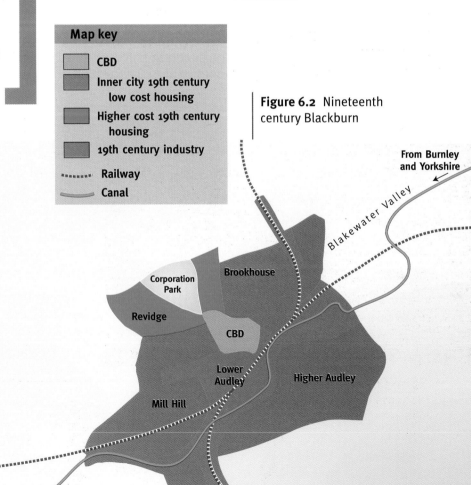

Figure 6.2 Nineteenth century Blackburn

In areas like Higher Audley and Brookhouse, terraced housing was built close to the factories so people could walk to work. Each house was small with a back yard and opening directly on to the street at the front (**Figure 6.3**). The housing was built in straight rows and the streets formed a gridiron pattern.

This working class housing formed almost a complete **ring** around the industrial areas. Today the area occupied by the nineteenth century factories and terraced housing is known as the **inner city**.

In 1827 Corporation Park opened on the north west side of the town. It was the first public park in Blackburn and formed a **sector** of open space, close to which houses occupied by wealthier residents, such as mill owners, were built. The houses were large with gardens, and built of red brick. By locating on higher land to the north west of the town they were above the air pollution which collected in the Blakewater valley. They were upwind of the smoke and close to the open space of the public park. These residents were able to live farther from the factories than their employees because they could afford carriages to travel to work. An example of this type of area is Revidge.

The **Central Business District (CBD)** occupied the centre of the town and consisted of public buildings, shops, offices and the railway station. It was the most accessible part of town and therefore the area most sought after. As a result there was competition for the land, so its value was high. Shops and offices were prepared to pay the increased costs to locate centrally because it was important for their customers to be able to reach them. Other functions such as industry were not prepared to pay the price demanded, and so they located slightly out of the town centre.

Figure 6.3 Terraced housing

Figure 6.4 Map of twentieth century Blackburn

Map key
- Motorway
- Main road
- Railway
- Canal

Map key
- CBD - shops and offices
- inner city 19th century low cost housing
- 1930s council housing
- modern council housing
- modern council housing (redevelopment)
- higher cost 19th century housing
- 1930s private housing
- modern high cost private housing
- 19th century industry
- modern industrial estates and out-of-town shopping areas
- ● Notre Dame Gardens
- Ⓜ Morrison's

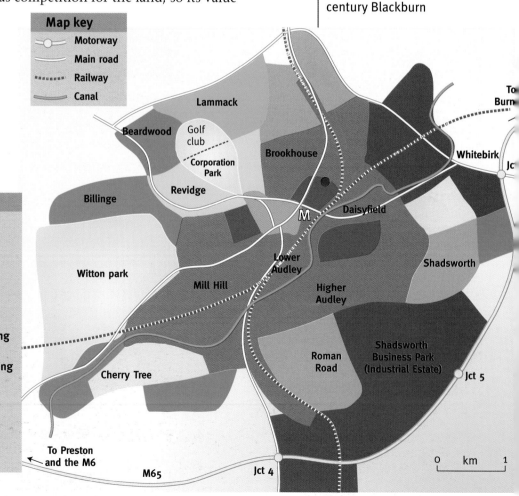

Twentieth century Blackburn

Figure 6.4 shows Blackburn in the twentieth century. Its features and morphology have changed. The rows of terraced housing are still there, but new types of housing were developed in the twentieth century.

1930s private housing (Figure 6.5)

These three-bedroomed semi-detached houses with gardens were built for private purchase. They are near Corporation Park in the north west of the town and form a sector of higher class housing in this area, which is known as Lammack. The housing is lower density than the nineteenth century development because people could afford more land and the road pattern contains crescents and cul-de-sacs, rather than a gridiron pattern. These houses were built on open land at the edge of the existing urban area. The development of bus transport and a suburban tram system meant that people could live further from the town centre and their work.

1930s council housing

These houses were built for people who could not afford to purchase homes (**Figure 6.6**). Areas such as the Cherry Tree estate (see **Figure 6.4**) developed in the south west of Blackburn, adjacent to the nineteenth century terraced housing. This resulted in a working class residential sector developing in this area.

The 1930s private and council housing areas are known as the **inner suburbs** and form an incomplete ring around the nineteenth century areas of Blackburn.

Figure 6.5 1930s private housing

Figure 6.6 1930s council housing

1960s–2000 private housing (Figure 6.7b)

This housing occupies areas like Billinge and Beardwood on the north west edge of Blackburn (see **Figure 6.4**). Its development extended the sector of higher class housing leading out from the CBD towards this side of the town. The housing is a mixture of semi-detached and detached houses and bungalows. Most properties have gardens and garages since the occupants own cars, which allow them to travel further to work and to the town centre. The road pattern is irregular, with words like 'Drive' and 'Close' appearing in the names. There are many cul-de-sacs and open spaces.

1960s–1980s council housing

Large council estates were built at the edge of the town in areas like Roman Road and Shadsworth (see **Figure 6.4**). These were built to house those people who rented property. They were needed partly to house the growing population of Blackburn, but also to accommodate some of the residents of the nineteenth century terraced housing areas. The housing in some of these areas was being cleared because it was old and too expensive to repair. Most of the new council estates were built adjacent to the nineteenth century working class areas. These council houses were an improvement on the terraced properties because they were larger, had gardens, inside toilets and bathrooms (**Figure 6.7a**). However, they were a long way from jobs and the town centre. Also many of the residents rehoused because of inner city clearance schemes were separated from neighbours and relatives so there was a loss of community spirit.

The housing developments which have taken place from 1960 onwards form a ring around the previously existing urban area. These newer residential areas form the **outer suburbs**.

> ## EXAM TIP
>
> Be able to recognise the different ages of the town from both photographs and street patterns on OS maps. See exercise 2 page 90.

Figure 6.7 a) Modern council housing b) modern private housing

To what extent does the morphology of Blackburn resemble the theoretical models?

A **model** is a theoretical pattern which can be used to help explain reality.

In the **Burgess model** the centre of the town is occupied by the CBD and there is a series of **concentric rings** around it. Moving out from the centre the housing age becomes newer and the occupants become wealthier.

Blackburn shows some of the Burgess pattern in that:

- The CBD occupies the centre.

- Housing is newer as you move outwards e.g. Shadsworth is newer than Brookhouse.

- Houses become more expensive as you move outwards, e.g. houses in Beardwood cost more than in Brookhouse.

However, there are some exceptions to this pattern, e.g. the Roman Road council estate on the southern outskirts of Blackburn is a poorer area, whilst Notre Dame Gardens is an area of more expensive housing found in the Brookhouse nineteenth century residential zone (**Figure 6.4**).

In the **Hoyt model** the CBD is also found in the centre. The remaining functions form **sectors** or wedges. This is because some functions are attracted to certain features, e.g. transport routes, whilst others are repelled, e.g. higher class residential areas do not want to be alongside industry.

In Blackburn the structure resembles the Hoyt pattern in that:

- The CBD occupies the centre.

- The nineteenth century industry and low class housing form a sector following the railway and canal (**Figure 6.2**), e.g. Lower Audley and Mill Hill.

- The cheaper housing of all ages forms sectors to the south west, south east and north east of the town (**Figure 6.4**) e.g. Mill Hill.

- The higher class housing forms a sector to the north west of the town (**Figure 6.4**) e.g. Beardwood.

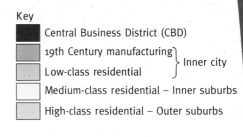

Key

Central Business District (CBD)

19th Century manufacturing } Inner city
Low-class residential

Medium-class residential – Inner suburbs

High-class residential – Outer suburbs

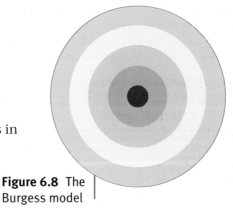

Figure 6.8 The Burgess model

Key

Central Business District (CBD)

19th century manufacturing } Inner city
Low-class residential

Medium-class residential – Inner suburbs

High-class residential – Outer suburbs

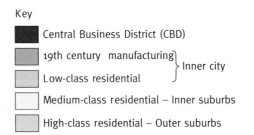

Figure 6.9 The Hoyt model

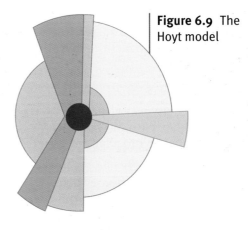

> ## EXAM TIP
> You are unlikely to be asked about individual models, but should be able to apply the models to your individual town.

Inner city decline in Blackburn

Causes

1 The closure of the mills and engineering works in areas such as Lower Audley.

These factories closed because:

- They were old with out-of-date machinery, so production costs were high.

- There was competition from new products, particularly from goods being made in cheaper labour cost locations overseas, e.g. India.

- The factories were on congested sites with no room to expand.

- The Leeds and Liverpool Canal and the railway are no longer used for transport. Instead articulated lorries are used, but the inner city roads are too narrow.

Today industrialists want single storey buildings with access to major roads, so they choose motorway junction sites on the edge of town, e.g. Shadsworth Business Park next to the M65 (**Figure 6.4**).

2 The low quality housing.

- Many of the nineteenth century houses in areas like Brookhouse had fallen into disrepair, with broken gutters, crumbling brick and decayed pointing.

- Many of the terraced houses lacked basic facilities, e.g. no bathroom, inside toilet or hot water.

- The houses were small two-up, two-down, with no garages for cars or gardens for children to play in.

3 An unattractive environment.

- The inner city was visually unattractive, with old buildings (**Figure 6.10**) and a lack of green open space.

- In areas like Brookhouse there was serious air pollution from the factories which remained open.

Effects

1 Economic: There were high unemployment levels in areas like Lower Audley, particularly amongst the textile and engineering workers. With reduced incomes people no longer supported the shops and pubs, so these closed also. Residents could not afford to maintain their houses so these fell into disrepair.

2 Social: People with skills which could be employed elsewhere moved out of the inner city leaving behind low income groups, e.g. the elderly, single parents with young children, and the long term unemployed. In areas like Brookhouse immigrants moved into the terraced property and there have been instances of racial tension.

3 Environmental: As people left the inner city and factories closed, decline continued with many properties becoming derelict. The housing became damp, resulting in high levels of illnesses such as asthma, and the lack of job opportunities gave rise to depression. The canal became overgrown and rubbish was dumped into it. Vandalism and graffiti were common.

How have the inner city areas of Blackburn been renewed?

During the 1960s large areas of the terraced housing were pulled down in a **slum clearance** programme. Many people moved out to council estates such as Roman Road and Shadsworth. Other residents were rehoused in tower blocks. The flats had the advantage of modern facilities such as central heating, but the lifts were often broken, many of the flats were damp, and families with young children felt 'trapped'. **Comprehensive redevelopment** was carried out in other cities and involved the building of new housing and industry, together with roads and environmental improvement.

Figure 6.10 Old factories

Since the mid 1970s schemes to renew the inner city have had three elements:

1 Economically there have been attempts to improve job opportunities:

- In areas like Brookhouse small industrial units have been built with an attractive environmental layout, car parks and good road access.

- In areas such as Lower Audley some of the old mills have been converted into small, cheap industrial units (**Figure 6.11**).

Figure 6.11 A converted cotton mill containing smaller units

2 Social changes have been made by improving housing:

- People living in terraced housing in Brookhouse have received grants to improve their homes, e.g. to cover the cost of installing bathrooms, inside toilets and hot water, or to re-roof and install roof insulation and damp proof courses in walls. This is known as **housing renovation**.

- Where terraced property was too poor to upgrade, it was demolished and modern, low-cost housing has been built.

- In an attempt to attract higher income groups back into the inner city, private developers have been encouraged to build more expensive housing close to the town centre, e.g. Notre Dame Gardens in Brookhouse.

3 The environment has been improved in Brookhouse in the following ways:

- The terraced streets have been made safer and more attractive by making them one-way, providing parking bays and planting trees.

- Housing has been cleared to create open spaces, some of which have been grassed over, whilst others have been converted into play areas with secure fencing around them.

How successful has the renewal programme been?

Achievements

- Some jobs have been created.

- With an improved environment and modernised housing, fewer people are leaving the inner city.

- House prices have risen so people who own their homes feel more secure.

- With renewal rather than demolition, communities, relatives and neighbours are kept together.

- With some higher income groups moving into the area the population is more balanced.

Limitations

- Many of the jobs created require higher skills than those possessed by the inner city residents, so people who live in the outer city areas commute in to take the work.

- Social segregation exists; Brookhouse is dominated by Asians, whilst low income white families are concentrated in Mill Hill. The private development at Notre Dame Gardens in Brookhouse has a high wall around the estate and there is only one entrance. This separates it from the surrounding terraced housing.

The rural-urban fringe

The **rural-urban fringe** is where the edge of the built-up area of the town meets the surrounding countryside.

Communications: The M65 has been built to the south of Blackburn. It links to the M6 close to Preston and has made Blackburn more accessible from the British motorway network.

Industrial development: There are several new industrial developments on the edge of Blackburn. The factories tend to be single-storey and located on landscaped estates which have easy access to the motorway.

Figure 6.12 The M65 and Walker Industrial Park

For the factories on Walker Industrial Park (**Figure 6.12**) the advantages of this location are:

- Easy access from junction 5 of the M65 for lorries bringing raw materials and those taking finished goods elsewhere in Britain.

- The relatively flat, undeveloped land allows the building of large, single-storey premises, with loading bay areas for lorries and car parking for employees.

- The close proximity of the M65 makes it easy for employees to travel to work, either from other parts of Blackburn or from further afield.

Retail development: Retail parks, such as Peel Retail Park at junction six at Whitebirk (**Figure 6.4**), have also developed close to motorway junctions on the outskirts of Blackburn. They can be easily reached from many of the residential areas. The type of stores found are those selling do-it-yourself (DIY)

equipment, electrical goods, carpets and computer goods. The advantages of such locations are:

- Large, undeveloped areas are suitable for building the big single-storey showrooms with space for warehousing, delivery bays for lorries and plenty of car parking for customers.

- The short distance from the M65 motorway makes it easy for firms to make regular deliveries, limiting the amount of stock which has to be held at the store.

- There is easy access to the residential areas of Blackburn and via the M65 to other towns, e.g. Accrington, to give a large catchment area for customers.

- Being close to residential areas such as Shadsworth it is easy to recruit staff, many of whom work on a shift basis.

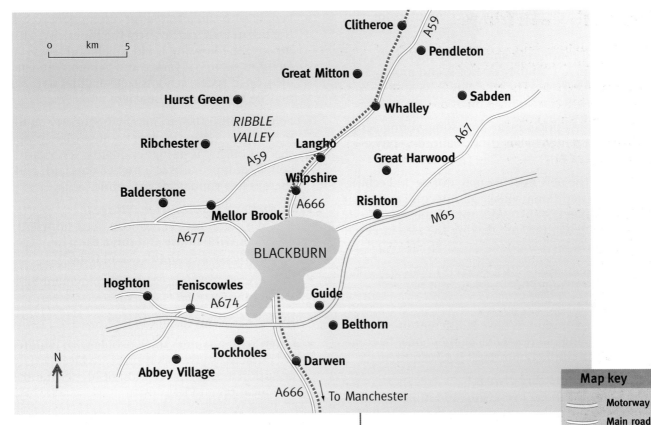

Map key

══════	Motorway
──────	Main road
‧‧‧‧‧‧‧‧	Railway

Figure 6.13 Location of commuter villages around Blackburn

Open space: **Figure 6.4** shows Witton Country Park in the west of the town and Blackburn Golf Course in the north, providing recreational areas in the rural-urban fringe. Many people prefer to see this type of development on the edge of towns rather than the expansion of urban functions such as housing, industry and retailing.

Suburbanisation is the continued expansion of residential areas such as Beardwood on the rural-urban fringe. Developments tend to be private, and whilst the housing is high quality the estates often lack services such as shops. Rather than live in one of these areas many people prefer to live in **commuter villages**.

Counterurbanisation and commuter villages

Counterurbanisation is the movement out of urban areas into a more rural environment. The growth of commuter villages is due to counterurbanisation. A **commuter** is a person who lives in one settlement and travels every day to work in another. A commuter village is where a high proportion of the residents are commuters.

Whalley is a typical commuter village (**Figures 6.13 and 6.14**). It is attractive to people working in Blackburn but wanting to live outside the urban area because:

- The A666 provides a fast route into Blackburn, which takes only 20 minutes.

- Whalley is situated in the Ribble Valley, which is scenically attractive.

- The village has many traditional features, e.g. an abbey, old residential property, small shops and public houses.

- There are essential services, e.g. doctors' surgery, supermarket and schools.

- Local schools with a good reputation provide education at a high standard.

Commuters have benefited Whalley in the following ways:

- They have brought money into the area and helped services such as public houses to survive.

- Their children attend the local schools so they have remained open.

- They participate in local social activities e.g. the Golf Club, so helping to maintain a community spirit.

- They have bought old property and improved it, making the area look better and providing local jobs.

- For people wishing to sell, house prices in Whalley have risen, giving local people a higher return.

There are some disadvantages of commuters for Whalley:

- Often the commuters shop where they work, e.g. Blackburn, and so they do not spend money in local butchers, bakers, etc., which have now closed.

- Rising house prices mean that some young people brought up in Whalley cannot afford to buy a house locally.

- Some of the new housing may not be 'in keeping' with the traditional village architecture and is built on open countryside around the village, destroying habitats and making the area more urbanised.

- There is increased traffic, often on narrow roads. This causes congestion, and air and noise pollution.

- Often the commuters have a different lifestyle from the original residents, so there may be some friction or conflict of interest between them.

Why has commuting grown?

- The increase in car ownership and improvements in roads and rail transport make it easier to live in one place and work in another. Commuters can now drive to Manchester along the M66. Whalley railway station has been reopened and trains take only 45 minutes to reach Manchester.

- The growth in the use of information technology (IT) means that more people do not have to travel into work each day but can do some of their work at home. This means they can live further from the office, travelling in on only a few days a week.

- With more offices and factories locating in the rural-urban fringe it is easy to live away from the main urban centres and travel to work.

- People who can afford a car often prefer to leave the urban area, particularly the inner city. This is because the housing is old, small and lacks facilities such as a garage and garden. There is little open space, schools lack facilities and crime may be higher than elsewhere.

- People with sufficient money frequently choose to live in a commuter area because there is open space, housing is of higher quality, schools are better equipped and of a higher standard, and there is less vandalism and crime.

Who moves to commuter villages?

To live in a commuter village you need sufficient money to buy the house and run a car. The characteristics of a commuter tend to be:

- A person in full-time, secure employment with a reasonable income.

- In the 25–50 age group.

- Often with a family, since people with children are attracted to the open space, reduced air pollution and the perception of higher standards of education and less crime.

What are the disadvantages of being a commuter?

- The high cost of running the car or purchasing a rail season ticket.

- The delays experienced due to traffic jams or an inadequate rail service.

- For someone used to urban life they may dislike the lack of leisure facilities in the village, e.g. cinemas, night clubs.

Recently, some professional people and their families have been returning to live close to the city centre. They buy older, substandard housing, and improve it so it is worth more. This is called '**gentrification**', but it is not yet happening in Blackburn.

Figure 6.14 Whalley, a commuter village

The location of the retail trade in Blackburn

Traditionally shops were found in four main locations:

1 **Corner shops** were found in the nineteenth century terraced housing areas. These were small, family-owned businesses which sold a wide range of **low-order convenience goods**, e.g. milk, bread, vegetables. Local residents walked to these shops, often visiting them on a daily basis.

2 **Shopping parades** were found in the suburban housing areas. They included some shops selling low-order convenience goods, e.g. small grocers, newsagents and shops providing a service, e.g. hairdressers. Again local residents used these shops on a daily basis, often walking to them.

3 **City centre** areas such as Blackburn are **high-order** shopping centres to which people travel by public transport or car to purchase goods such as clothes and electrical goods. Customers come from all over Blackburn or even further, probably visiting the centre once a week or less. This area is part of the CBD.

4 Whalley New Road, Blackburn, is typical of the type of shops found along the main roads leading out of city centres. They are low-order, e.g. newsagents, and serve a passing trade where drivers park their cars immediately outside the shop and make a rapid purchase.

How has the location of the retail trade changed?

The majority of low-order goods, particularly food, are now bought at supermarkets. There are two main locations for these stores:

- On cleared land at the edge of the CBD. This is where Morrisons in Blackburn is located (**Figures 6.4 and 6.15**). It was an area known as the **twilight zone** and consisted of nineteenth century factories and terraced housing which were demolished. This provided a suitable site which had a large area of flat land on which to build a single-storey shop and car park. It is next to the bus station so the shoppers can use public transport, and it is close to densely populated areas such as Higher Audley which provide a large customer base.

- On land at the edge of the urban area. Many higher-order stores, e.g. electrical firms, have relocated out of the city centre in retail parks at the edge of the urban area. An example of this is Peel Retail Park at Whitebirk in Blackburn.

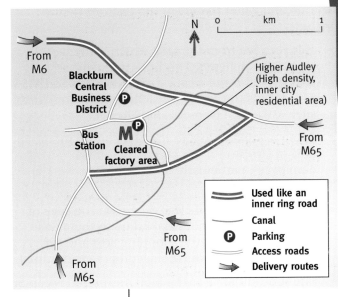

Figure 6.15 Location of Morrisons

These retail parks are known as out-of-town shopping centres because they are not within the built-up area of the city.

Regional centres such as the Trafford Centre in Manchester have developed (**Figure 6.16**). These serve a wide area, and people from Blackburn can travel to this centre in less than an hour.

The Trafford Centre, Manchester

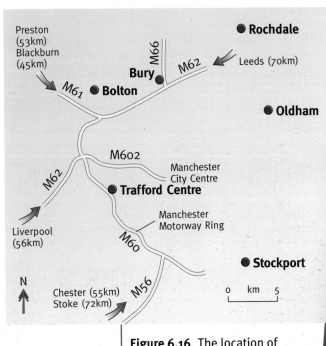

Figure 6.16 The location of the Trafford Centre

The advantages of the site of the Trafford Centre include:

- It is accessed from the M60 which is the motorway ringing Manchester. This links to the other motorways in the area, e.g. the M62, M6 and M56. This means the centre is reached easily from areas such as Leeds, Liverpool and Chester.

- Being relatively close to the Manchester suburban area of Urmston it has been easy to find employees, particularly those willing to work a shift system.

- It was a large area of cleared land on the edge of the Trafford Park Industrial Estate so there was sufficient space for the shopping area and car parking whilst planning objections were minimal.

- The short distance to the M60 means goods can be delivered quickly from the warehouses, many of which are located along the M6 and M62.

The Trafford Centre provides the following incentives to attract shoppers:

- Free parking, with special facilities for the disabled and its own bus station.

- Over 280 shops and 32 cafés. This includes a large number of national chain stores selling middle and high order goods.

- A 'market' feel is created, and throughout the complex there are street barrows selling a variety of goods.

- A crèche is available.

- The cafés stay open late and there is a cinema.

- The wide, tree-lined, air-conditioned malls provide a pleasant shopping environment.

- The complex stays open late and is open on Sundays to provide for people wishing to shop outside normal hours.

Why have these changes in retail location occurred?

1 The *expansion of car ownership*. This means that:

- People can buy in bulk and so are attracted to supermarkets.

- Customers need to be able to park the car close to the shopping outlet so stores are attracted to areas where there is enough cheap land available to build a large car park, e.g. the rural–urban fringe.

- Customers want to drive quickly to the stores, so favoured sites are near motorway junctions at the edge of residential areas.

Figure 6.17 A corner shop

2 *A change in lifestyle.* This means that:

- Working people want to purchase the food for a week under one roof. This attracts them to the supermarket.

- People want to shop at weekends and in the evenings so they visit stores and centres which are open at these times.

- Shopping is seen as a 'leisure' activity so centres which combine purchasing, cafés and entertainment are popular.

3 Retailers want to encourage custom whilst keeping costs low so they are attracted to:

- Out-of-town locations where land is cheaper and does not need to be cleared.

- Motorway junctions where customers can be attracted from a wider area than the immediate housing.

How have these changes affected the traditional retailing pattern?

- Many corner shops have closed because their customers now go to the supermarkets. Those that remain often open much longer hours ('8 till Late'), have joined **co-operatives** like Spar to reduce their overheads, and act as off-licences, video shops, or newsagents (see **Figure 6.17**).

- In many shopping parades outlets like bakers and grocers have closed or have changed their format in the same way as the corner shops.

- Many high streets and city centres have been affected badly by the development of out-of-town shopping areas. Retail outlets have closed, particularly on the fringe of the CBD as customers found it more convenient to travel by car to the edge of the urban area. Some city centres like Blackburn have begun to 'fight back', attracting customers by creating under-cover shopping centres with trees and cafes, pedestrianising main shopping streets, reducing parking fees for shoppers and encouraging late-night and Sunday opening. This attempt to attract shoppers back to the city centres is being helped by recent government restrictions on any further regional shopping centres.

- The line of shops on roads leading out of the city centre still exists. However, many takeaways, hoping for passing trade, are found now alongside the more traditional shops such as newsagents.

The effect of road transport on urban structure

- With the increased use of private cars and road transport for industry, Blackburn has expanded into the rural-urban fringe with the development of housing at Beardwood, industry at Walker Park and retail estates at Whitebirk.

- To enable vehicles to avoid the town centre and to reach these new developments an outer ring road and the M65 have been built.

- Motorway junctions 4, 5 and 6 on the outskirts of the town have become important areas for industrial and retail development, since they provide access for vehicles from a number of directions.

- The attraction of the rural-urban fringe due to the increased use of road transport has speeded the decline of city centre retailing and inner city industry and housing. This has led to redevelopment in the CBD and renewal in the inner city areas, such as Brookhouse and Audley.

- To improve road access in the centre of Blackburn an inner ring road is being built. This involves further demolition of town centre buildings. Whilst waiting for this development to take place, areas adjacent to it become 'blighted', so adding to the unattractive appearance of parts of the town centre.

- To encourage people to remain working and shopping in the town centre, large areas of land on the edge of the CBD have been converted into car parks. Much of this land was occupied previously by nineteenth century housing and industry.

How has the increased use of road transport affected the environment?

- Air pollution occurs at major road junctions, particularly during rush-hour (**Figure 6.18**). Locally pollutants can collect in the atmosphere to cause allergies and breathing difficulties. Under high pressure weather conditions the risk of **smog** can be increased, particularly as Blackburn is situated in a valley bottom. Globally, vehicle pollutants are a cause of acid rain and add to the 'greenhouse effect' (see Chapter 20).

- Noise pollution occurs along the major routeways into the town from the high number of cars, lorries and buses.

- Habitats are destroyed to build motorways.
- Car parks can detract from the appearance of city centres, whilst motorways can scar the countryside around an urban area.

How can the problems of traffic in towns be solved?

1 Reducing the amount of traffic entering the urban area. With less traffic in the city congestion and air pollution will be reduced. Schemes to achieve this include:

- Traffic-free zones, as in the centre of Blackburn where the shopping area is pedestrianised.
- Park-and-ride schemes.
- Inner and outer ring roads/motorways so that traffic does not have to pass through the city centre, e.g. the M65 around Blackburn.

2 Encouraging people to use public transport. With more people using public transport there will be fewer cars on the road and therefore less need to build extra roads and car parks. Schemes to achieve this include:

- Running a reliable, frequent bus service.
- Offering reductions in fares, e.g. season tickets.
- Developing 'bus only' lanes so that public transport is faster.
- Installing new rapid-transport systems, e.g. Manchester Metro.

3 By reducing air pollution from vehicle exhausts by:

- Enforcing the law on vehicle emissions.
- Using traffic control methods, e.g. computer controlled traffic lights, to reduce congestion at busy junctions.

Figure 6.18 Rush-hour

Conurbations

As many urban areas have continued to expand they have merged with their neighbours to give one continuous built-up area with no countryside in between. This is known as a **conurbation (Figure 6.19)**. For example, the Greater Manchester conurbation includes towns such as Oldham, Ashton, Rochdale, Bury, Bolton, Salford, Stockport, Tameside and Wigan.

Today local authorities try to prevent this happening by restricting building on the open land between the urban areas. In some cases the open space is protected by Act of Parliament and is known as a **green belt**.

The reasons local authorities wish to protect the green belt are:

- To give a separate identity to their own urban area.

- To preserve some open areas nearby for people living in the cities to use for recreation.

- To improve the urban environment by retaining areas of woodland and grass which help to absorb the carbon dioxide produced by fossil fuel burning in the cities.

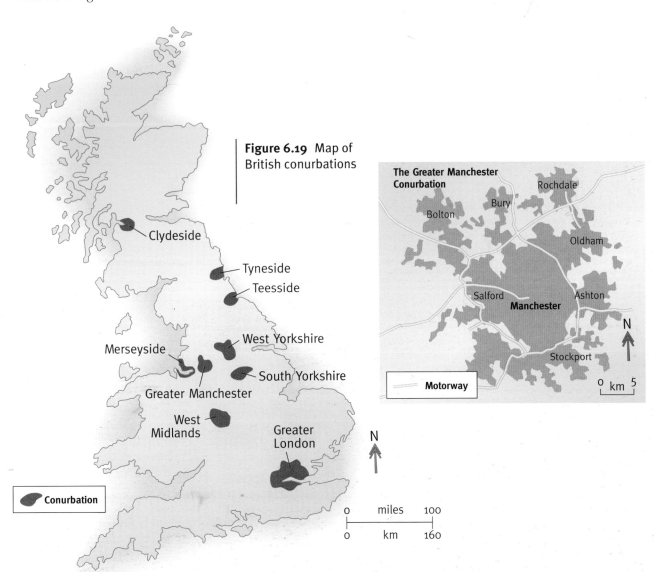

Figure 6.19 Map of British conurbations

1

Look at Figure 6.20 Describe and explain the changes shown.

2 *Pages 75–79*

Use the OS map extract of Birmingham (Figure 6.22) to locate the following:

Type of urban area	Grid Reference	Area named on map
Central Business District	to the north west of the map	
Inner City	0785	Highgate
Inner Suburbs	1181	Hall Green
Outer Suburbs	0878	Highter's Heath

a What evidence on the Ordnance Survey map suggests that Highgate is a multi-cultural area?

b Describe the different street patterns found in north west Highgate, Hall Green and Monkspath.

c Describe the type of housing (age and appearance) you would expect to find in each of the three areas.

d Explain why the type of housing changes with distance from the Central Business District which is north west of the map.

e Give three pieces of evidence that the area in 1084 is an industrial district.

3 *Pages 80–84*

Figure 6.21 shows a migration pattern typical of cities such as Birmingham.

a What are the push factors which encourage people to leave areas such as Highgate?

b What are the characteristics of the population (i.e. age, wealth, family structure) who make this move?

c How does the loss of this group of people add to the problems of the inner city?

Figure 6.20 A model of population change in industrial cities in United Kingdom

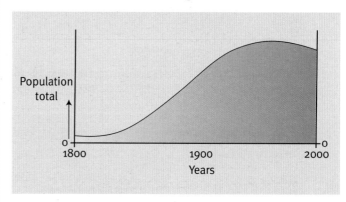

Figure 6.21 A migration pattern typical of Britain

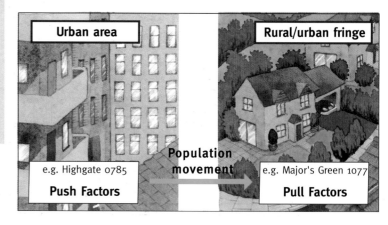

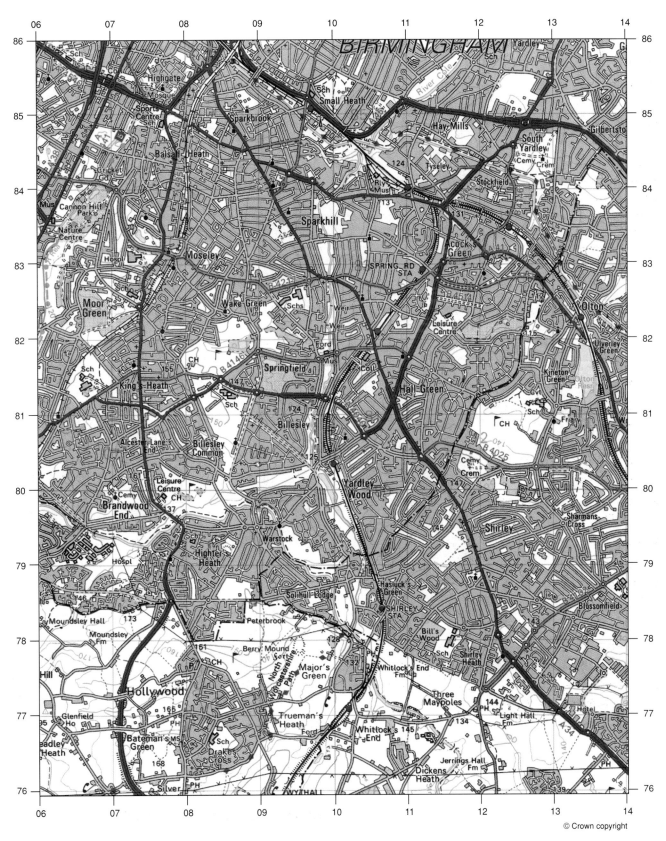

© Crown copyright

Figure 6.22 OS map extract of Birmingham 1:50 000

THE UNITED KINGDOM

4 *Pages 80–81*

Look at Figures 6.23A and B, which show inner city redevelopments.

a   Describe the redevelopments shown on photographs A and B.

b   Discuss how developments such as these can help to solve the problems found in inner city areas.

5 *Page 82*

1376 would be a suitable site for an industrial estate.

a   What are the advantages of this location?

b   Name one group who would be in favour of this location, and one group who would be against it, giving reasons for their attitude.

6 *Pages 82, 85–86*

A possible location for an edge-of-town retail park is in square 0777.

a   Why might this be regarded as a suitable site?

b   Name an edge-of-town retail park or centre known to you and explain why it is popular with customers.

c   Why might the residents of Hollywood decide to oppose the plan?

d   Birmingham city is rebuilding its shopping centre. For a city centre you know, describe the ways in which the city council is attracting customers back into the centre.

7 *Pages 83–84*

Figure 6.21 showed that some people living in Highgate (0785) might have chosen to move to Major's Green (1077).

a   What is the name given to people who live in Major's Green but travel to work in central Birmingham?

b   Why would Major's Green be attractive to people moving out of Highgate?

c   How might Major's Green have gained from people moving in?

d   Why might some residents of Hollywood (0876, 0877) and Major's Green object to newcomers moving into the area?

e   Name one other group who might object to this movement into Major's Green and explain why they would take this attitude.

Figure 6.23 Inner city redevelopments

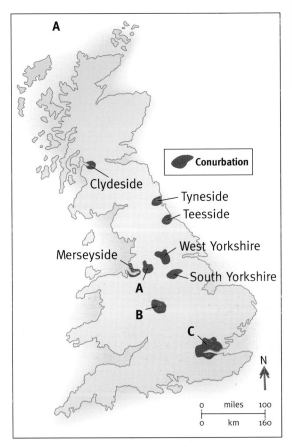

Figure 6.24a
Conurbations in Britain

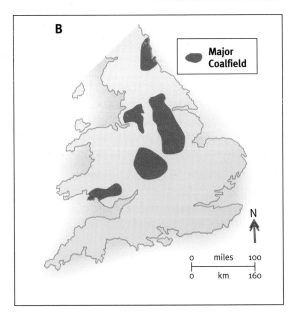

Figure 6.24b Major
coalfields in Britain

8 *Pages 87–88*

a   If large numbers of people were to move into Bateman's Green (0776) what impact would this have on the A435 nearby?

b   How would this affect people living along the route?

c   For a named town describe the ways in which attempts have been made to reduce traffic problems.

9 *Page 89*

Look at Figure 6.24 a and b

a   Name the conurbations marked A, B and C.

b   What is meant by the term 'conurbation'?

c   With reference to Figure 6.24a and b, describe the distribution of the conurbations.

d   What problems have been created on the rural/urban fringe by the expansion of conurbations?

e   How do local authorities try to limit the growth of urban areas?

7 Rich and poor regions in the European Union

Economic development within the European Union

Figure 7.1 shows the main area of wealth within the European Union (EU) running from south east Britain, through the Benelux countries, northern France, the Rhine and the Ruhr, to Milan and northern Italy. This is called the **Hot Banana** and forms the **core** area of the EU.

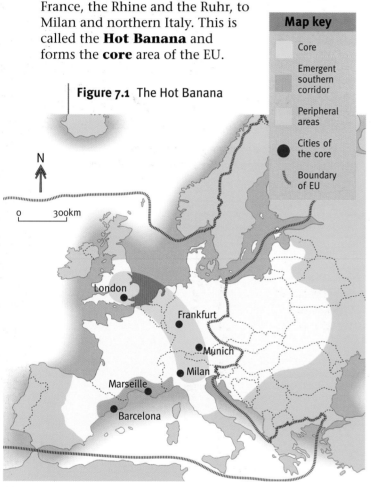

Figure 7.1 The Hot Banana

Map key

- Core
- Emergent southern corridor
- Peripheral areas
- ● Cities of the core
- ∙∙∙ Boundary of EU

The **peripheral** areas are geographically on the edge of the EU and include Greece, southern Italy, Portugal, Spain, Eire and Scotland.

Core areas

A **core area** is the richest part of a region with the highest level of development (**Figure 7.2**). The area marked on **Figure 7.1** accounts for only 10 per cent of the surface area of the EU but for more than 40 per cent of the total output. The **GNP** for most of the area is more than 20 per cent higher than the average for the EU.

Figure 7.2 Part of the core area: Canary Wharf, London

GNP/capita stands for **Gross National Product/person** and is the total income for an area for a year in $US (including income from overseas investment) divided by the number of people in a country.

The core area is likely to contain the major cities (e.g. Milan) and industrial areas (e.g. the Ruhr). It attracts the main transport and telecommunication links, so head offices and research facilities are drawn into the core zone. Services such as banking, insurance and government offices open, and as the levels of capital, technology and skilled labour increase, the region becomes more wealthy. It can then afford to provide higher quality schools, hospitals, shopping centres and housing. The economic and social advantages attract people from the surrounding areas and so the population grows.

Figure 7.3 Part of the peripheral area, a Greek farm

Peripheral areas

Peripheral areas are the poorest parts of an area and they often lie on the edge of a region (**Figure 7.3**). In the EU the periphery accounts for 60 per cent of the land area but only 20 per cent of total output. For much of the area the GNP is 40 per cent below the average for the EU.

Most of the peripheral areas are agricultural regions with poor transport links. There are limited job opportunities, which tend to be low paid. Services such as schools, hospitals, shopping centres and housing tend to be lower quality than in the core region. The lack of opportunities and poor services encourage people to leave the periphery and migrate to the core. Therefore the periphery has a low **level of development**.

How does the EU try to reduce the differences between levels of development in the regions?

The main approach is to give funding to areas where the standard of living is extremely low and where there is serious unemployment. The money is used to promote economic development to reduce the gap between the core and the periphery.

- The **Common Agricultural Policy** (CAP) gives money for farm modernisation, irrigation, intensification and training to improve the skills of farm workers. Chapter 8 looks in detail at this scheme.

- The **European Investment Bank** uses money from the member states to grant loans for projects in under-developed regions, e.g. to build the Taranto steelworks in southern Italy (see Chapter 8).

- **Structural Funds** are used to 'top up' regional national programmes where regions lag behind in development, are declining industrially, or are rural areas needing development. Such a scheme was used to finance the Integrated Mediterranean Programme (see Chapter 8).

1   What is meant by a 'core' area?

2   What is meant by a 'peripheral' area?

3   Using Figure 7.1 to help you, state which of the following are core areas and which are peripheral:
    - Northern Scotland
    - The Ruhr
    - South east England
    - The Milan area
    - Southern Spain
    - Southern Italy
    - The Rhine area
    - Rotterdam/Europoort.

Traditional farming in the Mezzogiorno

There are three main areas in the Mezzogiorno (southern Italy) (**Figure 8.1**).

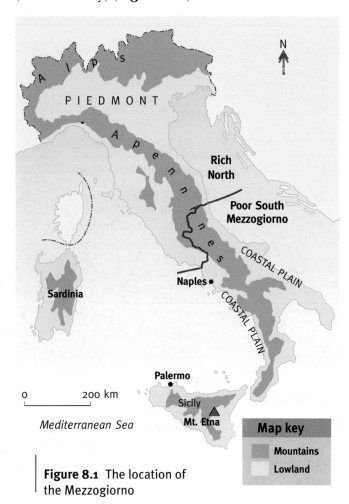

Figure 8.1 The location of the Mezzogiorno

1 **High mountains** formed of **limestone** rise to a height of almost 3000 m. Most of the land is between 200 and 1500 m high and divided into small ranges of hills. These are separated by deep, steep-sided valleys eroded by fast-flowing streams which have very small floodplains. The natural vegetation is **garrigue**, which is low bushes, e.g. rosemary. These are drought resistant and evergreen. This area is mainly used for grazing sheep and goats.

2 **Hillsides** originally vegetated with trees but now largely cleared. In many areas terraces have been cut into the hillside to increase the amount of level land. Wheat and vegetables are grown on patches of flat land in the valleys, with olives and vines grown on the terraces.

3 **Coastal plain** Flat land with thicker soils. This area is used for the commercial production of grapes, olives, citrus fruits and tobacco. Subsistence farming of wheat and fruit together with the grazing of sheep and goats also takes place.

Farm organisation

Traditionally farms were organised under a system called **latifundia**. This means that the land was divided into large estates owned by landlords who lived away from the area in the cities. Peasant farmers rented plots which were often small and scattered. This type of farming gave low yields because:

- The absentee landlords paid little attention to the land and did not invest in new farming techniques.

- After paying the rent the peasant farmers did not have the money to invest in the land.

- Since the peasant farmers did not own the land there was little incentive for them to improve it.

Relief, soils and climate influenced traditional farming practices in the Mezzogiorno as shown in **Figure 8.2**.

Relief

The steep slopes make farming difficult because:

- Soil is eroded easily by the rapid surface run off in the heavy winter rain.

- It is hard to use machinery so previously mules and donkeys were used.

- Only narrow, twisting roads can be built so the crops reach market in a poor condition, selling for a lower price.

Soils

Soils are thin and **alkaline**, formed from the underlying limestone. They result in low yields because:

- Roots cannot anchor in the shallow material.

- The thin soil contains few nutrients for crop growing and gives poor quality grazing for sheep and goats.

- With steep slopes, deforestation and sudden heavy rainstorms, soil on the hillsides is eroded easily.

- The eroded soil is deposited in rivers resulting in flooding.

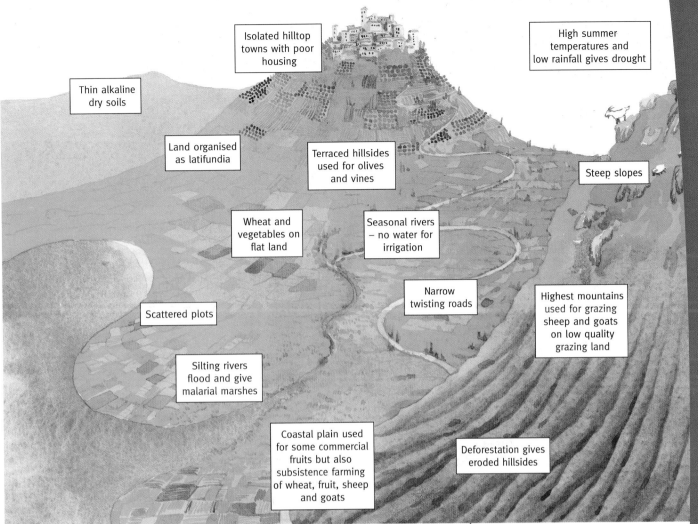

Isolated hilltop towns with poor housing

High summer temperatures and low rainfall gives drought

Thin alkaline dry soils

Land organised as latifundia

Terraced hillsides used for olives and vines

Steep slopes

Wheat and vegetables on flat land

Seasonal rivers – no water for irrigation

Narrow twisting roads

Highest mountains used for grazing sheep and goats on low quality grazing land

Scattered plots

Silting rivers flood and give malarial marshes

Coastal plain used for some commercial fruits but also subsistence farming of wheat, fruit, sheep and goats

Deforestation gives eroded hillsides

Figure 8.2
Traditional farming in the Mezzogiorno

Figure 8.3
Climate graph

Climate

Figure 8.3 shows features which are typical of the Mezzogiorno area:

- Hot summers (up to 25°C) because the Sun is at a high angle to the land.

- Dry summers because there is high pressure over the area from June to August.

- Mild winters (more than 10°C).

- Wet winters (more than 75 mm per month) because there is low pressure over the area and westerly winds from the Atlantic bring moist air to the region.

Climate affects the farming because:

- Low rainfall in summer (less than 10 mm per month) results in drought conditions so crops die and grazing is very poor.

- High summer temperatures evaporate much of the rain which does fall so it is not available to plants.

- Summer rainfall tends to be in the form of heavy **convectional storms** so water is lost rapidly as surface run off and is not available to plants.

- Low total rainfall (less than 750 mm per year) means rivers run dry early in the summer so water is not available to irrigate the crops.

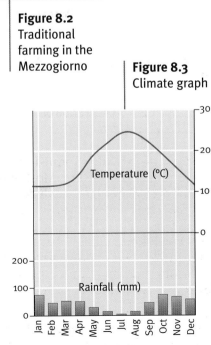

Temperature (°C)

Rainfall (mm)

Jan Feb Mar Apr May Jun Jul Aug Sep Oct Nov Dec

Migration to and from the Mezzogiorno

Over the last thirty years, each of the provinces forming the Mezzogiorno has experienced out-migration. The majority of this movement was to cities in the north of Italy e.g. Milan.

Push factors are those features which encouraged people to leave the Mezzogiorno. These factors can be divided into economic and social groups.

Economic factors:

- Low income from subsistence farming which meant people could not afford housing with modern facilities, transport, holidays, etc.

- Lack of jobs outside farming to provide an alternative income.

- A limited market to sell farming produce to because the population had a low income.

Social factors:

- Low quality housing lacking piped water and electricity.

- Lack of schools with a high educational standard.

- Lack of medical services including doctors and hospitals.

- Restrictive traditional culture which young people resented.

- Lack of entertainment, e.g. few cinemas, night clubs, etc.

Pull factors are those features which people expect to find in another area which they moved to (these features can be real or imagined). These factors can be divided into economic and social groups.

Economic factors:

- More jobs in manufacturing and services.

- Higher paid jobs.

Social factors:

- High quality housing with piped water and electricity.

- Schools with a high standard of education and universities.

- Modern hospitals and health clinics.

- Freedom from the traditional culture.

- More entertainment in the form of cinemas, theatres, night clubs, etc.

Land reform and changes in farming practices

Land reform and changes in farming practices have changed the traditional landscape of the Mezzogiorno as shown in **Figure 8.5**

Figure 8.5 The landscape after investment

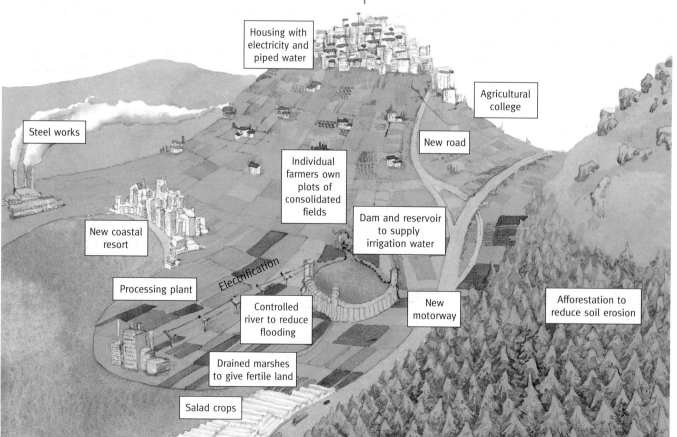

Housing with electricity and piped water

Agricultural college

New road

Steel works

Individual farmers own plots of consolidated fields

Dam and reservoir to supply irrigation water

New coastal resort

Processing plant

Electrification

Controlled river to reduce flooding

New motorway

Afforestation to reduce soil erosion

Drained marshes to give fertile land

Salad crops

Land reform

Land reform means to change who owns the land. It was administered by the 'Cassa per il Mezzogiorno' (Fund for the South) which was established in 1950. The Cassa took over the land of the absentee landlords and made the peasant farmers landowners. They then had an incentive to improve the farms and the land could be used as a security for loans. Each farmer was given enough land to be self-sufficient, and fragmented fields were consolidated so the farmers spent less time travelling and it was easier to irrigate and use machinery.

Changes in farming practices

- Higher yielding varieties of seeds have been introduced.
- Chemical fertilisers, herbicides and pesticides are used to increase yields.
- Irrigation is used so crops can be grown during the summer drought.
- New crops e.g. salad crops and citrus fruits are grown to be ready during the north European winter so they can command a higher value.
- Tractors are used which allows farming of a larger area.
- Bulk purchases to reduce costs and marketing takes place via co-operatives.
- More products are processed on the farm e.g. grapes are turned into wine so selling for a higher value.

How has funding improved the Mezzogiorno?

1 The **Cassa per il Mezzogiorno** was used for the following improvements (**Figure 8.6**):

Farming:
- To finance the land reform programme.
- To provide cheap loans for land improvements.
- To establish agricultural colleges to teach new farming skills.
- To reforest and build river control schemes to reduce flooding and soil erosion.

Infrastructure:
- To build roads linking the farming areas to the towns, and the South to the North of Italy so the farmers could get their produce to market in a fresher condition and to a wider area so increasing their income.
- To provide a water supply for domestic use so farmers would be healthier, and for irrigation so crop yields would be higher in summer, giving more income.
- To provide an electricity supply which could be used to work sprinklers and irrigation pumps.

Industrial development:
- To help build factories processing agricultural products e.g. tinned tomatoes. This increases the market for the farmer and provides employment for people living in the South who cannot find jobs in agriculture.
- To help build factories not related to agriculture e.g. Taranto steel works, to provide extra employment.
- To help develop tourism to provide additional jobs and a market for some of the agricultural produce.

Education and health:
- To improve schools so students would modernise farming and be suitable employees in the new industries.
- To improve medical facilities so that people are healthier and able to work harder.

2 The **Integrated Mediterranean Programme (IMP)** is used as shown in **Figure 8.7**.

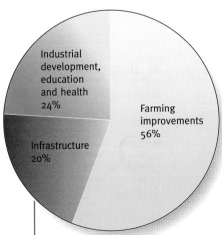

Figure 8.6 The use of the Cassa per il Mezzogiorno

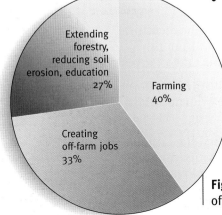

Figure 8.7 The use of the IMP fund

The aims of the IMP funding are:

- To improve the quality of olives, vines and animal products so they fetch a higher price.

- To improve marketing so the farmers can sell more produce.

- Other employment such as craft activities, small scale industry, small hotels, campsites, etc. receive money for development. Some of these enable farmers to diversify to increase their income so they can modernise, others encourage tourism so farmers will have a larger market, whilst others provide employment for family members who can return an income to the farm.

- Extending forestry and reducing soil erosion to produce more fertile farming areas which will increase yields.

- Education and training to teach farmers new practices.

Overall the funding has led to the following improvements:

- Agricultural productivity has increased and incomes have risen.

- More people are employed outside agriculture.

- Tourist developments are attracting an increasing number of visitors.

- Migration to the North has largely ceased.

However, there are limitations to the funding:

- The 5 hectares of land given to each farmer under the reform programme proved too small for many of them to make a profit so they have been forced to sell and have left the area.

- The amount given under the IMP fund is small compared with the subsidies available under the CAP for crops such as olives, so this has encouraged farmers to remain farming low quality produce which is in surplus instead of encouraging them to move to high quality produce for which there is a market.

- The improvements have been uneven with many of the steep mountain slopes suffering still from erosion and many hill farmers failing to modernise.

- The movement into citrus fruits and horticultural crops has suffered from competition from other Mediterranean countries, e.g. Spain.

- Many of the non-agricultural industries developed are state owned and there is little evidence that small scale private industry is growing.

- Much of the money has not reached the farmers but has been diverted to illegal organisations, e.g. the Mafia. There is still much unemployment and poverty in the region (**Figure 8.7**).

Figure 8.7 Poverty and unemployment rates in the Mezzogiorno

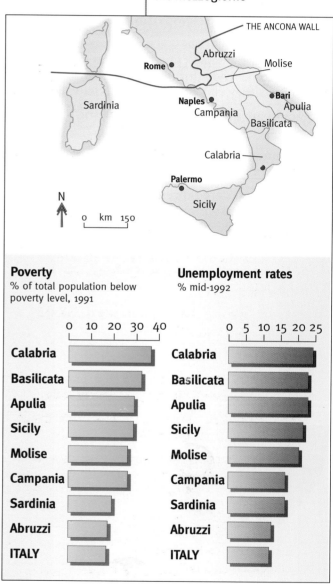

Questions

1 *Page 96*

a Copy Figure 8.8 and label islands A and B, mountains C, sea D and town E.

b What is another name given to southern Italy?

c Complete the following table to show the physical features and land use of the three main areas of southern Italy.

Area	Appearance	Land use
Mountains		
Hillsides		
Coastal plain		

2 *Pages 96–97*

a Identify three problems the physical geography of southern Italy creates for farmers in the region.

b Describe clearly how each problem limits yields and income for the farmers.

3 *Page 98*

a Using Figure 8.9 describe the pattern of farming employment in southern Italy in 1955.

b What does Figure 8.9 suggest about the level of economic development in southern Italy in 1955? Explain your answer.

c Suggest why large numbers of young people left southern Italy during the 1950s.

4 *Pages 99–100*

a Name the two funding programmes which were used to finance changes in farming in southern Italy.

b For each of the forms of funding, give an example of how the money was spent.

c Explain how these improvements have helped to raise the standard of living of farmers.

5 *Pages 96–100*

Compare Figures 8.2 and 8.5.

a Describe the changes shown.

b Suggest why some farmers claim that the Cassa per il Mezzogiorno and IMP funding has not helped them at all.

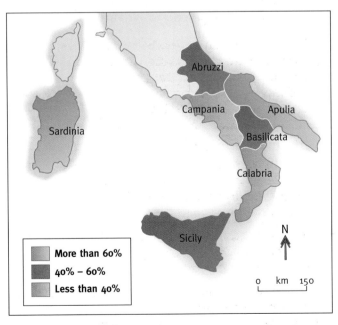

Figure 8.8 Outline map of Italy

Figure 8.9 Farming employment in southern Italy (in 1955)

What natural advantages does Spain have for a tourist industry?

The reasons why the tourist industry grew in Mediterranean Spain can be seen from a study of Benidorm on the Costa Blanca (**Figure 9.1**). The physical features and climate of the area are the main reasons for the growth of the tourist industry here.

Physical features

Benidorm has two long sandy **beaches** extending for 5 km. The Levante is to the north east, and the Poniente to the south west (**Figure 9.2**). Tourists can lie on the hot sand, and children can make sandcastles. The beach is wide enough for beach volleyball, and the small **tidal range** of the Mediterranean Sea of only 50 cm means that tourists do not have to walk far to the sea at low tide. The sea is shallow, which allows it to warm up quickly. It has no strong currents, so it is safe for tourists, especially children, to swim in.

To the north of Benidorm, between Altea and Javea there are high **cliffs**, and to the south there are many small sandy **bays** between rocky **headlands** (**Figure 9.2**). These are close enough to Benidorm for families to visit for a day.

The countryside around Benidorm attracts tourists on day trips. They can see the traditional Spanish building styles and way of life in small whitewashed villages, and in old towns such as Altea and Villajoyosa. They can go for a walk in the mountains, or take a ride on the 'Lemon Express', a small railway which passes through the olive, orange and lemon groves and the vineyards.

Figure 9.1 Location of the Spanish tourist industry

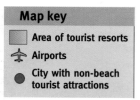

Map key

- Area of tourist resorts
- ✈ Airports
- ● City with non-beach tourist attractions

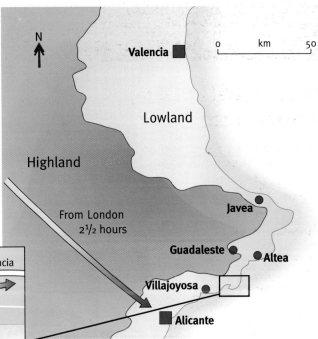

Figure 9.2 Location of the Costa Blanca and Benidorm

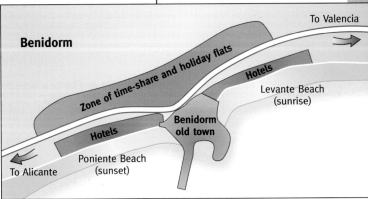

Climate

Summer temperatures: The average daily temperature in July and August in Benidorm is 27°C (**Figure 9.3**). This means it is over 30°C in the middle of the day, and over 15°C at night. Tourists can stay warm with little clothing most of the time, unlike in Britain, where London's average temperature in the same season is only 17°C, and tourists need warmer clothes.

Winter temperatures: The average temperature in January is 15°C in Benidorm, which is warm enough to sit outside, unlike in Britain, where the temperature in London is 6°C, and thick clothing is needed (**Figure 9.3**). Benidorm, therefore, attracts holiday-makers in winter, especially retired people who often stay for several weeks.

Sunshine: Benidorm has over ten hours of sunshine each day from May to August, which is four hours more than in London. This is because Benidorm has an area of high pressure (an **anticyclone**) over it in summer and this stops clouds forming. Tourists like the sunshine as it means they can lie on the beach, develop a suntan, and spend as much time outside as possible.

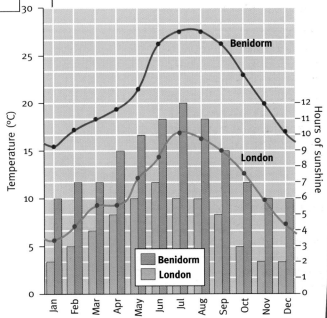

Figure 9.3 Temperature graphs of Benidorm and London

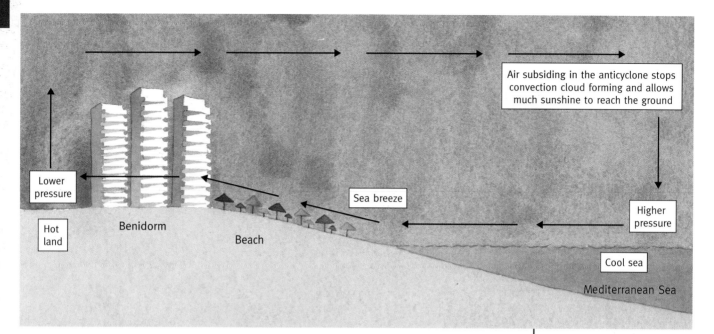

Lower pressure

Hot land

Benidorm

Beach

Sea breeze

Air subsiding in the anticyclone stops convection cloud forming and allows much sunshine to reach the ground

Higher pressure

Cool sea

Mediterranean Sea

Figure 9.4 The sea breeze on a summer's day

Sea breeze: Benidorm has a sea breeze on many days in summer (**Figure 9.4**). The land heats up faster than the sea, and this produces differences in air pressure which create a gentle wind. It is important because it blows traffic exhaust fumes and other air pollution inland away from the tourists on the beach. The clean air blowing in from the sea also allows more **ultraviolet light** to reach the beach and tan people's skin.

Rainfall: Benidorm has only 1–2 mm of rain in July and August, compared with 55–60 mm in each month in London (**Figure 9.5**). Tourists can be almost certain of a holiday without rain. The rain in Benidorm tends to fall in short, heavy showers, so tourists can soon resume their beach activities.

Figure 9.5 Rainfall in Benidorm and London

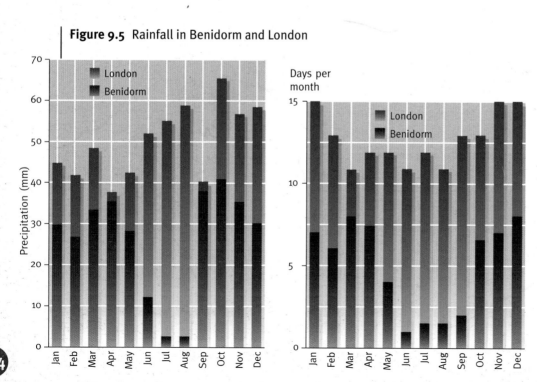

Economic factors leading to the growth of Spain's tourist industry

Package holidays

Going on holiday involves arranging transport from home to the airport, the flight, the journey to the hotel, accommodation, entertainment, day trips, and insurance to cover all these activities. When companies such as Thomas Cook and Thomsons began to arrange them so that the holiday-maker had just one payment to make in advance, they were called **package holidays**, and tourists bought them because they were convenient. The tour operators bought large numbers of holidays in Benidorm, and competition between them brought prices down. As a result, the number of visitors to Benidorm increased rapidly in the 1970s. Holiday prices were also low because the high unemployment and scarcity of jobs in other occupations such as manufacturing industry kept average wage rates low in Spain.

Transport

In general, people who have a holiday for one week do not want to travel for more than a day to get there. The development of large jet aeroplanes in the 1960s meant that tourists could travel faster and therefore further than previously. Alicante Airport is only two and a half hours' flying time from London, and it then takes only 30 minutes along a good road to reach Benidorm. Tourists could travel from anywhere in Britain to Benidorm in less than a day.

Since the 1950s, the economies of countries in northern Europe have grown rapidly. People have higher salaries and more money to spend. Their paid holidays have increased from one or two weeks to three or four, and this has encouraged more of them to travel abroad for their main summer holiday.

Holiday accommodation

High-rise hotels line Benidorm's beaches, and behind them are self-catering apartments and timeshare accommodation. Tourists want to stay only a few minutes' walk from the beach, and this they can do. A typical hotel (**Figure 9.6**) has a balcony for holiday-makers to sit on, a swimming pool, bars and entertainment in the evening.

Amenities

Many tourists in the 18–30 age range are attracted to Benidorm by its night life. There are bars in the old town, where tourists can experience Spanish culture in the form of flamenco dancing and cheap Spanish wine, as well as the more familiar disco music and English food. Families are attracted by leisure amenities such as the Terra Mitica theme park with its big dipper, water rides, and other attractions designed around the theme of the Ancient Egyptian, Greek and Roman civilizations.

Figure 9.6 Benidorm

Where do tourists in Spain come from?

Figure 9.7 shows where tourists travelled from to spend their holidays in Spain in 1996. Most tourists came from northern Europe, including 9 million from Britain and 12 million from Germany. Britain and Germany are rich countries where many people have more than two weeks of paid holiday per year and high salaries. They also have large populations of over 50 million. Smaller numbers (about 1 million) came from other countries which have small populations of less than 10 million. Russia is a poorer country, but its huge population of 200 million means that there are still many people (7 million) who can afford to travel to Spain.

More than 10 million visit Spain from Portugal because it is next to it. Travel costs are low as tourists can drive to the resorts where the sea is warmer than in the Portuguese resorts on the coast of the Atlantic. However, less than 1 million travel from Greece and Italy because they have the same climate and landscape as Spain. They visit their own Mediterranean resorts because their transport costs are lower and travel time is shorter.

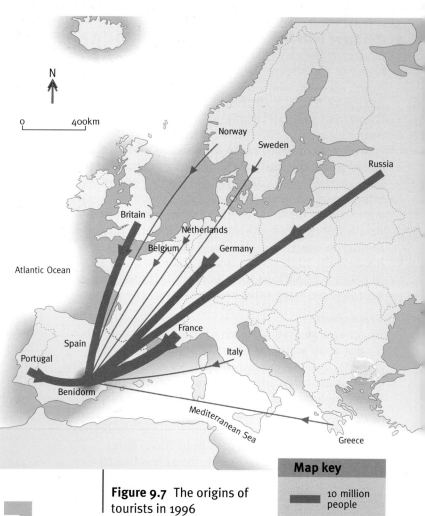

Figure 9.7 The origins of tourists in 1996

Map key	
▬▬	10 million people

EXAM TIP

When describing a map such as Europe, low marks are gained for naming each country in turn. Higher marks are awarded for grouping similar countries so that you describe patterns.

The main reasons for all these nationalities holidaying in Spain are:

- The Mediterranean climate of hot, dry, sunny summers.

- The opportunity to experience a different culture such as flamenco dancing, watching a bull-fight, and visiting historic places.

- The convenience and low prices of Spanish package holidays which are often cheaper than holidays in their own countries.

How has tourism affected the economy and environment of the region?

Employment
Before tourism grew, most people in the Benidorm area worked on small farms which had low incomes from selling wheat and olives (**Figure 9.8**). Many are now employed in hotels such as the Hotel Marina and in shops and other services. They have higher incomes than previously, but the employment is seasonal as there are fewer tourists in winter so many workers are unemployed at that time of year. The hotels try to attract more visitors in winter by offering very cheap holidays, especially for retired people. The Benidorm Fiesta week is held in November.

Figure 9.8 Changes in employment

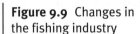

Figure 9.9 Changes in the fishing industry

There are fashions in the choice of holidays. As wages have increased in Benidorm, more tourists have chosen cheaper holidays in newer tourist areas such as Turkey, or long-haul destinations such as Florida and the Seychelles. Another trend is for tourists to use self-catering and timeshare accommodation, both of which are cheaper than hotels. Fewer waiters, cooks, etc. are employed as a result. Unemployment has increased in Benidorm to over 15 per cent.

Industry

Before tourism developed there was little industry. It was orientated to the needs of farming, such as repairing farm machinery. Now industries have grown in Benidorm to serve the needs of tourists. Examples include the making of souvenirs for tourists to buy, such as leather handbags and wickerwork baskets. Although these industries provide permanent employment, they are often craft-based and do not give rise to high volume goods which could be exported to the rest of the world.

Benidorm used to be a small fishing port where men fished the local waters and sold their catches to local people (**Figure 9.9**). The growth of tourism increased the demand for fish, leading to **over-fishing**, so there are now few fish in nearby waters and most boats have to sail further out to sea. The fishermen have diversified into taking tourists on trips along the coastline and on fishing trips.

Landscape

The Benidorm area used to be a small fishing village surrounded by wheat fields, grasslands, woods and olive groves, with mountains rising behind the coastal plain to 1000 m. Now, there are many high-rise hotels of ten storeys or more which extend along the coast for 5 km and inland for 2 km. They block the view of the mountains from the beach.

Pollution

Before hotels were built there was little pollution. Untreated sewage was put into the sea from the fishing village, but this had little effect on the environment because there were so few people there. The increase in tourists caused severe pollution from rubbish dropped on to the beach and from untreated sewage. The shallow sea and high water temperatures encouraged the growth of bacteria, and pollution lingered for a long time as the currents in the sea are weak. Many tourists became ill, and marine wildlife was damaged. Sewage works were built to treat the waste, and each night machines are used to sift the beach sand and remove litter dropped by tourists.

Cultural changes

Before tourism developed, the inhabitants of the Benidorm area had a typical Spanish culture of close knit extended families, a devotion to the Roman Catholic Church, and leisure activities such as flamenco dancing, football and bull-fighting (**Figure 9.10**). The area now has other cultural influences. British and German tourists wanted their own facilities, so there are British pubs, fish and chip shops and Bier Kellers.

In the 1980s and 1990s the formerly peaceful area of the old fishing village, where there are many bars, was taken over by drunken gangs of young British and German tourists, fighting and causing vandalism. The number of policemen on duty in this area is now higher to control such incidents.

Figure 9.10 Cultural changes

EXAM TIP

If you are asked to describe the views or attitudes of people to the development of tourism, make sure you name a specific person, e.g.

- A hotel waiter in Benidorm
- A fisherman in Benidorm
- A farmer near Alicante.

Try to describe ways in which they would be pleased about the development of tourism, and other reasons why they are not so happy about it.

Figure 9.11 Regional economic development

Regional economic development

The growth of tourist resorts along the Costa Blanca has created a demand for food. The dry coastal plain at Alicante only 40 km away used to grow wheat and graze sheep (**Figure 9.11**). Now it has been **irrigated** and grows **market garden crops** such as lettuce and tomatoes, providing more employment and much higher incomes. Polythene tents cover the ground in winter to grow crops such as salad crops and strawberries which can be exported to northern Europe.

The growth of the coastal resorts created a demand for people to fill the jobs in hotels, etc. Many young people migrated from the poor farming areas on the high, dry plateau called the Meseta which forms much of inland Spain. Older and less dynamic people

were left on the inland farms which led to problems similar to those in the farming areas of southern Italy (see Chapter 8).

With more people living on the coast and earning higher wages, demand for manufactured goods such as cars increased. This, together with the low wage rates compared with northern Europe, led to **transnational corporations (TNCs)** such as General Motors building car assembly factories at Valencia.

1 *Pages 102–104*

a Look at Figure 9.12 and name the following:
- Country A
- The sea B
- The group of islands C
- Capital city D
- Two of the costas E to I
- An important resort on each of the two costas you have named.

b Most tourists visit Spain in summer. However, 25 per cent of them visit during the winter months (October to March). Explain why so many tourists visit Spain during the winter. (Use the information in Figures 9.3 to 9.5 to help you.)

2 *Pages 103–106*

a Use the Internet to find views of Benidorm, for instance at http://www.athenea.com/benidorm.

b Look at Figure 9.13. It shows that, for example, in 1965, British people took 31 million holidays in Britain, and 4 million holidays abroad. State the figures for holidays taken in 1990:
- Holidays taken in Britain.
- Holidays taken abroad.

c Give four reasons why there has been an increase in holidays taken abroad in recent years.

d Study Figure 9.14.
- Describe the pattern of the origins of visitors to Spain
- Suggest reasons why the climate of Mediterranean Spain is attractive to tourists from Northern Europe

e Study the maps in Figure 9.15.
- Describe the distribution of visitors shown in Figure 9.15b
- Using the information in Figure 9.15a, suggest reasons for the distribution of visitors shown in Figure 9.15b.

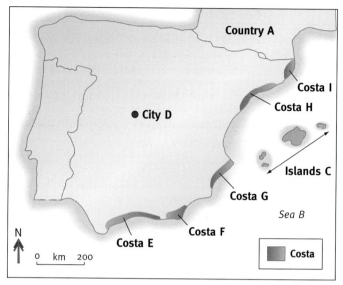

Figure 9.12
Some locations in Spain

Figure 9.13
Where do British people take their holidays?

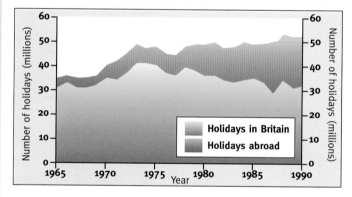

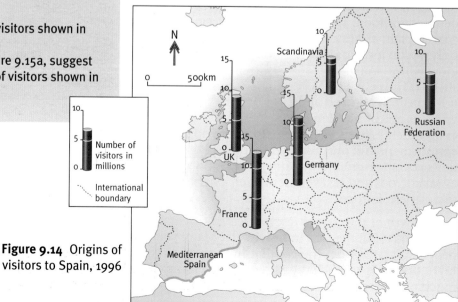

Figure 9.14 Origins of visitors to Spain, 1996

Questions

3 *Pages 106–109*

a Explain how the local economy, in and around a resort in Mediterranean Spain, benefits from tourism.

b During the last 30 years the area shown in Figure 9.16 has become a major tourist area. Describe the likely changes to the area and explain the effects of these changes on the local people

c Study Figure 9.17 which shows an imaginary area on the south coast of Spain. A new holiday development (including three large hotels, an apartment block, villas and a golf course) is proposed for the area at one of three possible locations marked A, B and C on the map.

- State one advantage of each location for such a development.
- State one disadvantage of each location for such a development.
- Eventually none of the locations A, B or C were chosen and the development was built at D instead. Suggest why D was considered to be more suitable.

d Describe and explain some of the effects of such a development on the local area in Spain.

e Tourism also brings problems to Mediterranean Spain. Describe some of these problems and explain how tourism has caused them.

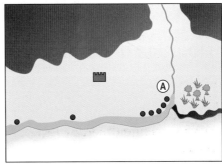
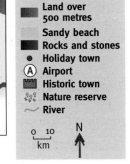

Map key
- Land over 500 metres
- Sandy beach
- Rocks and stones
- ● Holiday town
- Ⓐ Airport
- Historic town
- Nature reserve
- ∼ River

0 10 km

N

Figure 9.15
Features (a) and numbers of visitors (b) of a holiday area

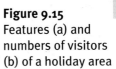

Map key

Number of visitors in August to the area shown above (9.15a)
- 50 000
- 40 000
- 30 000
- 20 000
- 10 000
- 0

0 10 km

N

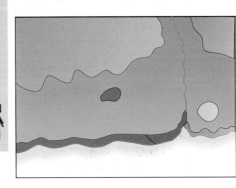

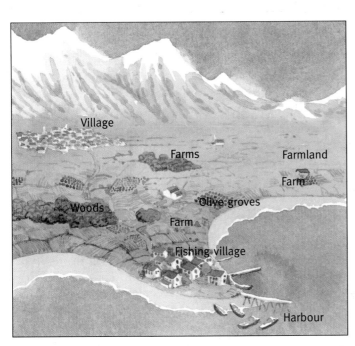

Village

Farms

Farmland

Farm

Woods

Olive groves

Farm

Fishing village

Harbour

Figure 9.16 An area of Mediterranean Spain before development

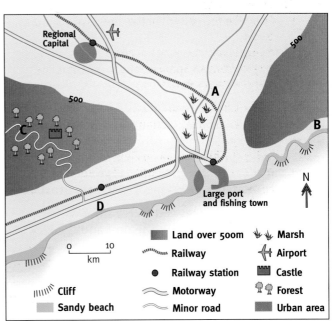

Regional Capital

A

B

C

500

500

D

Large port and fishing town

N

- Land over 500m
- Railway
- Railway station
- Cliff
- Sandy beach
- Marsh
- Airport
- Castle
- Motorway
- Minor road
- Forest
- Urban area

0 10 km

Figure 9.17 An area being considered for a holiday development

THE EUROPEAN UNION

111

The site and situation of Rotterdam/Europoort

Site

The **site** of a city is the land it is actually built on. The city of Rotterdam/Europoort is at the mouth of the River Rhine, although the centre of the old town of Rotterdam is 20 km from the sea (**Figure 10.1**).

Rotterdam/Europoort is on the **delta** of the River Rhine. A delta is the flat land formed by a river depositing its load of sediment just before it enters the sea. The land is often marshy. Much of Rotterdam/Europoort has been built on land which is below sea level; it has to be protected from flooding.

Before it reaches Rotterdam, the Rhine splits into its two main **distributaries**, the Rivers Lek and Waal, which both flow through Rotterdam. The River Maas (River Meuse in French) flowing from Belgium also reaches the sea at Rotterdam. The city therefore has a long waterfront on the banks of the rivers, and new harbours can be cheaply dug out of the soft **alluvium**.

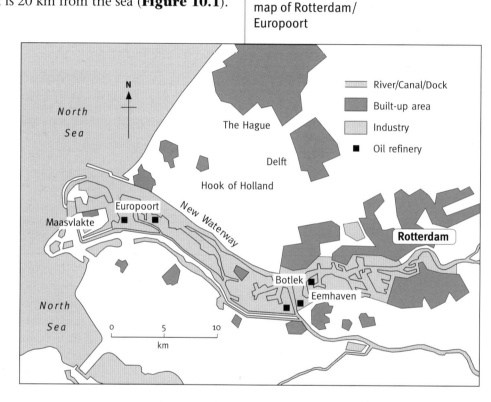

Figure 10.1 Site map of Rotterdam/Europoort

Situation

The **situation** of a city is its position in relation to the surrounding region. Rotterdam/Europoort is at the mouth of the Rhine **drainage basin** and has road, rail and canal links to cities and industrial regions in other drainage basins (**Figure 10.2**). All these form Rotterdam/Europoort's **hinterland**.

The hinterland of a port is the area from which goods are exported through the port and the area to which goods are imported through the port. Rotterdam's hinterland contains 80 million people. They create a huge demand for goods, many of them imported. Electronic goods, cars and other products from Japan and elsewhere in the world are imported through Rotterdam.

Industrial regions like the Ruhr and Frankfurt (**Figure 10.2**) need large quantities of **raw materials** such as iron ore for steelworks, and oil

and petroleum products for refineries and chemical works. Many of the raw materials are imported and the goods manufactured from them are exported through Rotterdam.

The reason for Rotterdam's growth to become one of the largest ports in the world is its situation at the mouth of the River Rhine. Large amounts of low value goods such as raw materials can be transported along it very cheaply to factories even if it is slower than by road and rail. All the industrial regions can be reached by river transport, and the barges are large, e.g. 7000 tonne barges can navigate to the Ruhr. A pipeline also transports crude oil from Rotterdam to refineries in the Ruhr. Transportation of bulky raw materials by rivers is very important in Europe. It is so cheap that the other main river systems have now been joined to the Rhine by

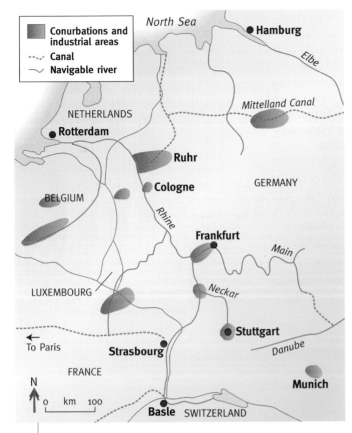

Figure 10.2 The location of Rotterdam/Europoort

canals. Rotterdam's hinterland has grown to include areas in other drainage basins such as the basin of the River Danube in south east Germany.

Manufactured goods are more valuable than raw materials, and are transported from factories by road and rail. These routes follow the Rhine Valley and its tributaries to Rotterdam for export. Rail transport has declined since 1950 but carries large heavy loads to areas not reached by barges. Road transport on motorways is the most important method of moving manufactured goods.

The growth of Rotterdam

- Rotterdam started to grow in the nineteenth century because of industrial development in the Ruhr and Saar coalfields in the Rhine drainage basin. These areas needed a port to import raw materials and export their products.

- The natural mouth of the River Rhine was twisty, with constantly moving sandbanks. In 1872 it was deepened to 23 m and straightened to make the 19 km long New Waterway so that big ocean-going ships could reach Rotterdam.

- The alluvium which forms the Rhine Delta can be dug out cheaply to deepen harbours and canals to take larger ships.

- The tidal range at Rotterdam is only 1.5 m so ships can enter and leave at any state of the tide. There is no delay which saves ship owners money.

- Rotterdam has grown because it is a **break-of-bulk** point. Ocean-going ships can unload there and barges can then take their loads cheaply up the River Rhine to the hinterland (**Figure 10.3**). For example, 100 000 tonne iron ore bulk carriers from Sweden unload into 7000 tonne barges which take the ore 170 km to steelworks in the Ruhr industrial region.

- A break-of-bulk point is the best place to process raw materials. 100 000 tonnes of crude oil can be carried cheaply in one ship from Saudi Arabia to Rotterdam. There it is refined and the hundreds of different products which have a higher value per tonne can be transported in smaller loads of a few thousand tonnes to chemical works at locations upstream on the Rhine, such as Mannheim

Figure 10.3 Break-of-bulk

- Ships have increased in size because of **economies of scale**. This means it is cheaper to transport 1 tonne of goods in a large ship than in a small ship, because labour and fuel costs are lower. However, bigger ships need bigger ports where they can load and unload. There was much cheap flat land on the banks of the Rhine between Rotterdam and the sea. The port of Rotterdam has therefore expanded westwards towards the sea. Botlek was opened in 1957 for oil imports and has oil refineries next to it (**Figure 10.1**). Eemhaven was opened in 1967 next to the New Waterway and was then the biggest container terminal in the world. Europoort was built in the 1960s and 70s by digging harbours out of the island of Rozenburg and using the clay to raise the land by 5 m to stop flooding. It handles mainly oil tankers and bulk carriers. Maasvlakte was reclaimed from the North Sea in 1974. It has a big container terminal and handles bulk carriers. There is little industry so far, but there is space for more development.

- Rotterdam/Europoort has also grown because of the Dutch willingness to use new technology to reduce costs for ship owners and win trade from other ports. All shipping movements in the port are controlled by computer.

- The integration of the EU economy by the removal of customs barriers at borders has extended Rotterdam's hinterland further.

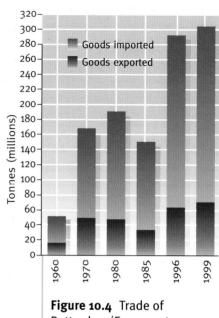

Figure 10.4 Trade of Rotterdam/Europoort

The functions of Rotterdam/Europoort

1 The **functions** of Rotterdam/Europoort are the types of work done there. The most important function is **trade**, the exporting of goods from the hinterland and importing of goods to it. **Figure 10.4** shows that the volume of imports is much greater than exports because the imports are mainly cheap bulky raw materials, while the exports are usually high value manufactured goods. The total values of imports and exports are more equal. Exports are often nowadays in containers.

Figure 10.5 Aerial photo of Rotterdam/Europoort

Rotterdam/ Europoort has built a big new container terminal on the Beer Canal where the deep water allows large ships to dock. Most of the old cargo ports in the old city of Rotterdam are now unimportant. Goods are also imported, stored and then exported; they are said to be in **transit**. These include, for example, iron ore from Sweden on its way to steelworks in Germany.

2 Rotterdam/Europoort has a second major function; **processing raw materials** in large quantities because it is at a break-of-bulk point. Examples include the many huge oil refineries and petrochemical works in Europoort (**Figure 10.5**).

The processing works need large areas of cheap flat land. Much was marsh or was reclaimed from the sea. Part of the need for land is to separate oil storage tanks to prevent fires spreading.

Very large supertankers of 200 000 tonnes need deep water to dock and enough room to turn around. The harbours have been dug cheaply from the alluvium. The processing works are next to the harbours to keep transport costs as low as possible.

Rotterdam/Europoort also has specialist harbours for bulky dry goods. Grain such as soya is imported in bulk carriers from the USA and is processed in flour mills next to the harbour. Iron ore from Sweden and Canada is unloaded into steelworks at the port.

3 A third function of Rotterdam/Europoort is **shipbuilding** and repair yards. They are next to the deep water of the New Waterway to launch ships (**Figure 10.1**). Most are near the old city of Rotterdam where there are engineering industries which have grown to make the parts. Many barges are built specifically for use on the Rhine.

4 A minor function of Rotterdam/Europoort is to transport vehicles and people. **RORO ferries** travel overnight between Hull and the Hook of Holland and between Rotterdam and Harwich.

Planning issues in Rotterdam/Europoort

Flooding by the North Sea and the River Rhine is a major issue which is affecting planning in Rotterdam/Europoort. Residents want to have their homes protected from the damage caused by floods but the port authorities and industrialists do not want anything done which would slow the working of the port or navigation along the River Rhine as it would reduce their profits.

Floods from the sea

The main purpose of Rotterdam/Europoort is to allow ships to dock to load and unload goods. However, the New Waterway along which ships pass is also the route that a high sea level could use to flood the city. In 1953 gale force winds from the north caused a **storm surge**. This raised the level of the North Sea by over 3 m and there were 3 m high **storm waves** on the top of that. The **dykes** built to keep out the sea in the southern Netherlands were broken. 1835 people were drowned in one night, and the city of Rotterdam was flooded. Could it happen again?

Global warming (Chapter 20) is causing storms to be more frequent and sea level is expected to rise by up to 80 cm in the next 50 years in the southern North Sea.

The Dutch solution has been the **Delta Scheme**. High dykes have been built, and the sea inlets south of Rotterdam have been dammed to stop the sea coming in. However, the New Waterway cannot be blocked. A frame has been built across it with a flood barrier which can be moved into place when the sea level rises to danger levels (**Figure 10.6**).

Floods from the land

The River Rhine flows through Rotterdam and is the route for much of the city's trade with its hinterland. However, it is also flooding more frequently. Rainfall has increased because of global warming, but the main reason for the floods is that water is flowing down the Rhine much faster than it used to. It reaches Rotterdam in larger volumes over a short time rather than in smaller amounts over a longer period which

Figure 10.6 The New Waterway storm surge barrier

would not cause a flood. The faster flow is because the river channel has been straightened by cutting off meanders to shorten journeys for barges. Deforestation, land drainage and the building of towns which have impermeable surfaces have all increased the speed with which rainfall can flow off slopes into rivers. The River Rhine can no longer spread out over much of its floodplain because towns and industry have been built there. Natural flooding has been prevented by embankments up to 4.5 m high.

The great Rhine floods of 1995 were caused by heavy rain and the rapid melting of snow in the Alps. Rotterdam was flooded but no lives were lost. There would have been a disaster if a storm surge had occurred at the same time because the water would not have been able to flow into the sea. The Dutch have started to tackle the problem by:

- Digging out new meanders to slow the flow of water (**Figure 10.7**).

- Building **wing dykes** into the river to slow it down.

- Moving people away from the river in some places to let it cover the floodplain in winter.

- Banning building on parts of the floodplain and protecting factories, homes, etc. with removable watertight walls made from aluminium girders which can be piled higher as the flood rises.

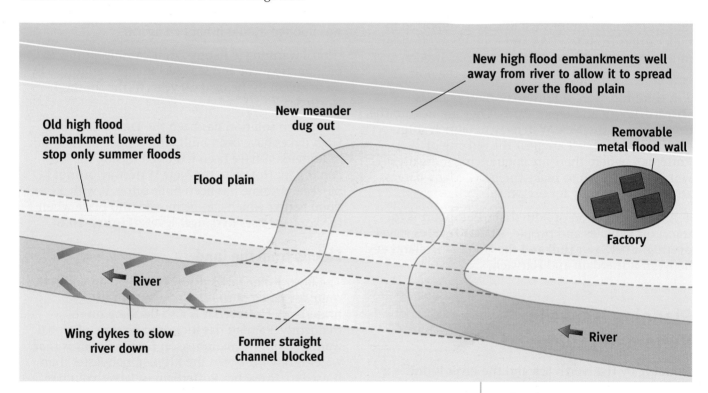

Old high flood embankment lowered to stop only summer floods

New meander dug out

New high flood embankments well away from river to allow it to spread over the flood plain

Removable metal flood wall

Flood plain

Factory

River

Wing dykes to slow river down

Former straight channel blocked

River

Figure 10.7 Methods to prevent the River Rhine flooding Rotterdam

EXAM TIP

For the AQA Specification B examination, study only one of the following conurbations:

- Rotterdam/Europoort.

- The Ruhr Conurbation.

- The Paris Region.

- The Milan/Turin/Genoa Industrial Triangle.

Questions

1 *Pages 112–115*

Figure 10.5 is a photograph of part of the site of Rotterdam/Europoort.

a   Using Figure 10.1 name the areas shown in the photograph.

b   Which of the following land use types would you find at letters A to D on the photograph?
   • Shipyard   • Houses
   • Grain storage   • Coal mine
   • Petrochemical works   • Ore terminal.

c   Figure 10.9 is a map of the Rhine and some of its tributaries. It tells you how many days it takes for a barge to travel to Rotterdam.

   • How many days does it take to travel from Duisburg to Rotterdam?
   • How many days does it take to travel from Basle to Duisburg?
   • It takes a barge seven days to travel from Basle to Rotterdam. However, it takes nine days for the barge to travel back to Basle. Explain why there is a difference in the journey times.
   • Figure 10.9 shows two waterway links to areas outside the drainage basin of the River Rhine. Explain how these links might affect Rotterdam's hinterland.

2 *Pages 112–115*

Give three detailed reasons why the area shown in Figure 10.5 is suitable for industrial development.

3 *Pages 112–115*

a   Use the Internet to study some of the functions of Rotterdam. A good site is at www.port.rotterdam.nl, which has a web-cam.

b   Describe the main functions of the port shown in Figure 10.8.

c   The port authorities have stated that: 'Rotterdam is not a Dutch port, but a European port. A true Gateway to Europe.' What are their reasons for making this statement?

d   Describe and explain the port functions of Rotterdam/Europoort.

Figure 10.8 The Rotterdam Europoort site

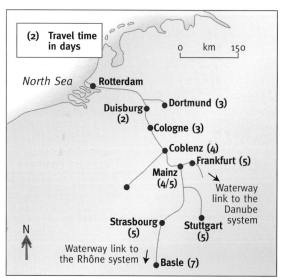

Figure 10.9 The Rhine waterway link to Rotterdam

11 Development of the European urban core – the Ruhr conurbation

The site and situation of the Ruhr conurbation

Site

The **site** of a city or conurbation is the land it is actually built on. The Ruhr conurbation lies in the **drainage basins** of three tributaries of the River Rhine, the Lippe, Emscher and Ruhr Rivers (**Figure 11.1**).

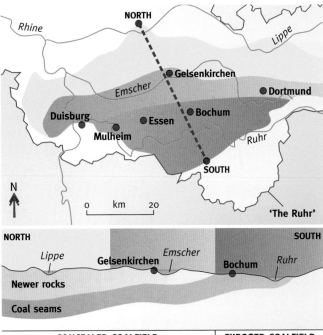

CONCEALED COALFIELD		EXPOSED COALFIELD
Coal at a depth of 1000m. Late 20th century mines. High investment and productivity. Few towns – mainly a rural area.	Coal at a depth up to 150m. Early 20th-century mines. Many closed since 1960.	Coal was at surface, now used up. 19th century mines now closed, mining towns decayed.

Figure 11.1 The site of the Ruhr conurbation

The conurbation is on the southern part of the Ruhr coalfield, Europe's largest deposit of coal. It still has huge reserves and much of it is the highest quality **coking coal** which is needed in iron and steelworks. The rivers on the coalfield have been made navigable and canals have been dug to transport the bulky, low-value raw materials such as coal and iron ore very cheaply.

Situation

The **situation** of a conurbation is its position in relation to the surrounding region. The River Rhine forms the western edge of the Ruhr conurbation and the large city of Duisburg at the **confluence** of the Rivers Ruhr and Rhine is the main port for the region (**Figure 11.1**). Industry has to import raw materials. They can be transported very cheaply from the port of Rotterdam (Chapter 10) on large barges of up to 7000 tonnes in weight along the River Rhine. These raw materials include iron ore and other minerals, timber and petroleum products. Barges up to 2000 tonnes in weight can sail down the River Rhine from Basle and bring large quantities of raw materials such as sand and gravel from southern Germany to use in construction (**Figure 11.2**). The rivers and canals are used to take manufactured goods such as petroleum products and steel to their markets. Railways and motorways join the Ruhr to other parts of Europe. With 18 million people, it is one of the most densely populated parts of Europe and is in the **core** area of the EU.

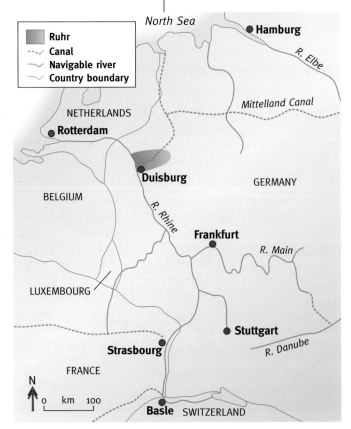

Figure 11.2 The situation of the Ruhr conurbation

The growth of the Ruhr conurbation

In the nineteenth century coal was the most important source of power for industry. Coal mining started in the valley of the River Ruhr where **coal seams** were exposed at the surface and the line of cities from Duisburg to Dortmund grew next to the mines (**Figure 11.1**). As the coal seams were exhausted, mining moved northwards to the deeper seams in the concealed coalfield. The number of mines decreased but the remaining ones were larger and more mechanised. The German government now subsidises coal mining so that Ruhr coal is still used in steelworks and in electricity power stations.

Coal was also used as the main raw material in the chemical industry during the **Industrial Revolution**. Important inventions were made in the Ruhr, such as how to make dyes for cloth. Oil is now used instead of coal but the chemical industry is still very important in the region.

Heavy manufacturing industries use large amounts of energy. Iron and steelworks grew in the Ruhr because they could keep their transport costs low by being next to the coal mines and they could get water from the rivers. There was also local iron ore, and when that was exhausted ore was transported cheaply along the River Rhine, first downstream from eastern France and then upstream from Rotterdam/Europoort. It was imported to there from Sweden, Canada and Australia.

EXAM TIP

The term 'heavy industry' includes coal mining.

The term 'manufacturing industry' does not include coal mining because coal mining does not make coal.

Heavy engineering industries which use a lot of metal set up near the steelworks. They made goods such as locomotives, bridges and armaments. Like all industries, they could also import raw materials cheaply along the Rhine and canals and export their products the same way. Transport by barge is cheaper than by rail or road even though it is slower.

The growth of so much heavy industry provided jobs for many people. These workers and their families needed other goods such as clothes and services such as education, health, public administration and leisure. The few basic industries which started because of the presence of coal, and the cheap transportation on rivers, therefore attracted other industries such as textiles. This is called **cumulative causation** and because of it the Ruhr became a core part of Europe.

The functions of the Ruhr conurbation

1 Before 1960 the Ruhr was Germany's main source of energy. Since 1956 **coal mining** has fallen to below 30 million tonnes (**Figure 11.3**). The oldest mines on the exposed coalfield were in the Ruhr valley and had closed by 1981. Larger pits in the Emscher valley have now closed and all the mining takes place at a few large efficient pits in the far north in the Lippe valley (**Figure 11.3**). The mines are deep and run at a loss; they are kept open by government subsidies to protect jobs. The coal is burned in power stations and steelworks. Demand for coal has decreased because of competition from oil, which is much cheaper and more convenient to handle. Natural gas is now imported from the North Sea, The Netherlands and Russia, and has replaced coal for heating homes; gas is cheaper, cleaner and more convenient. Germany has also built nuclear power stations along the River Rhine and North Sea coasts, so less coal is needed to generate electricity. Energy production is still a function of the Ruhr region but it is not as important as it used to be.

2 **Heavy industry** is still a function of the Ruhr, but it also has declined. In 1981 there were seven large integrated steelworks, mostly in the west so they could import raw materials along the Rhine from Rotterdam. There were also five old small steelworks, mainly in the Ruhr valley near their supplies of coal. By 1998, 10 out of the 12 had been closed because the cheapest location for steelworks is now at **break-of-bulk** points such as Rotterdam, where raw materials can be unloaded from large bulk carrier ships. The two remaining integrated steelworks in the Ruhr are near Duisburg and Dortmund (**Figure 11.4**). Demand for the products of heavy engineering has decreased because of competition from other materials, e.g. construction now uses concrete instead of steel for bridges. Aluminium and plastics have also replaced steel in many products.

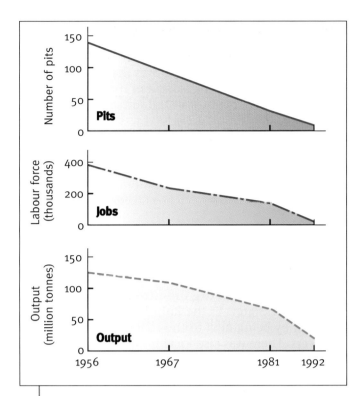

Figure 11.3 Changes in coal output

3 **Light industry**: The main function of the Ruhr is still industry, but in the last 50 years the large heavy industries have been replaced by hundreds of small firms producing a huge range of products, often involving high technology.

Figure 11.4 The Ruhr steel industry 1983–98

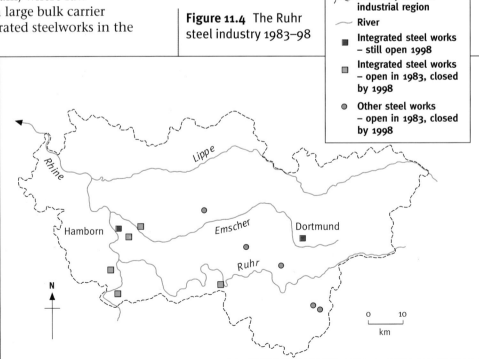

Planning issues in the Ruhr

How can the environment of the Ruhr be improved while industry is being developed?

By the 1980s, the Ruhr conurbation was decaying, with two major problems:

- A polluted environment.
- The closure of heavy industry and high rates of unemployment.

The polluted environment

As coal mining and heavy industry declined, the environment was left polluted with derelict mines and factories as shown in the table below.

The Ruhr Planning Authority (SVR) set up the **Ruhr Plan**, which had two broad aims for the environment:

- To encourage firms to reduce pollution. The chemicals company Bayer now filters out 122 000 tonnes of sulphuric acid from waste water each year, which helps to clean the River Rhine. Ruhrkohle, which owns coal fired power stations, has fitted 'scrubbers' into chimneys to remove sulphur dioxide from waste gases in order to reduce acid rain. The technology needed to remove pollution has led to the growth of many environmental technology companies in the Ruhr.

- To provide open spaces which can be used for leisure. They are at three scales:

1 Small spaces on the edges of cities. For example, the Graf Bismarck Pit between Gelsenkirchen and Bochum closed in 1966, and the 2.6 km² of derelict land and waste tips has been reclaimed to form dry ski slopes, sports pitches, woodland and nature reserves.

2 Green wedges are preserved between the cities (**Figure 11.5**).

3 Large forested areas surround the whole conurbation. The Naturpark Hohe Mark covers 1040 km² on the northern edge of the conurbation (**Figure 11.5**). Footpaths, car parks and cafes have been made in the forest. There are water sports on the reservoirs, and buses and trains connect the area to the conurbation.

Environment	Type of pollution and its cause	Effects
Land	Lakes and marshes caused by mining subsidence	Unsightly, dangerous
	Slag and waste heaps from steel works and coal mines	
	Derelict factories and mines	
Water (rivers)	Chemicals from chemical works and factories	Poisonous to fish
	Hot water from power stations and factories	De-oxygenation of water
	Sewage from burst pipes	Algal growth leads to eutrophication
	Oil washed from roads	Damage to birds' feathers
Air	Acid rain from burning fossil fuels	Acidification of soil and water; damage to buildings
	Smoke from burning coal	Blackening of buildings
	Photochemical smog from vehicle exhausts	Diseases, e.g. asthma

Table 11.1 The polluted environment

Figure 11.5 Environmental projects in the Ruhr

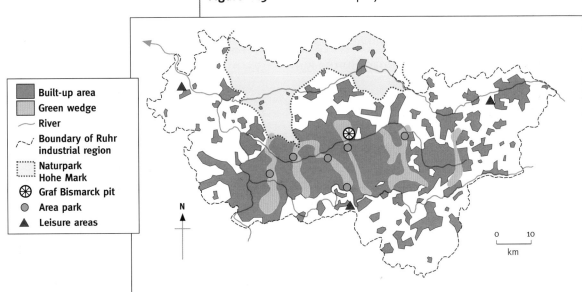

Legend:
- Built-up area
- Green wedge
- River
- Boundary of Ruhr industrial region
- Naturpark Hohe Mark
- Graf Bismarck pit
- Area park
- Leisure areas

0 10 km

High unemployment

As the demand for coal decreased and the coal seams in the Ruhr valley were exhausted, mining was increasingly concentrated on pits in the north. There, the mines were more mechanized and needed fewer workers. The number of jobs declined enormously (**Figure 11.6**) and no mines were left in the conurbation by 1990.

The steelworks also became unprofitable as large new works were built at deep water ports such as Rotterdam. The number of jobs has decreased by three-quarters (**Figure 11.6**). Other heavy industries such as chemicals and engineering also declined because of competition.

As unemployment rose, people had less money to spend, so those employed in the service sector such as in shops and hairdressers were also laid off, making unemployment even higher. Unemployment rose from 1 per cent in 1970 to 15 per cent in 1987. Many people moved out of the Ruhr to jobs in the growing cities in southern Germany, such as Frankfurt and Munich.

Reduction of unemployment

The Ruhr planners had to make changes so that new **footloose** industries such as electronics, vehicles, aircraft, light chemicals (such as drugs) and ICT industries would be attracted to the Ruhr. These modern industries are footloose because they use few raw materials and much skilled labour. They tend to locate where there is:

- A good environment, leisure facilities or climate.

- A good infrastructure of roads, airports, etc.

- A good supply of skilled labour.

- A number of universities or research institutes to help industries develop new products.

- A market to buy their goods.

- A supply of cheap labour to assemble products.

The following changes have been made in the Ruhr in order to attract new industries:

- The environment has been improved and leisure facilities have been created (see page 121).

- Over 500 km of new motorways have been built to link the cities in the conurbation (**Figure 11.7**).

- Buses, trains and trams now form an integrated public transport system with co-ordinated timetables to encourage people to use them rather than cars, which cause congestion and delay as well as air pollution.

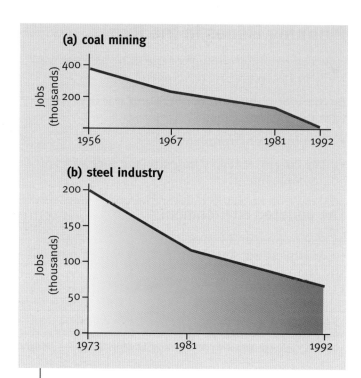

Figure 11.6 The decline of jobs in (a) coal mining and (b) steel industries

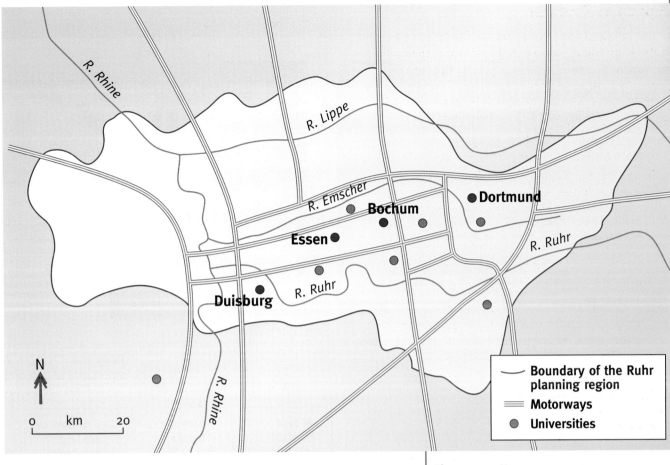

Boundary of the Ruhr planning region
Motorways
● **Universities**

Figure 11.7 New infrastructure in the Ruhr

- Three new universities have been opened in Munster, Marburg and Cologne. They teach science and technology courses to increase the supply of skilled labour. They also conduct research for industry. The government has set up Technology Transfer Centres to improve links between companies and research institutions. Firms have ideas for new and improved products and production methods and they are developed further by working with researchers at the universities.

- Since the union of communist East Germany with the West in 1990, many people have moved from the East and have been able to settle in the Ruhr where they supply cheap labour.

- The government has provided grants to companies to encourage them to set up factories in areas of high unemployment. Opel (now General Motors) built a car factory at Bochum after the coal mines closed.

EXAM TIP

For the AQA Specification B examination, study only one of the following conurbations:

- Rotterdam/Europoort.

- The Ruhr Conurbation.

- The Paris Region.

- The Milan/Turin/Genoa Industrial Triangle.

Questions

1 Pages 118–120

Figure 11.8 shows a factory system.

a How many different inputs are shown?

b Which one of the outputs may bring little income to the factory?

c Describe what the line marked A shows for the factory system.

d Make a large copy of Figure 11.8 leaving out the words. Label the factory 'iron and steel works at Duisburg'. Using the information on pages 119–120, fill in these boxes for this steel works; remember to name the places where inputs come from and where outputs go to.

e Write a paragraph on each of the following topics to give reasons for the growth and importance of heavy industry in the Ruhr:
- Energy supplies.
- Transport of raw materials and manufactured products.
- Markets for the products.

2 Pages 122–123

Use Table 11.2 to answer the following:

a State the two industries with the greatest change in position between 1950 and 1995. For one of these industries, suggest reasons for the change.

b From column C:
- Name two companies operating in the tertiary (service) sector.
- Name the company that is a primary industry.

c Give evidence for the following:
- Heavy industry was still important in 1995.
- The tertiary sector has increased in importance.

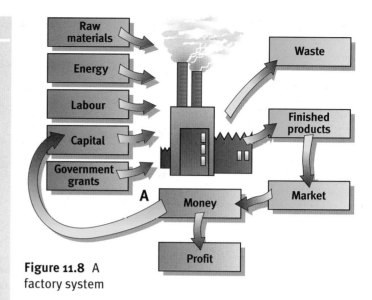

Figure 11.8 A factory system

Table 11.2 Changes in importance of different industries

A. 1950 Top eight industries	B. 1995 Top ten industries	C.1995 Ten largest companies
1 Textiles	1 Chemicals	1 Veda AG – chemicals
2 Coal mining	2 Machinery	2 RWE – energy
3 Food	3 Food	3 Telekom – telecom-munications
4 Steel and heavy metals	4 Electronics	4 Bayer – chemicals
5 Chemicals	5 Motor vehicles	5 Thyssen AG – steel and machinery production
6 Construction	6 Construction	6 Metro-gruppe – trading
7 Machinery	7 Steel and heavy metals	7 Rewe gruppe – retailing
8 Electronics	8 Petroleum-refining	8 Aldi-Gruppe – trading
	9 Coalmining	9 Ruhrkohle AG – mining
	10 Textiles	10 Mannesmann AG – machines and electronics

Questions

Figure 11.9
The Rhine at Duisburg

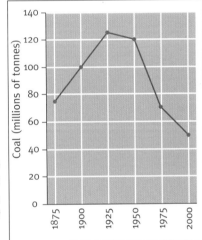

Figure 11.10
Coal production in the Ruhr, 1875–1999

3 *Pages 121–123*

a Look at Table 11.1 which lists some of the ways in which the environment of the Ruhr has been polluted.
  • Study Figure 11.9. Describe and explain how the local environment on the photograph may be damaged.
  • Explain how environmental damage may affect a much wider area.

b Explain how planners in the Ruhr region have tried to reduce the harmful effects of industrial development.

4 *Pages 119–120*

Describe and explain the changes shown on Figure 11.10.

5 *Pages 121–123*

Unemployment in the Ruhr has been reduced by the growth of new light manufacturing industries and service industries. Use information from pages 121–123 to complete Table 11.3.

6 *Pages 120–123*

In the 1960s the major employers in the Ruhr were the textile, iron, steel and chemical industries. In the 1990s there was a great variety of manufacturing industries.

a Identify the main changes to manufacturing industry in the Ruhr.

b Select any two changes and explain why they have happened.

Table 11.3 Factors affecting industrial growth

Factors	Named places	Why this factor encourages industry to grow
good environment and leisure facilities		
good infrastructure, roads, airports, etc.		
skilled labour		
universities and research institutes		
market		
cheap labour		

Figure 12.1 The Île de la Cité

The site and situation of Paris

Site

The **site** of a city is the land it is actually built on. The original site of Paris was on the Île de la Cité, which is an island in the River Seine (**Figure 12.1**). The island provided protection for the town and an easier crossing point over the river. As the urban area grew it expanded on to the surrounding valley sides of the River Seine. Further growth was along the valleys of the River Seine, River Marne and River Oise and on to the surrounding plateau areas (**Figure 12.2**).

Situation

The **situation** of a city is its position in relation to the surrounding area. Paris occupies a central position within the Paris Basin which is the major agricultural area of northern France. It is an important route centre with:

- France's major airport, Roissy Charles de Gaulle, lying to the north of the city, and the second major airport, Orly, lying to the south (**Figure 12.2**).

- The navigable River Seine linking the English Channel to the River Rhine via the River Marne and the Marne-Rhine Canal. The River Seine also links south to the River Rhône via the Centre Canal.

- Road and rail links north to the Channel ports such as Calais and the Channel Tunnel, east to Strasbourg and the River Rhine, and south to the Rhône valley and Mediterranean coast.

The functions of Paris

- The capital city where the parliamentary buildings and government offices are found.

- A financial and commercial centre with nearly all the major French banking, insurance and company head offices located there. They are mainly found in the City area, e.g. Montmartre.

- An industrial centre producing 30 per cent of the output of the aircraft industry, 40 per cent of French cars, and about 50 per cent of all precision, electronic, radio and television products. The nineteenth century industry was primarily located on the banks of the Seine around Argenteuil and in the inner suburbs of St. Denis and Aubervilliers-Bobigny, whilst the newer high-technology industries are located in the outer suburbs, e.g. Poissy, Massy and Creteil (**Figure 12.2**).

- An educational centre with the largest French university, The Sorbonne, located there.

- A cultural centre, with art galleries such as the Louvre, and numerous theatres and restaurants.

- A major retailing centre with many fashion houses, e.g. Gautier and shopping streets.

- A tourist centre with large numbers of French and overseas visitors visiting attractions such as the Eiffel Tower and Notre Dame Cathedral.

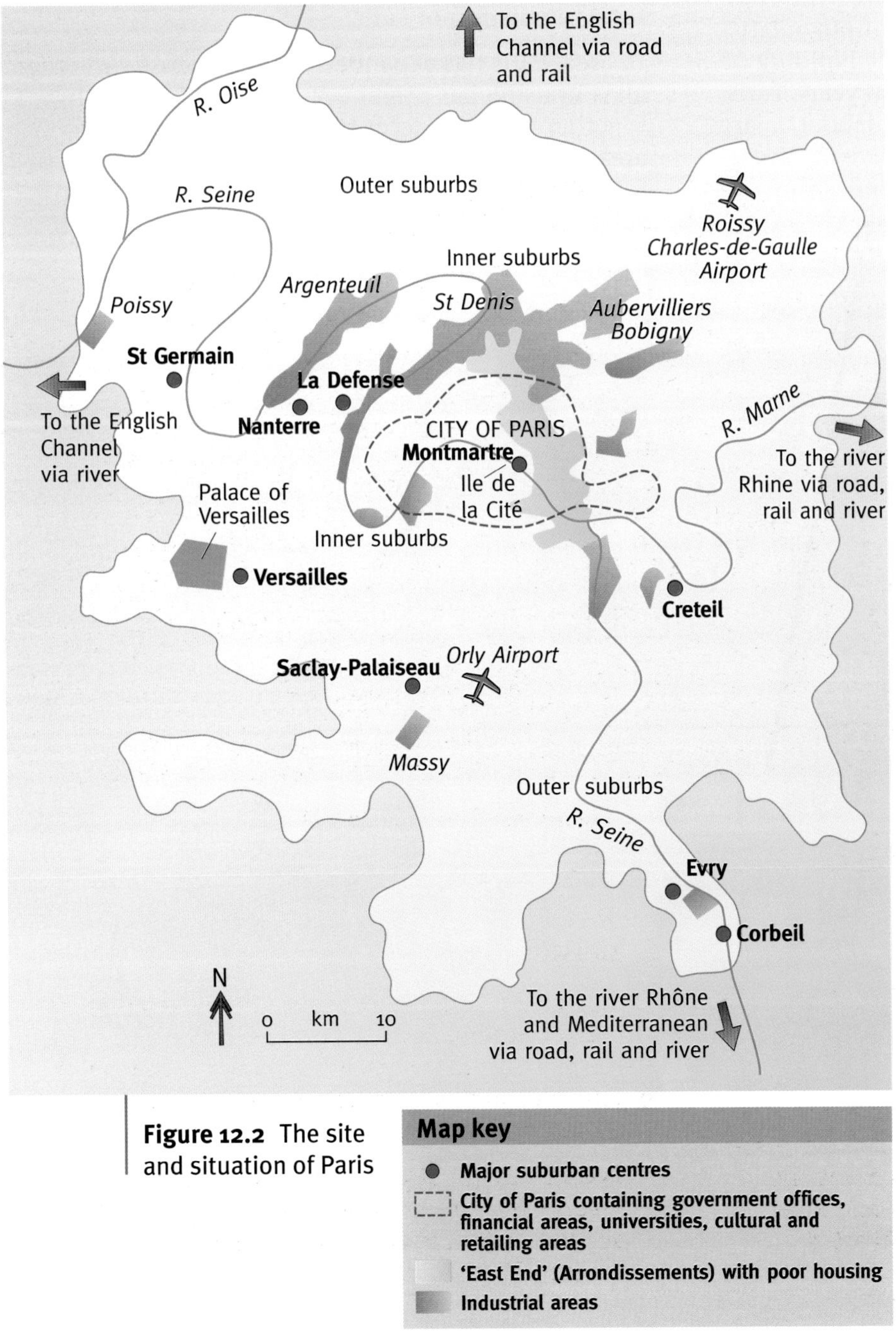

Figure 12.2 The site and situation of Paris

Map key

- ● Major suburban centres
- ⌐ ¬ City of Paris containing government offices, financial areas, universities, cultural and retailing areas
- 'East End' (Arrondissements) with poor housing
- Industrial areas

EXAM TIP

For the AQA Specification B examination, study only one of the following conurbations:

- Rotterdam/Europoort.
- The Ruhr Conurbation.
- The Paris Region.
- The Milan/Turin/Genoa Industrial Triangle.

The growth of Paris

From the 1600s until the mid twentieth century French policy was to centralise power in the capital city, Paris. As a result it became the focal point for the major roads and railways and its position as a route centre has encouraged the growth of Paris. As the capital city, Paris became a major administrative centre, leading to a growth of banking and insurance firms. Nowadays a high proportion of the professional service employment opportunities in France are found in Paris.

During the nineteenth century Paris developed as an industrial centre because of its excellent transport links, which meant that raw materials could be brought into Paris. This attracted workers into the city and **secondary** (manufacturing) employment opportunities have continued, with the building of high-technology factories in the last 30 years. Paris has the advantages of a pool of skilled labour, a large market (20 per cent of French people live in the city) and financial institutions to support new industry. 65 per cent of French research workers and 48 per cent of the total qualified engineers are employed in the area.

With a large population, many of whom are highly educated and well paid, there are a large number of jobs in the service industries. As a cultural centre, staff are needed in the museums and theatres, as a retail centre shop assistants are required, and the growth of Paris as a tourist centre has provided employment opportunities in cafes and bars. During the last 30 years many jobs in the low-paid sector of the **tertiary** (service) industry have been taken by immigrants. Some of these immigrants come from neighbouring countries, e.g. Portugal, but many come from former French colonies in North Africa, e.g. Algeria. They have moved to live in the inner city areas, e.g. St Denis (**Figure 12.3**), adding to the total population of Paris.

In area, Paris has expanded as lower density middle-class housing has been built in the outer suburbs, together with the decentralisation of industry to areas such as Creteil. Many previously independent settlements such as Versailles have become outer suburbs of the city.

Figure 12.3 The inner city area of St Denis

Planning issues in Paris

How can the inner city areas be revitalised whilst encouraging economic growth in the surrounding Paris Basin region?

The problems

- The **economic and social decline** of the inner city areas is a major problem. This has been caused by the decline of traditional industry in these areas and resulting high unemployment levels. The more skilled have left for job opportunities in the suburbs, leaving behind a low-income population. The old housing has deteriorated and much of it lacks basic facilities. It is in a decayed condition and overcrowded. This is particularly the case in the 'East End' part of Paris (**Figure 12.3**).

- With a high concentration of employment in the city area, **traffic congestion** is a serious problem. There are 3 million daily commuters, of whom 35 per cent travel by private car and for whom a major problem is parking. 15 per cent of commuters travel short distances on foot, but 50 per cent rely on public transport. The Metro (underground system) only goes as far as the inner suburban ring. At this point commuters travelling to the outer suburbs have to transfer to the municipal bus service or to the RER (Réseau Express Regional) which is the high speed suburban rail service (**Figure 12.5**).

- There is concern that towns in the commuter zones such as Versailles are being absorbed into the outer suburbs. This means the amount of green land around Paris is declining as this area is built on.

- Other towns in the Paris region such as Reims and Orleans are smaller than might be expected. This is because the population and industry have become too concentrated in Paris.

The solutions

1 *New developments* were built in the inner city areas, e.g. La Défense, just to the west of the city centre (**Figure 12.4**). La Défense contains shops, offices and public buildings. The purpose is to provide employment and attract private offices and factories to the inner city areas.

2 To reduce congestion in the city centre the following *improvements in transport* are being made:

Figure 12.4 La Défense

- The Metro system is being expanded into the outer suburbs (**Figure 12.5**).

- The RER system is being expanded to give a new fast suburban railway line which goes east-west and has two north-south lines which connect Orly with Roissy Charles-de-Gaulle Airport.

- Three ring motorways, one at 20 km, one at 15 km and the Boulevard Peripherique around the city centre have been constructed. These link with radiating motorways out of the city centre.

3 To preserve green land, **growth axes** parallel to the River Seine were designated, preserving open land along the river (**Figure 12.6**). **Green wedges** have been identified and in these areas the agricultural and forest land on the periphery of the city cannot be built on.

4 To reduce the concentration of population and industry in Paris, **growth points** have been identified. Five new towns, e.g. Evry, have been built up to 35 km from the city centre, and historic towns such as Reims and Orleans have received government support to attract industry.

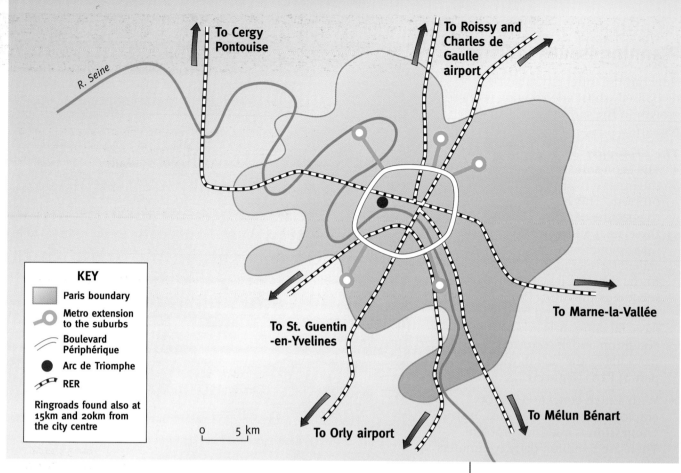

KEY

Paris boundary

Metro extension to the suburbs

Boulevard Périphérique

● Arc de Triomphe

RER

Ringroads found also at 15km and 20km from the city centre

0   5 km

To Cergy Pontouise

To Roissy and Charles de Gaulle airport

To Marne-la-Vallée

To St. Guentin -en-Yvelines

To Mélun Bénart

To Orly airport

Figure 12.5 New transport routes around Paris

Figure 12.6 Growth axes of Paris

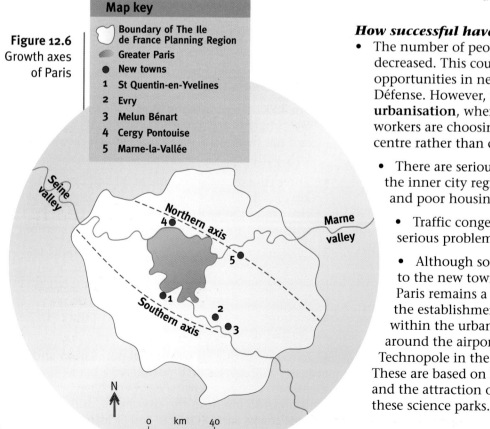

Map key

Boundary of The Ile de France Planning Region

Greater Paris

● New towns

1 St Quentin-en-Yvelines

2 Evry

3 Melun Bénart

4 Cergy Pontouise

5 Marne-la-Vallée

Seine valley

Northern axis

Marne valley

Southern axis

N

0   km   40

How successful have the solutions been?

- The number of people leaving the inner city has decreased. This could be because of improved job opportunities in new developments such as La Défense. However, it could also be because of **re-urbanisation**, whereby some more affluent workers are choosing to live close to the city centre rather than commute.

- There are serious social problems remaining in the inner city region with high unemployment and poor housing in areas such as St Denis.

- Traffic congestion in central Paris remains a serious problem.

- Although some firms have been attracted to the new towns and cities such as Orleans, Paris remains a 'magnet'. This has resulted in the establishment of two new growth areas within the urban zone. These are at Roissy around the airport and the Saclay-Palaiseau Technopole in the south-west (**Figure 12.2**). These are based on higher education institutes and the attraction of high technology firms to these science parks.

Questions

1 *Page 128*

Look at Figure 12.7

a   Describe the change of population in the Paris Region as a whole.

b   Describe the changes in the different areas of the Region.

c   Discuss why people move into the Paris Region.

2 *Page 129*

Describe four problems resulting from the growth of Paris.

3 *Page 129*

Several ways of relieving the problems of Paris are shown in Figure 12.7. List these, and discuss how two of them would help to solve the problems of Paris.

4 *Pages 129–130*

Describe how the problem of traffic congestion in Paris is being tackled.

5 *Page 130*

How effective do you think the Paris Regional Plan has been? Give reasons to support your answer.

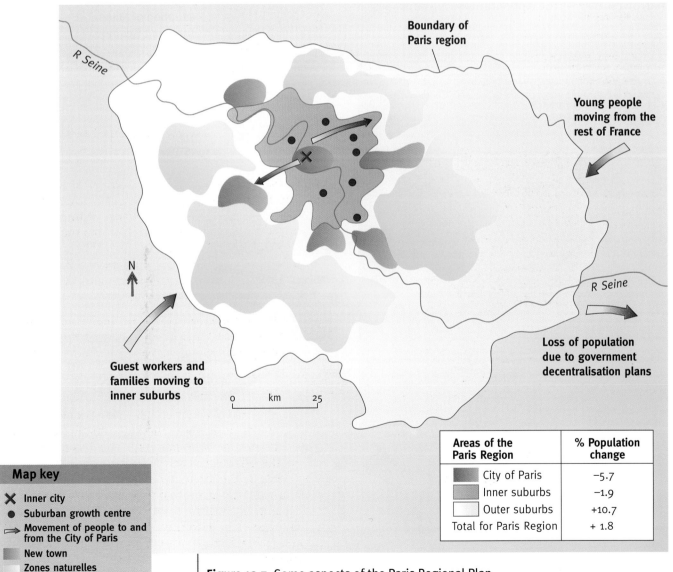

Areas of the Paris Region	% Population change
City of Paris	−5.7
Inner suburbs	−1.9
Outer suburbs	+10.7
Total for Paris Region	+ 1.8

Map key

✕ Inner city
● Suburban growth centre
⇒ Movement of people to and from the City of Paris
   New town
   Zones naturelles (protected countryside)

Figure 12.7 Some aspects of the Paris Regional Plan and population change in the Paris region

13 Development of the European urban core – the Milan/Turin/Genoa industrial triangle

The site and situation of the Milan/Turin/Genoa industrial triangle

Site

The **site** of a place is the land it is actually built on. The industrial triangle is on the wide lowland which is the western end of the River Po valley. It is an area of sand and alluvium which favours intensive farming. The three cities are at sites where important routes meet. Turin is at the confluence of the Dora Riparia and Po rivers. Milan is on the Lombardy plain and Genoa has a deep water port next to the lowest narrowest part of the Appennine Mountains

Figure 13.1 Site and situation of Milan, Turin and Genoa

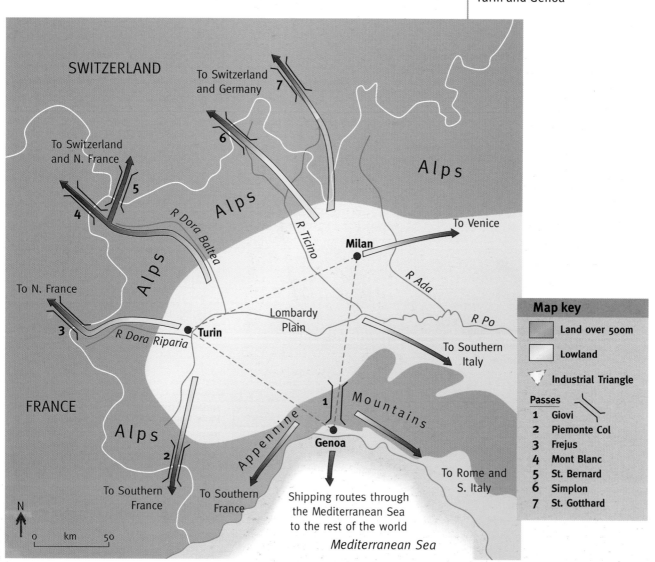

Situation

The situation of a place is its position in relation to the surrounding area. Looking at **Figure 13.1** it can be seen that Milan has route links to Venice, Turin and Genoa in Italy. It also has access to Switzerland via the Simplon and St. Gotthard Passes. Turin links to Milan and Genoa in Italy. The St. Bernard Pass leads to Switzerland and the road via the Mont Blanc tunnel goes to France. Genoa has a coastal route to France and southern Italy. The Giovi Pass provides a link to Turin and Milan. The coastal location gives direct access to the Mediterranean shipping routes.

The network of **communications** makes this part of Italy very accessible to the other member countries of the EU. This has helped develop the region as the most economically significant area of Italy.

The functions of the Milan/Turin/Genoa industrial triangle

- The area is the major industrial region of Italy. Milan is important for food processing, textiles and engineering. Turin is a major car manufacturing centre with the Fiat works located in the town (**Figure 13.2**). Genoa has steel making and oil refining industries.

- Genoa is an important port.

- Milan is a major financial centre.

- Tourism is a major industry along the Ligurian coast.

- Intensive agriculture takes place across the whole region.

The reasons for the growth of Milan

- Milan is the focus of road and rail routes within the Lombardy Plain.

- HEP is generated in the nearby Alps and natural gas is available to provide energy for industrial development.

- The population is well educated and enterprising.

- The highly productive local farming provides the raw materials for food processing leading to activities such as cheese-making, e.g. Gorgonzola, Parmesan.

Figure 13.2 Fiat factory

- Local cotton and wool provide the basis for the textiles industry.

- Chemical industries providing dyes for the textile industry and pharmaceuticals for the large local population developed here.

- Engineering firms opened, using local scrap metal. They made goods to supply the textile and vehicle industry.

- Car manufacturing e.g. Alfa Romeo is located here.

- The town became a major financial and commercial centre because of the large industrial development in the area. A major trade fair to promote Italian products was opened.

The reasons for the growth of Turin

- It is a route centre particularly for roads coming from Paris to the west and Switzerland to the north.

- Natural gas is located nearby.

- HEP can be generated to provide energy for local industries.

- The establishment of major factories e.g. Fiat and Lancia cars (**Figure 13.2**), Olivetti typewriters, led to the attraction of other electrical and engineering industries.

The reasons for the growth of Genoa

- It is a major port. Oil amounts to two-thirds of the tonnage imported, and an oil pipeline runs from Genoa to Milan. Other major imports are coal, mineral ores, grain, tropical foods, chemicals and textile fibres.

- Steelworks developed as they use the imported raw materials e.g. scrap iron, West African ore and coal.

- The steel is used in the shipbuilding and heavy engineering works which subsequently developed.

- Food processing plants based on imports have also been built, e.g. flour mills, sugar refineries.

- Good road and rail links north to Turin and Milan mean that imports e.g. textile fibres can be sent to provide the raw materials for the factories in these towns.

How did the growth of Milan, Turin and Genoa lead to the establishment of an industrial triangle?

As the three towns became major economic centres the area became a **core** region of the EU. This happened because:

- Some factories supplied raw materials for others, e.g. the steel works in Genoa supplied the Fiat car factory in Turin.

- Road and rail routes were built to make it easier to move goods around the region.

- There was a high demand for workers, so people moved to the area for employment especially from southern Italy (Chapter 8).

- The high concentration of industry and population in the area created a demand for services such as banking, education and retailing. These generated further employment.

- The area is attractive to live in, with the Alps to the north and the Mediterranean to the south. This encouraged industrialists to invest in the area because it would be easy to attract highly skilled employees.

EXAM TIP

This is a classic example of a core area. Link the characteristics of core areas from Chapter 7 to the features of the Milan/Turin/Genoa industrial triangle. You could contrast this with the peripheral features detailed in Chapter 8 on southern Italy.

Planning issues in the industrial triangle

How can economic development in the Milan/Turin/Genoa triangle be maintained without the area becoming environmentally damaged?

Problems

This core area has proved extremely attractive for economic investment. This has encouraged migration into the area, giving a rapid population growth. As a result:

- Small, attractive towns in the rural areas have been absorbed into the main urban zones, e.g. despite being 18 km away from the city centre, Gorgonzola is now within the built-up area of Milan.

- Within the cities many of the areas of open space and parkland have been replaced with blocks of flats, housing estates and new roads.

- There is serious air pollution. This is caused by car exhaust fumes which build up during the frequent traffic jams. The large amount of factory smoke adds to the pollutants. The situation is particularly serious in winter when the polluted air is trapped by cold winds descending from the surrounding mountains.

- The oil refining and petrochemical industry along the Ligurian coast at Genoa means there is a high risk of water pollution in the Mediterranean Sea.

Solutions

- Planning controls to restrict further building on green land have been put in place.

- Environmental laws to reduce factory air and water emissions are being strictly enforced.

- Public transport is being improved to reduce the number of cars on the road.

- Regional policies have been put in place to encourage industrial development in other parts of Italy. This would then reduce migration from these areas to the north.

- In the south (Mezzogiorno) agricultural reform and investment in both large state industries (e.g. the steel works at Taranto) and private manufacturing (e.g. the Fiat car works at Melfi) has taken place (see Chapter 8). In the area of the country known as the 'Third Italy' (**Figure 13.3**)) financial support has been given to small specialist firms.

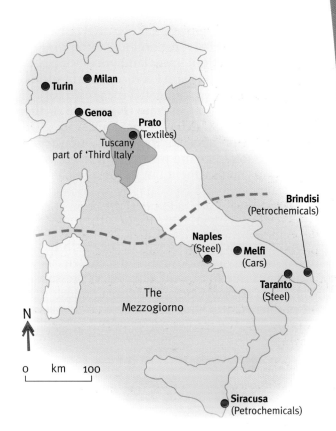

Figure 13.3 Regions developed to relieve pressure on the Milan/Turin/Genoa Industrial Triangle

How successful have the policies been?

Fewer green areas are being built on, but this reduces the building land available so prices rise. With improved transport and pleasant countryside relatively near, e.g. the Alpine foothills, some of the more affluent population are moving to these areas and commuting in to the cities. However, the poorer people cannot afford to do this so they remain in the older housing, increasing the social problems of the urban area.

Industrial air and water emissions are being controlled, but with more commuting the number of cars has increased, giving higher levels of air pollution from vehicles. The improvements in public transport have not kept pace with the rise in commuting, so traffic congestion is still a serious problem.

Some manufacturing growth has occurred outside the north. In the 'Third Italy' region local enterprise, high levels of education, lower land prices than Milan, Turin and Genoa and good communications to major markets, have stimulated the growth of small firms. For example in Prato (**Figure 13.3**) there are a large number of textiles firms, constantly developing new products for the fashion industry. In the south the steel, car and petrochemical works have provided some employment but the area remains economically depressed (see Chapter 8), encouraging migrants to move north, adding to the population pressure.

Although manufacturing growth in the north has slowed down, service industries and commercial activities continue to expand. This places pressure on land and also attracts workers, adding to housing and traffic problems.

EXAM TIP

For the AQA Specification B examination, study only one of the following conurbations:

- Rotterdam/Europoort.
- The Ruhr Conurbation.
- The Paris Region.
- The Milan/Turin/Genoa Industrial Triangle.

Figure 13.4 The growth of the Milan/Turin/Genoa triangle

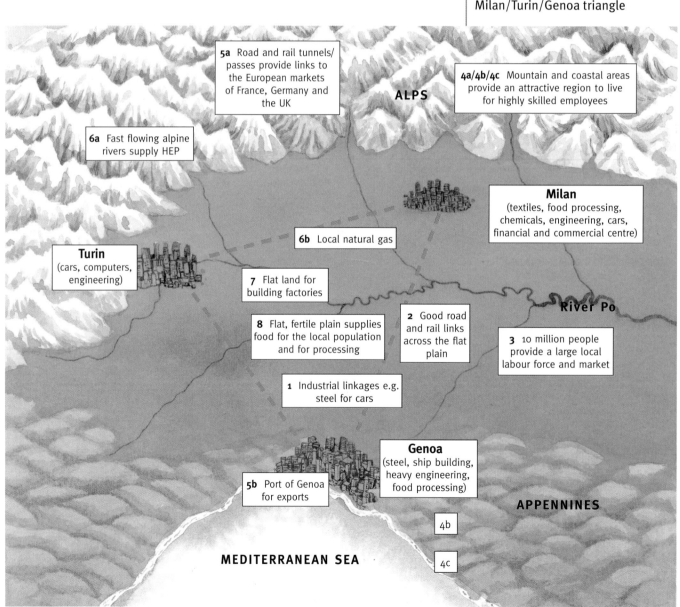

Questions

1 *Pages 132–134*

Look at Figure 13.4 on page 136. Use the labelling on this map to explain:

a   Why industry has been attracted to this area. You should use the numbers on the map to help you.

b   Why people have been attracted to move to the Milan/Turin/Genoa area. Use the following side headings to help you.
- Employment
- Communications
- Environmental attractions

2 *Pages 135–136*

a   Copy Figure 13.5.

b   Complete the following table. The first problem has been done for you.

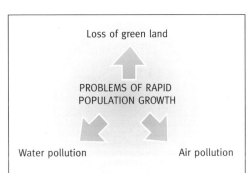

Figure 13.5
Problems of rapid population growth

PROBLEM	DESCRIPTION OF PROBLEM	SOLUTION	HOW DOES THE SOLUTION WORK?
Water pollution	The large numbers of factories, particularly oil-refining and petro-chemical works at the coast, pollute rivers and the Mediterranean sea	1. Strict environmental laws 2. Encourage firms to locate elsewhere, e.g. Mezzogiorno	1. The heavy fines mean the companies are prepared to invest in prevention. 2. There are fewer factories polluting the water.
Air pollution			
Loss of green land			

3 *Pages 135–136*

How effective do you think the policies put in place to address the problems of the Milan/Turin/Genoa area have been? Give reasons to support your answer.

The Hinterland of Dover

The **hinterland** of a port is the area from which goods are exported through the port, and the area to which goods are imported through the port. The whole of Britain forms part of Dover's hinterland. **Figure 14.1** shows where the highest population densities in Britain are, and large numbers of people from these areas travel to Europe each year, either on business or on holiday.

Most people and goods travelling to Dover go on motorways (**Figure 14.1**). This is because:

- They usually have three lanes so vehicles can overtake safely and go fast to save time.

- The junctions have slip roads so traffic does not have to slow down when reaching them.

- Hills and corners are gentle so heavy lorries are not slowed down.

- Parking is not allowed, and vehicles which have broken down have to move on to the hard shoulder so they do not cause accidents.

Dover is joined to the motorway network by the M20/A20 and M2/A2. Other east coast ports such as Felixstowe are joined by the A12/A14 dual carriageways.

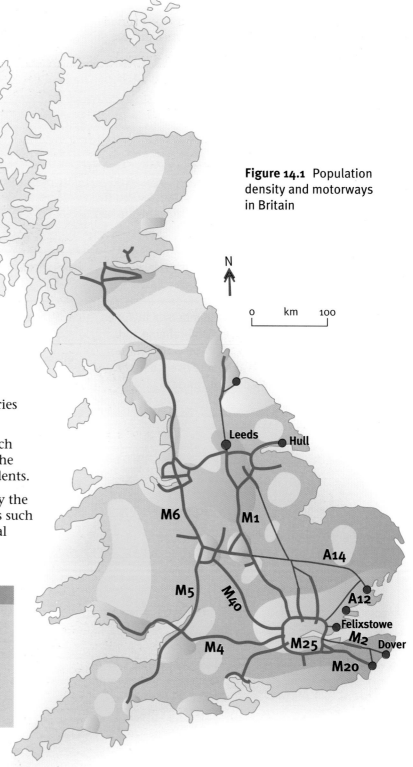

Figure 14.1 Population density and motorways in Britain

Map key
- Motorway
- Other road (selected)
- East coast port
- Many people (over 100/km²)
- In between
- Few people (less than 20/km²)

The infrastructure of the Port of Dover

The infrastructure is the facilities which make it possible to operate the port e.g. roads, cranes, and management.

Ships need calm water in order to load and unload. **Breakwaters** have been built to provide this at Dover (**Figure 14.2**). Dover has facilities for four types of ship:

- Roll-on/roll-off (RORO) ferries.
- Container ships.
- Pleasure boats.
- Cruise ships.

RORO ferries

These are ships which cars, coaches and lorries can drive on to and off. At Dover they use the Eastern Docks (**Figure 14.2**). A road leads down on to the quay and there are large parking areas where vehicles wait for the next ship. Loading time is quick. This is important because ferries need to make as many crossings as possible to France each day to make the maximum profit. The usual number is ten crossings (by each RORO ferry), each of which takes 90 minutes. However, Dover has two fast RORO ferries (catamarans or Sea-Cats) which make the journey in only 50 minutes. Most ferry passengers want the shortest and quickest route to Europe, so there are over one hundred crossings each day by 12 RORO ferries from Dover to Calais. Single ferries also cross to Dunkirk in France and Ostend and Zeebrugge in Belgium. Once there, drivers can go straight on to the French and Belgian motorways (**Figure 14.3**).

Map key

Chalk cliff	
Sea	

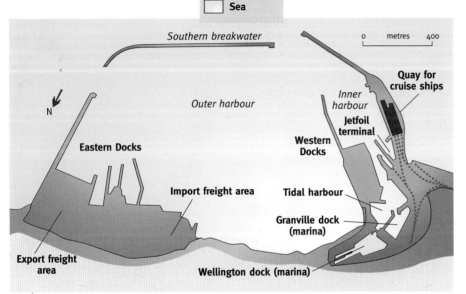

Figure 14.2 Dover docks

Figure 14.3 Links across the channel

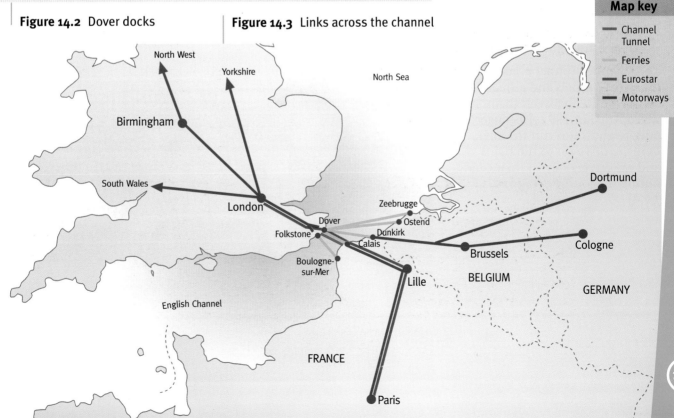

Map key

Channel Tunnel	
Ferries	
Eurostar	
Motorways	

Container ships

Containers are steel boxes built to a standard size. Their advantages are that:

- They can be filled and sealed at the factory to prevent theft.

- They can be transported by road, rail and sea.

- They can be quickly moved from lorries and trains to storage areas next to the dockside. Cranes load them on to container ships. The use of cranes for loading and unloading means that the operation employs few workers and it takes only a few hours, rather than the several days which were needed before containers were invented.

Dover is now one of the leading ports for fresh food imports especially fruit, which is stored in a temperature-controlled warehouse.

Pleasure boats

The Western Docks provide a harbour for yachts and other small pleasure boats. They are kept away from the larger ships so that they do not delay their timetables.

Cruise ships

Because of the increase in cruise ships in recent years, Dover now has two cruise terminals. The many passengers can be quickly taken by coach on short sight-seeing tours in Kent and London.

The Channel Tunnel

The Tunnel runs from Cheriton near Folkestone to Calais (**Figure 14.3**). It was built here because:

- It was almost the shortest route, which was important to keep building costs down and it means that travel time is very short.

- It is in the Chalk Marl, a clay which is impermeable and is soft so that it was easy to tunnel through.

The Channel Tunnel is actually two large tunnels and a small service tunnel between them. It was opened in 1994. Passenger and freight trains run through. Vehicles drive on to the trains and car drivers stay in their cars during the journey (**Figure 14.4**).

Figure 14.4 The Shuttle Train

The advantages of the Tunnel are:

- The travel time is only 35 minutes (90 minutes by ferry).
- Crossing the Channel is not delayed by bad weather as ferries often are.

However, the Tunnel has increased competition with nearby ports such as Dover, where fewer people are now employed and two of the ferry companies have merged.

Eurostar (passenger) trains travel between London and Paris in three hours, and between London and Brussels in two hours. Each train can carry up to 766 passengers, and 12 trains leave London each day. They have reduced the number of air flights between the cities.

The Shuttle Trains (for vehicles and passengers) travel between the two ends of the Tunnel. On the British side, they can join the M20 motorway and then travel to all parts of the country. On the French side, vehicles get on to the A26 motorway which links to the rest of the motorway system in Europe (**Figure 14.3**).

The trade of Dover

Dover is by far Britain's most important ferry port. In 1999, 18.2 million passengers, 3.3 million cars, 156 000 coaches and 1.5 million lorries travelled through it (**Figure 14.5**). The total number of passengers, cars and coaches travelling on the surface to Europe has risen sharply over the last five years. However, as **Figure 14.5** shows, only the number of lorries passing through Dover has increased during this time. This indicates that the Channel Tunnel is taking the increased number of journeys to Europe but is not yet harming Dover's trade.

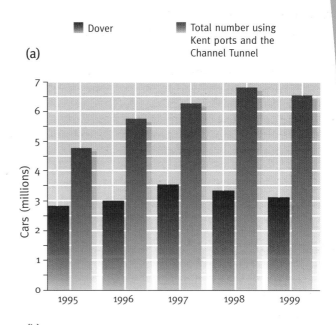

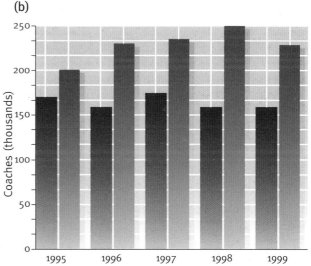

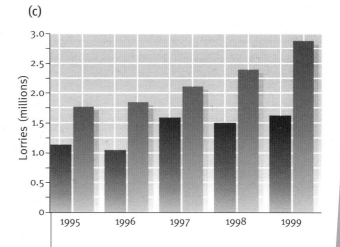

Figure 14.5 Transport on Dover's ferries: (a) cars, (b) coaches and (c) lorries

Questions

1 Page 138

Look at Figure 14.1.

a List the numbers of the motorways you would use on a journey from Leeds to Dover travelling only by motorway.

b Describe two advantages which Dover has over Felixstowe for passengers.

c Give several reasons why travelling by motorway is faster and cheaper than using normal A class roads.

d Give two reasons why north and central Wales form an unimportant part of Dover's hinterland.

e Suggest two reasons why East Anglia is also an unimportant part of Dover's hinterland.

2 Pages 138–140

Figure 14.6 is a vertical aerial photograph of part of the docks at Dover. Using this and Figure 14.2:

a Which direction is north on the photograph?

b To where does the main road on theright go?

c To where does the main road at the centre bottom of the photograph go?

d If you were driving an articulated lorry from the M20, which road would you use to reach the dock?

e What are the names of areas A, B, C and D?

f What types of ship dock at these points?

g What are these ships used for?

3 Pages 139–140

a What is a 'roll-on/roll-off' (RORO) ship?

b Figure 14.7 shows another type of ship which uses British ports.
  • Name the type of ship.
  • Explain in detail why there has been an increased use of this type of ship for carrying cargoes.

4 Pages 140–141

a Give two reasons why some passengers and freight continue to use the ferries across the English Channel instead of using the Channel Tunnel.

b What have been the effects of the Channel Tunnel on the port of Dover?

c People have different views about the building of the Channel Tunnel. Three are shown below:
  • **Sailor on a ferry** – 'The Tunnel is seriously affecting my work'.
  • **British tourist** – 'The Tunnel has greatly improved the quality of my family's life'.
  • **Someone who lives in Dover** – 'The Tunnel has had mixed effects on me and my family'.

Explain why these people have different attitudes to the Channel Tunnel.

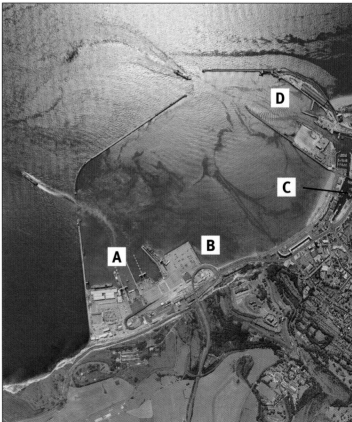

Figure 14.6 Part of Dover Docks

Figure 14.7
A type of ship

15 Amazonia – development in the rainforest environment

The location and climate of Amazonia

Amazonia consists of the **drainage basin** of the River Amazon and its **tributaries** in Brazil. The river rises in the Andes in Peru and flows east to the Atlantic Ocean. Many tributaries, e.g. the Negro, Madeira and Xingu join it so that its drainage basin is extremely large (**Figure 15.1**). Most of the basin lies in northern Brazil and it is a low-lying, flat area.

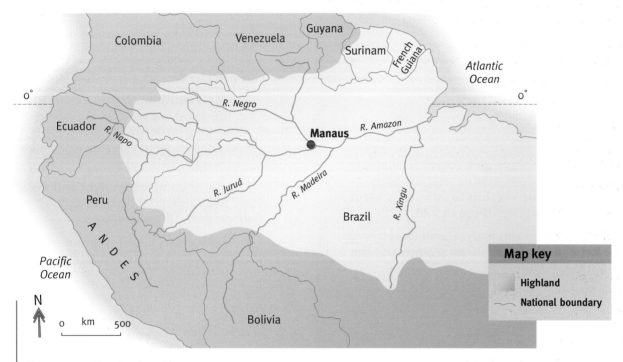

Figure 15.1 Map to show the location of the Amazon

The temperatures in Amazonia are high (about 27°C) throughout the year with a low annual temperature range (about 3°C) (**Figure 15.2**).

The temperatures are high because the Sun is directly overhead (over the **Equator**) in March and September and almost overhead in the intervening months. In June the Sun is overhead at the **Tropic of Cancer** and in December it is overhead at the **Tropic of Capricorn**. This means the rays are concentrated over a limited area, and since the rays pass through only a small section of the Earth's atmosphere little heat is lost before they reach the Earth's surface (**Figure 15.3**).

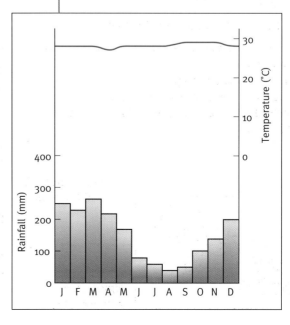

Figure 15.2 Climate graph for Manaus

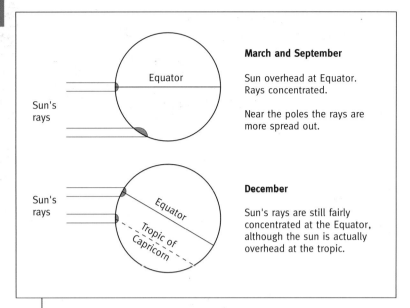

Figure 15.3 The effects of the Sun's rays at the Equator

March and September

Sun overhead at Equator. Rays concentrated.

Near the poles the rays are more spread out.

December

Sun's rays are still fairly concentrated at the Equator, although the sun is actually overhead at the tropic.

The rainfall is high in this region (over 1500mm per year) because there is low pressure, and the high temperatures cause **convection** to take place, giving heavy rainfall on most days (**Figure 2.4**).

The high temperatures and high rainfall exist throughout the year as there are no seasons and the area is extremely humid.

The relationship between climate, soil and vegetation in the rainforest ecosystem

An **ecosystem** is the way in which the plants, animals, soils and climate interact with each other in an area. In Amazonia the natural vegetation of the area is **tropical rainforest**, which can also be called **selva**. The natural vegetation is one that grows in response to the climate and soils of an area and has not been altered by humans.

The constantly high temperatures and high rainfall mean a large number of plants can grow and there is a wide variety of species. There are no seasons so plant growth is continuous throughout the year, i.e. the forest is **evergreen**. Individual plants may be deciduous but there is never a period of time in the year when all the plants shed their leaves.

The plants compete for light and this gives rise to a number of features and adaptations (**Figure 15.4**):

- The vegetation forms layers:
  Layer A = A disjointed layer of

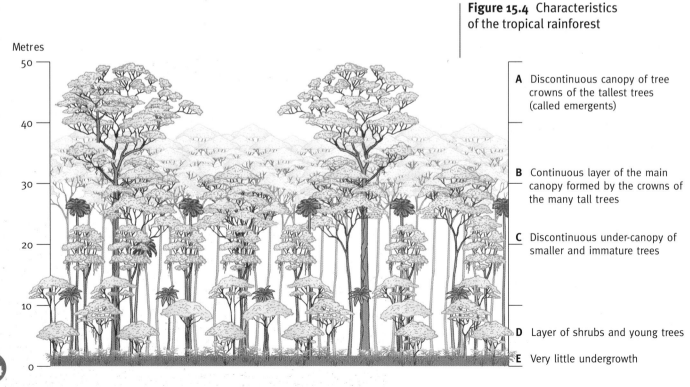

Figure 15.4 Characteristics of the tropical rainforest

A Discontinuous canopy of tree crowns of the tallest trees (called emergents)

B Continuous layer of the main canopy formed by the crowns of the many tall trees

C Discontinuous under-canopy of smaller and immature trees

D Layer of shrubs and young trees

E Very little undergrowth

emergents at a height of about 45 m. Layer B = A more continuous layer at about 30 m where the crowns of the trees spread out to form a **canopy**, blocking out the light below.
Layer C = An **undercanopy** at about 20 m formed of smaller or immature trees. Layer D = A shrub layer at about 5 m. Layer E = Very little undergrowth because no light gets through except in clearings and along rivers.

- Some vegetation uses other plants to reach the light, e.g. **epiphytes** grow on branches of trees where water and leaf litter collect, whilst **lianas** (climbers) reach up to the light by twisting around tree trunks.

- The individual trees have few branches because their main aim is to reach the light. With most of the nutrients contained in the **leaf litter** or near the surface of the soil, the root system is shallow. With tall trees and shallow roots there is the possible risk of the trees falling over, so **buttress roots** grow out of the trunk to act like a prop to secure the tree. The bark is thin since the tree does not have to be protected against the cold, and leaves have **drip-tips** and **leathery cuticles** to shed excessive rain water so that the plant is able to take in carbon dioxide and to photosynthesize more efficiently.

The soils in Amazonia are known as **laterites**. They are coloured red by the iron and aluminium in them and are infertile. They contain only a few nutrients in a shallow layer near the surface.

Cycles within the tropical rainforest ecosystem

1 Carbon dioxide and oxygen (Figure 15.5a)

- Plants take in carbon dioxide from the atmosphere during the process of photosynthesis.

- When leaves and dead wood fall to the forest floor they decay rapidly to release carbon dioxide which returns to the atmosphere.

- During the process of photosynthesis oxygen is released in to the atmosphere.

Figure 15.5 Cycles within the tropical rainforest: (a) carbon/oxygen, (b) water and (c) nutrients

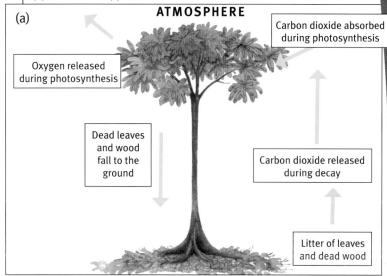

(a) ATMOSPHERE

Oxygen released during photosynthesis

Carbon dioxide absorbed during photosynthesis

Dead leaves and wood fall to the ground

Carbon dioxide released during decay

Litter of leaves and dead wood

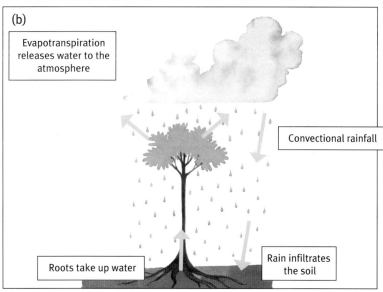

(b)

Evapotranspiration releases water to the atmosphere

Convectional rainfall

Roots take up water

Rain infiltrates the soil

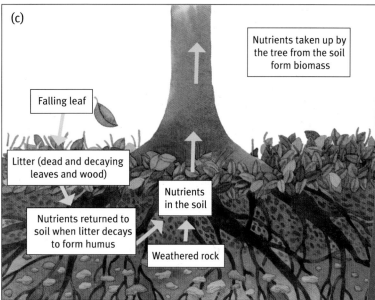

(c)

Nutrients taken up by the tree from the soil form biomass

Falling leaf

Litter (dead and decaying leaves and wood)

Nutrients in the soil

Nutrients returned to soil when litter decays to form humus

Weathered rock

2 Water (Figure 15.5b)

- Rain falls on to the ground and **infiltrates** the soil.

- Tree roots take up water from the soil.

- Water passes from the soil and trees to the atmosphere by **evaporation** and **transpiration**.

- The water in the atmosphere returns to the surface as convectional rainfall.

3 Nutrients (Figure 15.5c)

- Nutrients in the soil are formed from weathered rock and humus, which is decayed plant and animal material.

- Nutrients on the ground are found in the leaf litter, which is the dead and decaying leaves and wood which fall to the ground from the trees.

- The plants take up these nutrients to form **biomass**.

- When the plants die they are returned to the litter which decays to form humus which returns nutrients to the soil.

In the tropical rainforest the decay of dead material and the take-up of nutrients is very rapid in the hot, wet climate. This means a large number of the nutrients are stored in the plants (biomass) so if the trees are removed, nutrients are also removed from the system.

People in Amazonia – the Yanomami

There are about 9000 members of the **Yanomami** tribe living in a remote area of Amazonia. The tribe is divided into villages of 25–400 people. Each group has a clearing in the forest occupied by a **yano** which is a large doughnut-shaped house built of trees and thatched with palm leaves (**Figure 15.6**). The yano is located close to running water and flat land suitable for farming.

The Yanomami do not trade with outsiders. Instead, they practise subsistence farming, which means they produce food only for themselves with no surplus to sell. The food is obtained in two ways:

1 **Hunting and gathering** accounts for about 20 per cent of the food, but it provides the bulk of proteins, vitamins and minerals. Vegetable drugs are used to stun fish, whilst the women gather wild nuts, fruits and small creatures such as frogs and caterpillars. A particular favourite is honey, of which the Yanomami know 15 different kinds.

2 **Slash and burn** agriculture provides 80 per cent of the food. Clearings called *chagras* are used to grow crops (**Figure 15.6**).

- Approximately 5 ha of forest and undergrowth is cleared using stone axes and machetes, leaving some of the larger trees standing.

- After the felled trees have 'dried out' they are burned. This helps to provide extra nutrients as the ash is spread on the soil.

- Holes are made in the soil with a pointed stick.

Figure 15.6
A Yanomami clearing

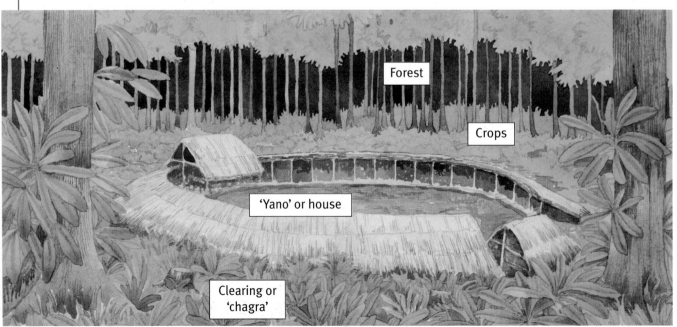

Forest

Crops

'Yano' or house

Clearing or 'chagra'

- Cuttings and seeds of crops such as cassava, sweet potatoes, bananas, plantain, maize and papaya are planted and the hole is filled in. In all, about 60 crops are grown. 20 are for food, the rest for medicine, and religious ritual.

- The hot, wet climate means crops grow quickly, but so does other vegetation so the area has to be constantly weeded.

- The crops are harvested by hand when they are needed, and as the climate allows crop growth all the year round the plantings are timed to give a continuous supply of food so storage is not necessary.

- After three or four years the crop yields decline, so the Yanomami move to another area of the forest.

Shifting cultivation

The Yanomami practise **shifting cultivation** i.e. the tribe leaves one clearing after three or four years of cultivation, clears another by the 'slash and burn' method, and then cultivates that area.

The tribe does this because after this time the soil has begun to lose its fertility so crop yields decline. The soil nutrients decrease because the trees have been removed and so no more nutrients are being added to the soil. The growing crops have used the limited supply of soil nutrients and no fertilisers or manure are used to replace them. Also, with fewer trees the high rainfall is able to **leach** nutrients from the soil, which means that the nutrients are taken down to levels in the soil which the plant roots cannot reach. By leaving the area after three or four years the damage is not permanent and the forest is able to recover so eventually the tribe can return.

Shifting cultivation does not cause permanent damage because:

- In 'slash and burn' agriculture, not all the trees are removed. Also the clearings have a lot of vegetation on them which is not removed. This means that some nutrients are being returned to the soil, the soil is partly protected from the rainfall so not all the nutrients are washed away, and when the clearing is abandoned the forest can grow back quickly.

- With some vegetation protection, the rain cannot erode the soil and the wind cannot blow the ash away.

- The clearing is surrounded by existing forest so the area is re-seeded quickly.

- No chemical fertilisers or herbicides are used so the soil structure is not destroyed and the indigenous forest plants remain to grow back.

- Using hand tools, e.g. a pointed stick rather than large machines means only the surface soil is disturbed with the underlying rock still being weathered to supply more nutrients.

If the trees are removed the soil loses its fertility due to the following factors:

- In the tropical rainforest most of the nutrients are stored in the trees so if the trees are removed there are few nutrients returning to the soil (**Figure 15.7**).

- With no protective tree cover the high rainfall rapidly leaches the remaining nutrients from the soil.

- With no vegetation cover there are no tree roots to hold the soil or organic material within the soil, so the high rainfall can easily erode it, carrying the fertile material away to the rivers.

Figure 15.7 How the tropical rainforest loses its soil fertility

High rainfall

Cleared trees so no nutrients are returned to the soil via the litter

High rainfall erodes the soil into the rivers

High rainfall leaches nutrients from the soil

Modern farming and development in Amazonia

In the Amazon trees are removed for:

- Modern farming.

- Timber extraction.

- Mineral extraction.

Modern farming
Peasant farming plots in Rondônia

Migrants who had no land to farm in north east Brazil moved into the Rondônia area, particularly after 1984 when the Trans-Amazonian highway was paved (**Figure 15.8**). They settled on a small piece of land which was cleared by cutting and burning. This removal of trees is known as **deforestation**. Food crops such as maize were planted whilst cash crops like sugar and coffee were also grown. The land soon became infertile and so the farmers had to clear more land.

Figure 15.8
Developments in Brazil

Cattle ranching in Mato Grosso

From 1970 onwards many foreign **transnational corporations (TNCs)** set up large ranches on which cattle were kept to produce beef. Each animal requires a large area of pasture (two cattle per three hectares). This grazing land is provided by cutting or burning the forest. Soil fertility is rapidly reduced so that the grazing becomes too poor to support the animals and more forest has to be cleared.

Timber extraction
Logging at Paragominas

The loggers search the forest for suitable trees to cut. The required trees are scattered through the forest, but in total 100 different species are suitable for cutting and selling. The trees are felled with chain saws and then collected by skidders (bulldozers) to be taken to the sawmills in Paragominas (**Figure 15.8**). Much of the wood is sold in Brazil but high quality timbers, e.g. mahogany, are exported through Manaus and Belem.

The environmental damage caused by this logging includes the following:

- When a selected tree crashes down it brings down surrounding trees not needed by the logging company.

- The bulldozers which remove the selected tree destroy more surrounding vegetation.

- Trees do not grow back along the tyre trails and the wind channelled along the trails brings down more trees.

- With no protecting canopy, the leaf litter on the forest floor dries out, increasing the risk of fire.

Mineral extraction
Mining in the Carajás region

Mineral reserves include 18 million tonnes of iron ore (the world's largest reserve), 150 tonnes of gold, significant deposits of silver, manganese, copper, molybdenum, nickel, cassiterite and bauxite.

The method of mining for the iron ore in Carajás is **open-cast**. A large excavation hole 4.1 km long, 300 m wide and 400 m deep has been dug out in 15 m high step-like benches. The operations are computer controlled, with 38 bright yellow 240-tonne trucks (the largest in the world) delivering the 66 per cent pure iron ore to the nearby crushing and processing plant. Other developments in the region include transport and processing plants, a railway line to the coast and the Tucurui HEP scheme.

Markets for the iron ore are mainly Europe and North America, although Japan is the most important purchasing country.

The 'Grand Carajás' mining programme has had the following impacts on the local Indians:

- A large section of the rainforest which was home to several thousand Indians has been changed into a large mining and industrial area.

- Hundreds of Indians died as a result of 'imported' diseases, e.g. measles.

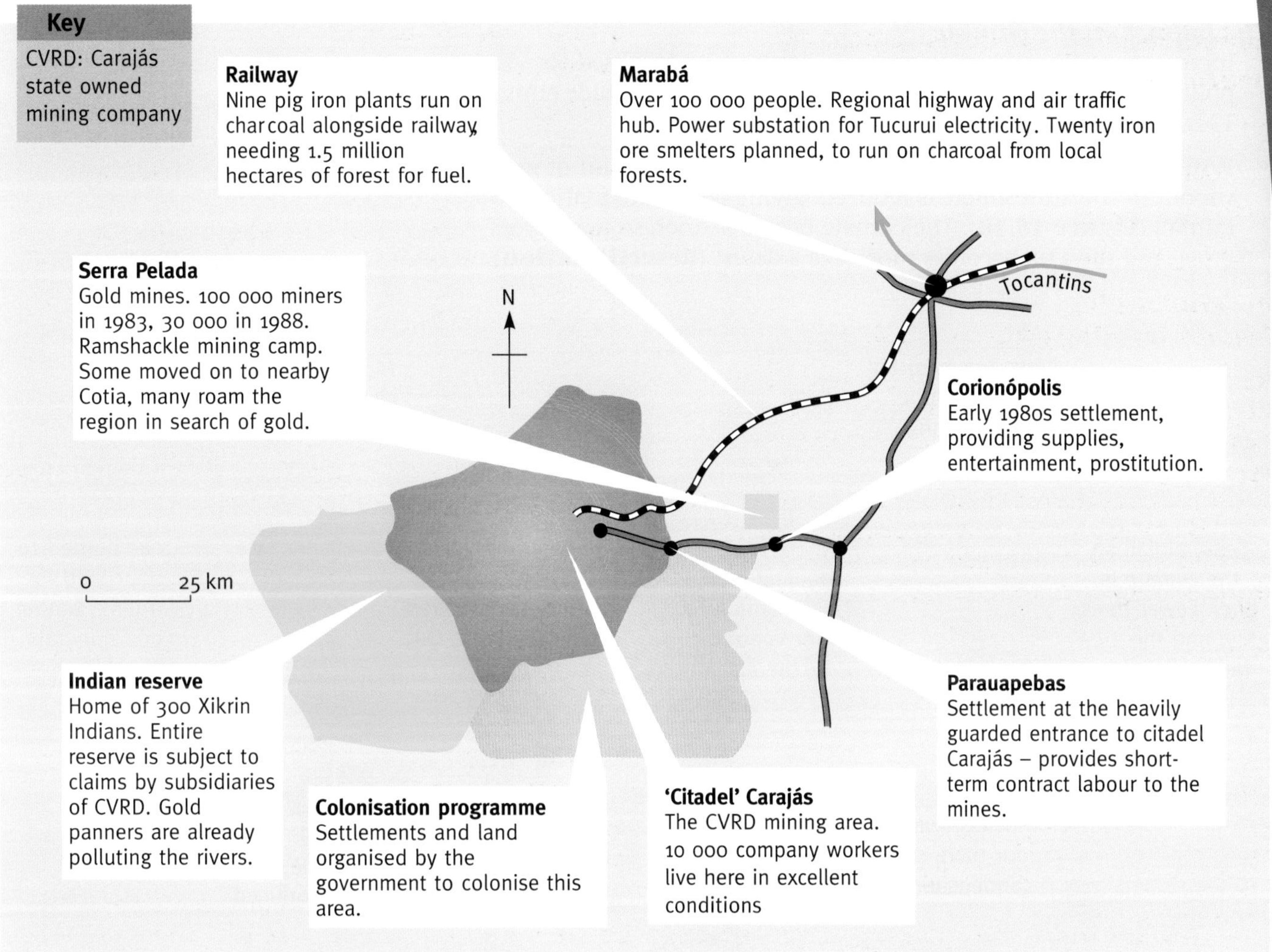

Key

CVRD: Carajás state owned mining company

Railway
Nine pig iron plants run on charcoal alongside railway, needing 1.5 million hectares of forest for fuel.

Marabá
Over 100 000 people. Regional highway and air traffic hub. Power substation for Tucurui electricity. Twenty iron ore smelters planned, to run on charcoal from local forests.

Serra Pelada
Gold mines. 100 000 miners in 1983, 30 000 in 1988. Ramshackle mining camp. Some moved on to nearby Cotia, many roam the region in search of gold.

N

Tocantins

Corionópolis
Early 1980s settlement, providing supplies, entertainment, prostitution.

0   25 km

Indian reserve
Home of 300 Xikrin Indians. Entire reserve is subject to claims by subsidiaries of CVRD. Gold panners are already polluting the rivers.

Colonisation programme
Settlements and land organised by the government to colonise this area.

'Citadel' Carajás
The CVRD mining area. 10 000 company workers live here in excellent conditions

Parauapebas
Settlement at the heavily guarded entrance to citadel Carajás – provides short-term contract labour to the mines.

Figure 15.9 The Grand Carajás programme

- In the Xikrin Indian reserve (**Figure 15.9**), independent miners have moved into the area and polluted the rivers with mercury which is used to separate gold after panning.

- The railway line to the coast was built through the Gavioes Indian reserve, against their wishes.

The impact of modern farming, timber extraction and mining on the environment

The impact on the forest
- Clearance of large numbers of trees.

- Loss of soil fertility and increased soil erosion so trees cannot grow back.

- Some plant species, e.g. mahogany, are becoming endangered.

- Many animals and birds are losing their habitat so they become endangered.

- Many modern medicines, e.g. quinine for malarial treatment, came from the rainforest. There may be others which have not yet been discovered.

- Soil erosion adds silt to the rivers, making them more liable to flooding.

The impact on the climate

- Increased use of machinery and vehicles leads to localised air pollution in the form of carbon, sulphur and nitrous oxide emissions. This can increase local acid damage to plants.

- With fewer trees there is less transpiration, so the amount of water vapour in the atmosphere is reduced, giving less condensation and rainfall (**Figure 15.10**). The climate becomes drier, so fewer trees grow, and the area becomes more like a desert (**desertification**).

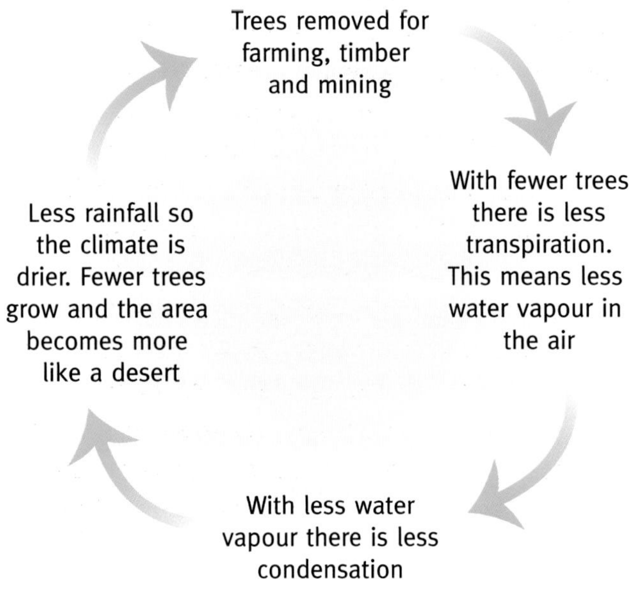

Trees removed for farming, timber and mining

With fewer trees there is less transpiration. This means less water vapour in the air

With less water vapour there is less condensation

Less rainfall so the climate is drier. Fewer trees grow and the area becomes more like a desert

Figure 15.10 Why rainfall decreases after deforestation

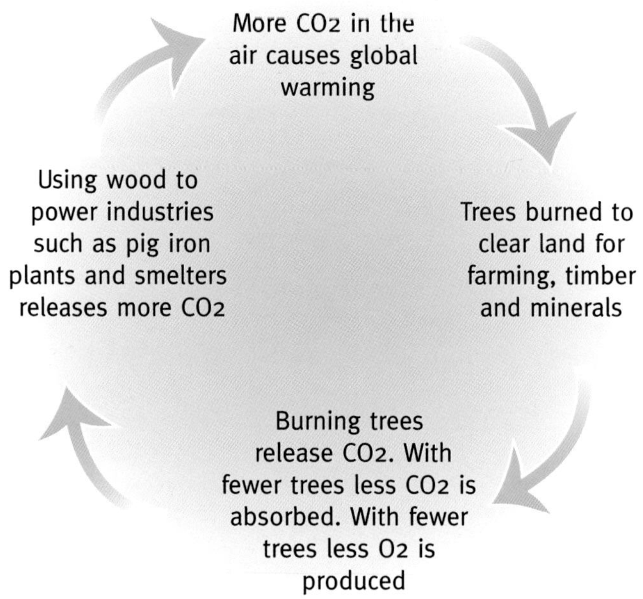

More CO$_2$ in the air causes global warming

Trees burned to clear land for farming, timber and minerals

Burning trees release CO$_2$. With fewer trees less CO$_2$ is absorbed. With fewer trees less O$_2$ is produced

Using wood to power industries such as pig iron plants and smelters releases more CO$_2$

Figure 15.11 Atmospheric change due to deforestation

- Deforestation could increase **global warming**. The clearing of the land by burning trees adds carbon dioxide to the atmosphere (**Figure 15.11**). With fewer trees growing, less carbon dioxide is removed from the atmosphere. These two processes increase the amount of carbon dioxide in the air, which traps heat trying to leave the Earth so raising its temperature (see Chapter 20).

- With fewer trees producing oxygen the amount in the atmosphere could be reduced.

The impact on the Indians

As land is taken for developments the Indians have less forest to use for 'slash and burn' subsistence farming or for hunting and gathering supplementary food. This can have the following consequences:

- Some Indians retreat further into the forest.

- With less land for farming, the tribe have to return to a chagra before it has had time to recover, so food supplies are reduced causing starvation.

- Some Indians leave the tribe to beg along the road or to look for work in the towns. For many this is very difficult as they do not have the skills needed for the type of jobs available in urban areas.

Ecotourism in the Amazon

Ecotourism is where people travel to natural areas to understand the culture and natural history of the environment. They take care not to upset the ecosystem and provide money to help conserve the natural resources so that these are of benefit to the local people. Ecotourism has developed as people now recognize the need to preserve the rainforest and understand how traditional tourism (e.g. large hotels) can damage it.

The characteristics of ecotourism shown by the Alta Floresta Project (**Figure 15.12**) are:

The Alta Floresta tourist project

'Alta Floresta, a town in the highlands of the Amazon rainforest, is the home of an innovative research centre and ecotourist project. The research centre was set up to study sustainable ways of using the forest and to teach people in the area how to use these new practices. The project is centred on community involvement, setting up schools, hospitals and training programmes. Local people are trained in sustainable farming practices and the harvesting of non-timber forest products. In addition, instead of being forced out of the economy, they are trained to work at the tourist centre, thereby becoming an integral part of the whole project. The tourist centre also educates travellers on the ecology of the rainforest and causes and effects of its destruction. This project is a positive example of how an ecotourism centre can be set up.'

Rainforest Action Network

Figure 15.12 The Alta Floresta ecotourism project

- The money raised at Alta Floresta is used to educate tourists on rainforest ecology and threats to it, i.e. awareness of the importance of conservation is raised.

- Tourist finance helps to support the research centre, i.e. it enables the protection of natural habitats and endangered species.

- The community school, hospital and education of farmers in sustainable farming practices are helped by money from tourism, i.e. local people gain economically and socially.

- The residential lodge can be accessed only by boat, i.e. the tourist development does not add further stress to the ecosystem by building roads.

FACT FILE

The Cistaline Jungle Lodge

- ◆ Forest reserve

- ◆ Brazilian natural heritage site

- ◆ Ecologically sustainable lodge accessible only by boat

- ◆ Internationally renowned for rare birds

- ◆ Opportunities for bird watching, trekking, swimming, canoeing, fishing

1 Pages 143–144

Look at Figure 15.13.

a   Name ocean A and ocean B.

b   Name latitude C and latitude D.

c   Name rivers E and F.

d   Name town G.

e   Name the range of mountains H.

f   Name the type of natural vegetation you would expect to find in shaded area J.

2 Pages 143–144

Use the information in the list below to complete the following paragraph (you do not need to use all the information).

5	10	20	500	1000	1500
HIGH	LOW	CONVECTION	WET	FRONTAL	
WARMS	COOLS	RAIN	CLOUDS	OVERHEAD	

The climate of the Amazon Basin is very regular, changing very little throughout the year. The annual temperature range is usually less than ....°C. As the sun is almost always .... in the sky the temperatures are generally high and the daily build up of heat causes huge .... currents of warm air which rise in the early afternoon. As this warm air rises it .... and large cumulonimbus .... form, leading to a heavy downpour of .... each afternoon. As a result, the annual rainfall total is almost always over .... mm.

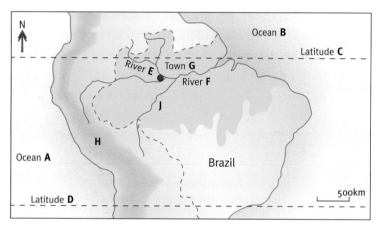

Figure 15.13 Map of the Amazon

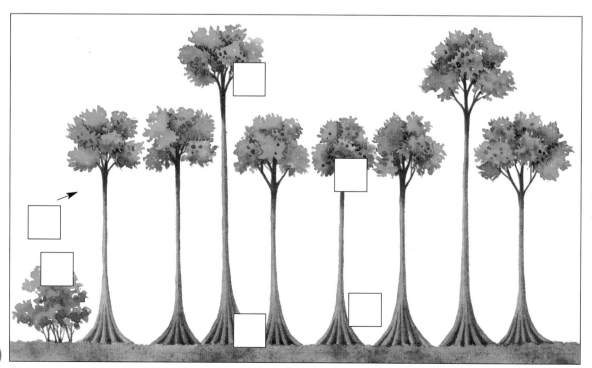

Figure 15.14
Natural vegetation of Amazonia

Questions

THE WIDER WORLD

3 *Pages 144–146*

a   Copy Figure 15.14

b   Study the list below and label the diagram by putting each letter in the correct box:
A Not much undergrowth
B Buttress Roots
C Emergents
D Leaves with drip tips
E Crowns spread to form a canopy
F Dense undergrowth in clearings

c   For each label, explain why this feature has developed

d   Explain why the Amazon rainforest is evergreen

e   Why are the high rainfall and high temperatures important to the rainforest ecosystem?

f   Explain why the rainforest ecosystem is described as a stable ecosystem

4 *Pages 146–147*

a   Copy and complete Figure 15.15 with the following labels:
• Harvest
• Weed
• Move on to a new area
• Sow crops
• Burn vegetation to clear the forest
• Select suitable area in the forest (S on diagram)

b   What is meant by 'subsistence' farming?

c   Explain why farmers have to move to a new farming area every three or four years

d   This traditional type of farming causes little damage to the rainforest ecosystem. Explain why.

e   What happens to a system of shifting cultivation as the farming population increases?

5 *Pages 148–150*

a   Describe changes that may have taken place in the area shown in Figure 15.16, as a result of economic development since 1950.

b   Explain why these changes have taken place.

c   In what ways have the changes helped:
• The local people
• The country of Brazil?

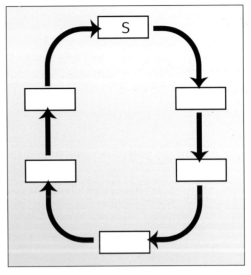

Figure 15.15
A shifting cultivation system

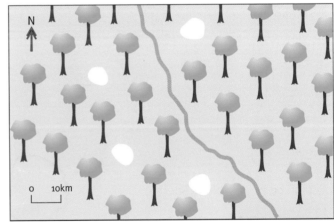

Figure 15.16 The Amazon rainforest in 1950, before economic development

Map key

Area inhabited by shifting cultivators

Dirt track

Rain forest

6 *Pages 149–150*

a   Copy Figures 15.17a and 15.17b. Complete Figure 15.17b by adding suitable labels or symbols and a key to show the main changes in the forest ecosystem.

b   Explain the effects of changes in the Amazon rainforest on:
   • The local environment
   • The global environment.

7 *Page 151*

a   From Chapter 16, page 160, explain what is meant by the term 'sustainable' development.

b   What are the characteristics of 'sustainable' development?

c   In what ways can the Alta Floresta tourist project be described as 'sustainable'?

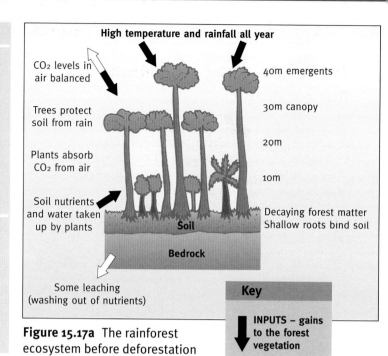

Figure 15.17a The rainforest ecosystem before deforestation

Key	
↓	INPUTS – gains to the forest vegetation
⇧	OUTPUTS – losses from the forest vegetation

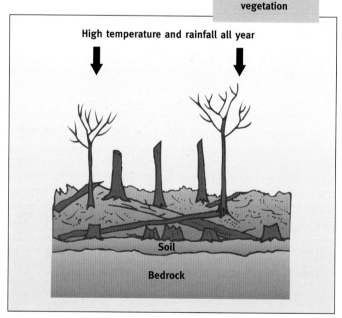

Figure 15.17b The rainforest ecosystem after deforestation

16 ## The Ganges Delta – dense population in a high-risk environment

The location and formation of the Ganges Delta

The River Ganges rises in the Himalayas and flows through northern India towards the east before turning south to flow into the Bay of Bengal. As it turns south it flows into Bangladesh and divides into a number of channels which form the **delta**. A delta is a flat, triangular, low-lying area of marshy land at sea level.

Map key

--- National border

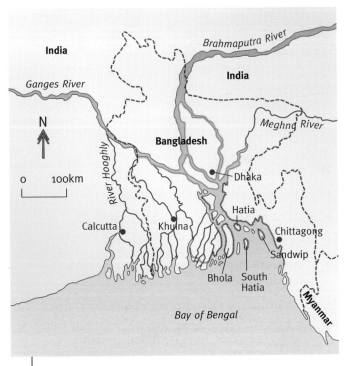

Figure 16.1 Map of the Ganges Delta

The River Ganges forms a delta because it carries a large **load** (sediment). As it approaches the Bay of Bengal the gradient of the river decreases and the load is deposited, blocking the river channel. The blocked channel divides into two channels, called **distributaries**. This process is repeated, and gradually the delta is built out to sea and the River Ganges enters the Bay of Bengal via a large number of distributaries.

The climate of the Ganges Delta

This region experiences a **tropical monsoon climate**. The delta is just north of the Equator so the Sun is at a high angle throughout the year, giving high temperatures. The highest temperatures are from April to June as the Sun moves almost directly overhead. From November to February the overhead Sun is south of the Equator so it is at a lower angle, giving reduced temperatures.

In summer, as the land mass of Asia heats up, the air above is heated and rises, forming a region of **low pressure** air. Moist air is drawn into this low pressure area from the south west and passes over the Ganges Delta bringing rain onshore (**Figure 16.2a**). This is known as the **south west (summer) monsoon**.

In winter the Sun is at a lower angle. The land mass of Asia cools down, and the air above is cooled and

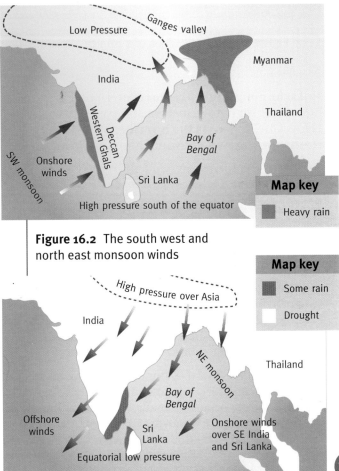

Map key

▇ Heavy rain

Figure 16.2 The south west and north east monsoon winds

Map key

▇ Some rain

☐ Drought

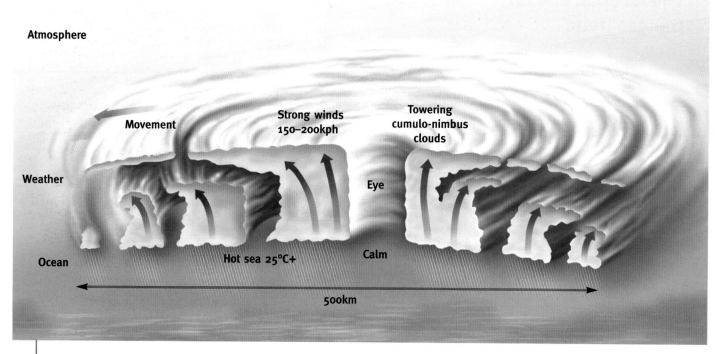

Atmosphere

Movement

Strong winds 150–200kph

Towering cumulo-nimbus clouds

Weather

Eye

Ocean

Hot sea 25°C+

Calm

500km

Figure 16.3 Cross-section of a tropical cyclone

sinks, forming **high pressure** air. Dry air is forced out of this high pressure area and passes over the Ganges Delta. This is the **north east (winter) monsoon** and is a dry wind, bringing no rain.

Tropical cyclones are frequent in the Ganges Delta region **(Figure 16.3)**.

Tropical cyclones form when air is heated above the warm sea and the warm moist air rises to a high level. A deep low pressure system is formed and air is drawn in to replace the rising air. This air forms winds up to 150–200 km/h which circulate in an anticlockwise direction for up to 400 km from the centre. **Cumulonimbus** clouds form around the centre and high rainfall of 100 mm in 24 hours often occurs. In the centre (**eye**) of the cyclone the air is sucked downwards giving an area of calm.

In May 1985 a tropical cyclone hit the coastal area of Bangladesh, claiming the lives of 40 000 people. Severe flooding occurred, made worse by a 9 m high storm surge which extended 150 km inland. A local official claimed that 6000 people were washed out to sea, and survivors clung on to roofs and the tops of palm trees in the 180 km/h winds.

The **primary** or initial effects were:

- Flooding of villages and farmland.
- Loss of houses, animals and crops.
- People drowned.
- Communication links such as roads and telephone wires broken.
- Contaminated drinking water.

Secondary or later effects were:

- With communication links destroyed the rescue services could not get to the area so people died due to lack of food, clean water, shelter and the injuries they had sustained.
- With food crops destroyed people starved and had no seed to plant for the next year.
- Contaminated water caused the spread of diseases such as cholera.
- With no crops to sell the people had no income to repair houses or buy new seeds to sow.
- People experienced trauma as they lost family and friends.

Why does flooding occur so often in the Ganges Delta?

Climatic influences

- The high rainfall is concentrated into a few months so the ground becomes saturated, giving a rapid surface runoff.

- Tropical cyclones increase the amount of rainfall.

- The high winds associated with cyclones bring storm surges which flood the coastal area (**Figure 16.4**).

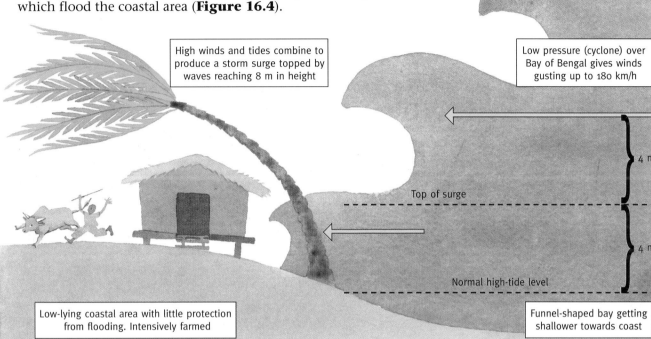

High winds and tides combine to produce a storm surge topped by waves reaching 8 m in height

Low pressure (cyclone) over Bay of Bengal gives winds gusting up to 180 km/h

4 m

Top of surge

4 m

Normal high-tide level

Low-lying coastal area with little protection from flooding. Intensively farmed

Funnel-shaped bay getting shallower towards coast

Figure 16.4 A storm surge

Relief influences

- Much of the delta is low lying, some below sea level. The rivers are contained by **levées** above the level of the surrounding land so when they burst their banks the surrounding area is quickly covered with water.

- The land is flat so flood water rapidly flows across the area.

Human influences

- Deforestation, particularly in the Himalayas, increases the speed of surface runoff and soil erosion. With more silt in the rivers the channels are quickly blocked, giving further flooding.

- There is a lack of money for protection measures, e.g. barrages.

The Bangladeshi authorities and international aid donors have devised a **Flood Action Plan** which includes the following measures to reduce the severe impact of tropical storms:

1 *Flood prevention*: Reinforcing the coastal banks to protect land and people. This is expensive for a poor country like Bangladesh.

2 *Flood preparation*:

- Improving satellite weather forecasting, to give better prediction so that people can remove themselves from the danger.

- Raising the mounds that people live on so that they are above the level of the highest floods.

- Building concrete storm shelters so people are protected.

- Improving roads so that aid can be delivered more easily.

3 *Effective relief* for flood victims:

- In the medium term it is necessary to prevent the spread of disease by providing shelter, food and clean drinking water.

- In the long term the people need help to return to their homes and farms. They need to be provided with seed to plant next year's rice crop and animals to replace lost cattle. This is essential if the area is not to become dependent on foreign aid.

Rice farming in the Ganges Delta

Rice farming takes place mainly on a subsistence scale in this region (**Figure 16.5**). The Ganges Delta is suitable for rice farming for the following reasons:

- Rice seeds have a growing season of five months with temperatures above 21°C, and the monsoon climate gives 10 months above 21°C.

- Rice needs an annual rainfall of over 2000 mm with at least 120 mm falling in each month of the growing season, and the monsoon climate gives five months of sufficient rainfall. Additional water can be obtained by digging irrigation canals from the many distributaries.

- There is a dry sunny period in November and December for ripening and harvesting.

- The delta gives a large amount of flat land which can be flooded to create the padi fields. Mud banks (**bunds**) are built by hand to enclose the fields.

- The **topsoil** is fertile as each time the Ganges floods, fertile alluvium is laid down over the delta area.

- It has an **impervious** subsoil of clay to stop water draining away.

- The delta area is densely populated, providing the large labour force required for the manual work.

INPUTS	STORES	PROCESSES	OUTPUTS
High temperatures High rainfall Flat land Fertile alluvial soil Large labour force Hand tools Animal dung Rice seed	2 hectares land 1 ox few chickens	Manuring Ploughing Planting Weeding Harvesting	Rice Eggs Chickens } Consumed by the family

Figure 16.5 Rice farming

> **EXAM TIP**
>
> Compare the subsistence rice farming system with the commercial farming system in Chapter 2.

The Rice Farmer's Year

MONTH	CLIMATE	PROCESS
May	Hot, dry	Nursery beds are prepared above the flood level and manured
June	Beginning of the hot, wet season	• Rice seeds are planted in the nursery by hand. • Bunds (banks) are built to create a padi field. • Fields are manured with compost or animal dung. • A water buffalo pulls a wooden plough to turn the soil. • The mud is levelled. These jobs are done by the men.
July/August	Hot, wet season	• Rice seedlings are transplanted by hand into the padi fields by the women and children.
September/October	Hot, wet season	• Constant weeding by hand.
November/December	Warm, dry season	• Water is drained from the fields. • Rice is cut by hand with a sickle. • Rice is dried in the sun, threshed, winnowed and dried again to put into storage.
January	Warm, dry season	• If irrigation water is available, a second crop of rice is planted.

Many of the human inputs into the rice farming system are poor, e.g. hand tools needing repair, insufficient animal dung, rice seed from last year's crop is used even though it may be diseased. It is labour intensive with a large number of workers for each hectare of farmed land and it is hard work, with most of the processes being done by hand. Each farm is small and often composed of plots scattered throughout the village. It is therefore subsistence farming, i.e. the output of rice is sufficient only to feed the family, with none left to sell. This means the farmer has no money to invest in improving his farm.

The Green Revolution

The aim of the **Green Revolution** was to use technology to increase food production so that it would keep pace with population growth. This meant that people would not starve and there would not be any famines. There were four technological changes introduced during the Green Revolution:

- New strains of high-yielding seeds known as **HYV** or **miracle rice**. They are **hybrid seeds** bred by crossing different varieties of rice.
- Chemical inputs e.g. fertilisers, pesticides, herbicides.
- Increased irrigation.
- Increased use of machinery.

The successes of the Green Revolution are as follows:

- A large increase in food production. HYVs give increased yields, are more resistant to wind, rain and disease, and are faster growing, allowing an extra crop to be grown each year.

Figure 16.6 Miracle rice

- The higher yields mean other crops e.g. vegetables can be grown, so adding variety to the local diet.
- The increase in yields led to a fall in food prices at the market, helping consumers.
- The well-off farmers who could afford seed, fertilisers, irrigation and machinery have become richer.
- The reduced demand for farm labourers provided a work force for the new factories being built in the towns.

There are also failures of the Green Revolution including:

- Some of the HYVs are more susceptible to pests and diseases.
- Excess chemical fertilisers are washed in to water supplies causing **eutrophication** (see Chapter 2).

Figure 16.7 Salinisation of water

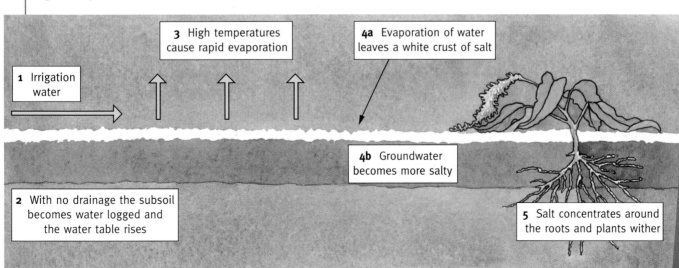

1 Irrigation water

3 High temperatures cause rapid evaporation

4a Evaporation of water leaves a white crust of salt

4b Groundwater becomes more salty

2 With no drainage the subsoil becomes water logged and the water table rises

5 Salt concentrates around the roots and plants wither

- The increased use of irrigation can cause **salinisation** of drinking water supplies and kills crops (**Figure 16.7**)

- Mechanisation has increased rural unemployment

- The poorer farmers cannot afford the seeds, fertilisers and machinery so their yields do not increase. Also, with the fall in the market price of rice their income fell and so many have had to sell their farms

- There has been an increase in rural to urban migration, putting pressure on services such as housing in the towns (see chapter 18).

How sustainable is the Green Revolution?

Sustainable development is development which can continue without causing any harm to the environment.

Sustainable development makes use of **intermediate technology**. Intermediate technology is a means of improving production by using methods which are low-cost, use local materials, fulfil a local need and suit the skills and knowledge of the local people. One example is a hand-operated well (**Figure 16.8**). This would bring the following benefits to a society:

- The wells are cheap to build.

- Local bricks or locally made concrete can be used to line the well.

- The hand pump is easily operated so a high level of skill is not needed.

- The production of farm crops is increased because there is water for irrigation and the women have time to help with the farming now they do not have to walk several miles to fetch water.

- Clean water reduces the risk of diarrhoea and dysentery which often kill children. The women are healthier as they no longer carry heavy buckets for several miles.

Figure 16.8
Intermediate technology

Sustainable development is progress which can continue without harming the environment.

FEATURE	IN SUSTAINABLE DEVELOPMENT	IN THE GREEN REVOLUTION
Labour	Uses local skills and employs local people	Needs new skills and displaces workers with machinery
Capital	Uses limited amounts of money	Large amounts of money are needed to buy seeds, fertilisers and machinery
Technology	Uses low cost technology e.g. hand tools, hand operated pumps	Uses diesel pumps and diesel-driven tractors which are complicated and expensive
Environment	Protects the environment e.g. uses compost made from kitchen waste, encourages natural predators to eat the insects which feed on crops	Uses chemical fertilisers and pesticides which damage the water supply

Birth rates and death rates in Bangladesh

The **birth rate** is the number of babies born for every thousand people in a country per year. In Bangladesh the birth rate is currently 36 live births/thousand/year which can be written as $36^0/_{00}$ per year. In the United Kingdom the birth rate is only $14^0/_{00}$ per year. It is high in Bangladesh because:

- People do not practise family planning. They expect some of their children to die so they have a large number of babies hoping that one or two will survive. They need children to work on the farm or to go to the town to earn money in the factories (i.e. they are an **economic necessity**). Parents need children to support them in their old age as there is no pension scheme.

- There is a young population so there are a lot of women in the child-bearing age range.

The **death rate** is the number of people dying out of every thousand people in a country per year. In Bangladesh the death rate is 13 deaths/thousand/year, which can be written as $13^0/_{00}$ per year. In the UK the death rate is $10^0/_{00}$ per year. This is also high in Bangladesh because:

- Health care is poor, with a shortage of doctors, nurses and medicines.

- Drinking water supplies may not be clean, and without piped sewerage systems the water becomes contaminated, leading to diseases such as cholera.

- Houses are overcrowded so disease spreads rapidly.

These conditions lead to a high **infant mortality rate** and a low **life expectancy**. Infant mortality is the number of babies dying before they reach their first birthday. In Bangladesh it is $118^0/_{00}$ compared to $7^0/_{00}$ in the UK. Life expectancy is the average age that people in a country live to. In Bangladesh the figures are 54 for men and 52 for women compared to 73 for men and 79 for women in the UK.

These features can be seen on the **population pyramids** for Bangladesh and the UK in **Figure 16.9**. For further explanation of population pyramids see Chapter 18.

The **demographic transition model** (**Figure 16.10**) helps to explain how the total population alters as a result of changes in birth rates and death rates.

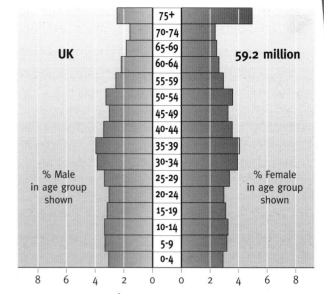

Figure 16.9 Population pyramids for (a) UK and (b) Bangladesh

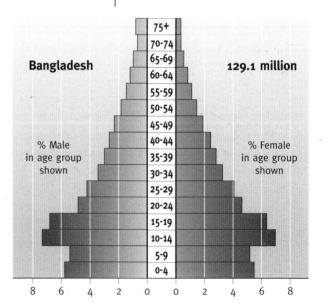

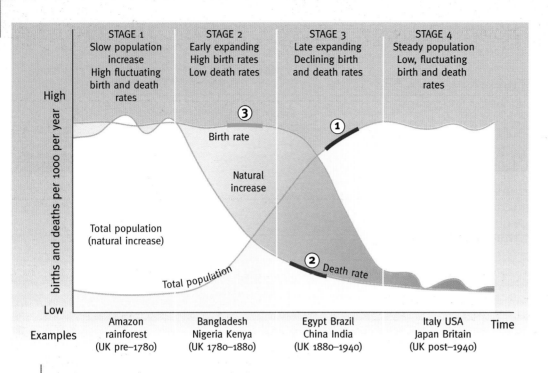

Figure 16.10 The demographic transition model

In **stage 1**, the birth rate is high because:

- Parents produce a large number of children because some will die and they need some to survive to support them in their old age.

- Children are needed to work the land.

- There is no knowledge of birth control or willingness to practise family planning.

The death rate is also high because:

- Unreliable food supplies lead to famine and malnutrition.

- A lack of piped clean water or sewage disposal leads to the spread of diseases such as cholera.

- There is a lack of medical resources, i.e. few doctors, immunisations, medicines, etc.

There is very little change in the overall population as high birth rates are balanced by high death rates.

An example is provided by the Yanomami tribe in the Amazon rainforest (Chapter 15).

In **stage 2**, the birth rate remains high because parents still expect children to die. The death rate falls because of:

- Improved food supplies.

- Cleaner drinking water and improved sanitation.

- Improved medical care e.g. doctors, vaccinations, drugs.

There is very rapid population increase as the birth rate is much higher than the death rate.

Bangladesh is in stage 2 of the demographic transition.

In **stage 3**, the birth rate falls because:

- Parents begin to realise that children will survive so they have fewer.

- Mechanisation on farms means fewer labourers are needed.

- Women enter the paid labour force so do not want time off to have children.

- People choose to spend money on material goods e.g. cars rather than large families.

- People have access to and understand about family planning.

The death rate continues to fall slowly.

The population increases slowly as birth rate falls and death rate is fairly low, e.g. Brazil.

In **stage 4**, the birth and death rates remain low. There is very little change in population as both birth rates and death rates are low, e.g. the UK.

Questions

1 *Page 155*

Look at Figure 16.11.

a   Name the following:
  • Country A
  • Country B
  • Bay C
  • River D
  • City E

b   From Figure 16.11, describe the location of the Ganges Delta

c   Describe the appearance of the Ganges Delta

d   Read the section about the formation of the delta, and use this information to explain the appearance of the delta.

2 *Pages 155–156*

a   Copy the maps and diagrams shown in Figure 16.12

b   On the maps, label:
  • High pressure (twice)
  • Low pressure (twice)
  • South westerly winds
  • North easterly winds

c   On the diagrams label:
  • High pressure (twice)
  • Low pressure (twice)

d   Label the winds on diagrams C and D by writing 'wet' or 'dry' on the dotted lines.

e   Explain when and how the dry season occurs.

f   Explain when and how the wet season occurs.

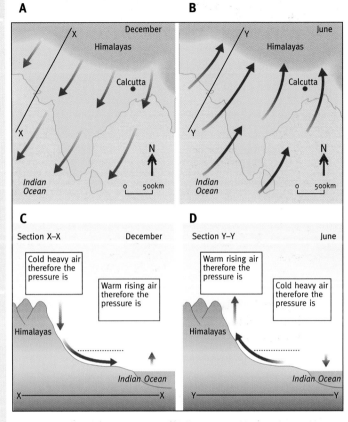

Figure 16.12 A tropical monsoon climate

Figure 16.11
Map of the Ganges Delta

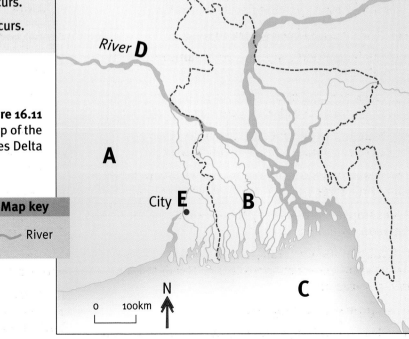

Questions

THE WIDER WORLD

3 *Page 156*

a Copy the cross section of the tropical cyclone shown in 16.13

b Match the following labels to the letters:
- Warm moist air rising
- Cumulo-nimbus clouds
- Eye
- Strong winds moving in an anticlockwise direction
- Low pressure
- Descending air
- Calm
- Heavy rainfall.

4 *Pages 156 – 157*

Look at Figure 16.14.

a Give at least five reasons why flooding may be so severe that people have to find higher ground before the storm arrives

b Why must people not leave their shelters when the 'eye' of the storm arrives?

c After a storm, what kind of short term aid could a foreign country provide?

d What are the problems of getting aid to those areas of the country where it is most needed?

e Describe some of the longer term solutions needed to reduce the damage caused by tropical storms.

5 *Page 158*

a Look at the climate graph (Figure 16.15) and put the correct label to the correct letter:
- Monsoon rains occur. Rice seedlings transplanted into the padi-fields
- Rice harvested in the drier weather
- Seeds planted in nursery beds before the rains begin
- Ploughing and manuring
- Constant weeding.

b What will be the problem if the monsoon rains fail?

c How could the farming be affected if a cyclone occurs in September?

6 *Page 158*

a Copy Figure 16.16. Add four more inputs to the 'physical' arrow and two inputs to the 'other' arrow.

b Why is the system described as 'subsistence'?

c Give four reasons why the yields per hectare in the traditional farming system are low.

7 *Pages 159–60*

a What are the benefits and problems of using mechanised farming on the Ganges Delta? (Figure 16.17)

b List the other three technological changes introduced during the Green Revolution and explain how each of them would help to increase yields.

c Study the list of the successes and failures of the Green Revolution. Do the successes outweigh the failures? Write out your opinions and conclusion in detail.

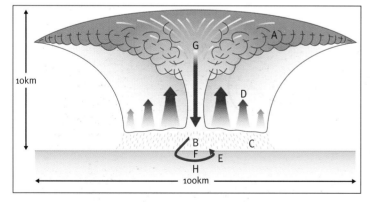

Figure 16.13
Cross section of a tropical cyclone

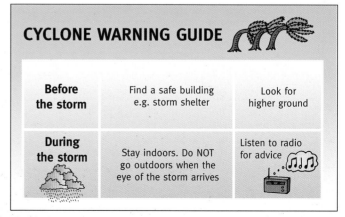

Figure 16.14 Cyclone warning guide

164

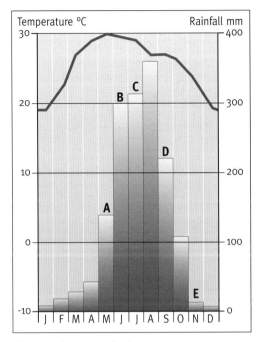

Figure 16.15 Tropical monsoon climate

8 *Page 160*

Look at Figure 16.18.

a How will the biogas unit help the farmers?

b What other advantages will it give the villagers?

c How can the biogas unit be described as 'sustainable'?

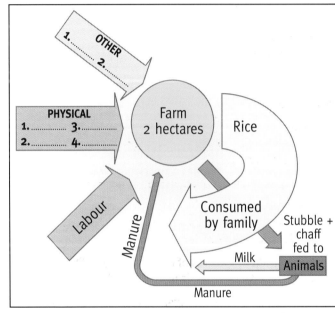

Figure 16.16 The farm system

Figure 16.17 Mechanised farming on the Ganges Delta

Figure 16.18 Bio gas unit in Ganges Delta

9 *Pages 161–62*

Copy the following table which is based on Figure 16.10. Complete the boxes by putting the words 'high', 'low', or 'falling rapidly' into the spaces.

	Stage 1	Stage 2	Stage 3	Stage 4
Birth rate				
Death rate			Falling slowly	
Rate of population increase		Increasing rapidly	Increasing more slowly	

b   What is meant by the infant mortality rate?

c   How can the infant mortality rate be reduced?

d   What is meant by life expectancy?

e   Why are life expectancy rates about twenty years higher in the UK than in Bangladesh?

f   Look at Figure 16.19. Describe how the factors shown on the diagram can help to reduce the birth rate.

Figure 16.19 Factors which help to reduce birth rate

17 Japan – urbanisation and industrialisation

The physical geography and climate of Japan

Japan has four main islands, the largest of which is Honshu (**Figure 17.1**). All four islands have a mountainous interior and coastal lowlands.

The mountainous areas

The mountainous areas have low population densities of less than 70 people per km². This is because they have deep, narrow forested valleys with steep sides and thin soils. Winter temperatures are below 0°C and summer temperatures are also low (less than 10°C). Rainfall is very high (more than 2000 mm per year) (**Figure 17.2**).

Rice is the main food in Japan. It is grown in flooded fields and requires fertile soils. These conditions do not exist on the steep mountains, where the growing season is also too short for arable farming. The narrow valley floors provide little flat land for building on, and the costs of constructing roads and railways are very high. These areas are far from markets in the cities. Industry is not attracted to them, so there are few jobs for people, and population densities are therefore low.

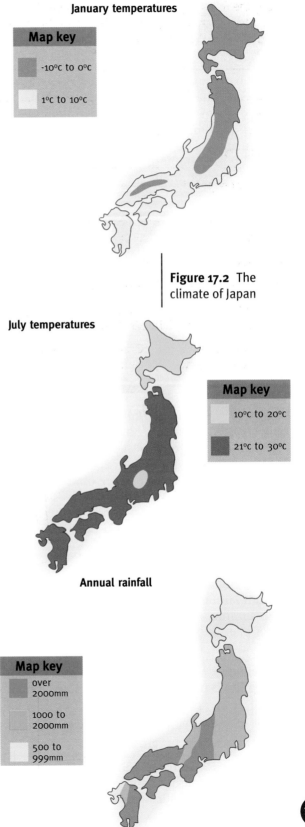

January temperatures

Map key

-10°C to 0°C

1°C to 10°C

Figure 17.2 The climate of Japan

July temperatures

Map key

10°C to 20°C

21°C to 30°C

Annual rainfall

Map key

over 2000mm

1000 to 2000mm

500 to 999mm

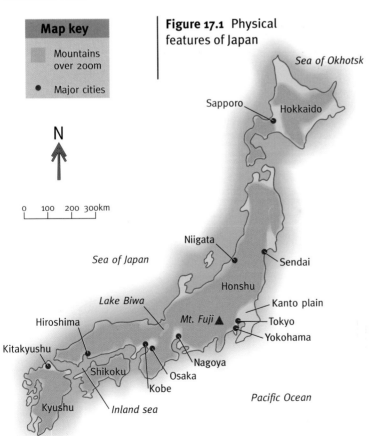

Figure 17.1 Physical features of Japan

Map key

Mountains over 200m

• Major cities

N

0   100   200 300km

Sea of Okhotsk

Sapporo
Hokkaido

Niigata
Sendai
Honshu
Lake Biwa
Sea of Japan
Kanto plain
Mt. Fuji ▲
Tokyo
Yokohama
Hiroshima
Nagoya
Kitakyushu
Osaka
Shikoku
Kobe
Kyushu
Inland sea
Pacific Ocean

Lowland Hokkaido

Most of the lowlands of Hokkaido have population densities of less than 100 people per km², and there is only one industrial area around the main city of Sapporo. Farming cannot support as many people as in the rest of Japan because it is not as intensive. This is because of climatic constraints (**Figure 17.2**). Only one rice crop is possible because winters are long and very cold (less than 0°C in January), summers are cool (10–20°C), and annual rainfall is low (less than 1000 mm). Coal mines have been closed as the coal seams have been exhausted, and mining costs have risen due to deeper mining. Little industry has spread to Hokkaido because it is separated by the sea from Honshu and is 700 km from the Tokyo industrial area, with mountainous terrain and poor transport facilities between them.

EXAM TIP

Do not make simple statements like 'there are few people here because the land is mountainous'. You should give details of how the physical environment prevents many ways of making a living.

Lowland Honshu, Shikoku and Kyushu

All lowlands in Honshu, Shikoku and Kyushu have high population densities of over 100 per km². Population density is highest (more than 200 people per km²) in the industrial zones where there are many jobs. Farms are small and very **intensive**. Before industry was developed, the lowlands grew so much food that high population densities could be fed. This is because:

- The growing season is long (up to ten months) in the south, which means that two crops can be grown each year. High summer temperatures (20–30°C in July) and high rainfall (more than 1000 mm per year), which falls in summer from the **monsoon**, mean that conditions for plant growth are ideal.

- The land is flat in the lowlands, or it has been **terraced**. Fields can be flooded for rice growing, and farming is mechanized. This results in large crop yields.

- Soils in the lowlands are usually **alluvium**, which is the fertile silt and clay deposited by rivers. It is rich in nutrients for plant growth.

- Rural areas also have high population densities because many of the farmers are part-time, working in factories in nearby cities during the week and on their farms at the weekends.

Industrial zones in Japan

There are five main industrial zones, four of which are along the south coast of Honshu (**Figure 17.3**). Industry has concentrated here for several reasons:

- Modern manufacturing industry uses assembly lines and continuous processes for which one-storey buildings are needed. They require much flat land. Japan has little of this, so industry grew on the largest of the small areas of lowland.

- Because of the scarcity of land, prices are very high, so buildings in towns tend to be crowded together. In recent years land has been reclaimed from the sea for industry (**Figure 17.4**).

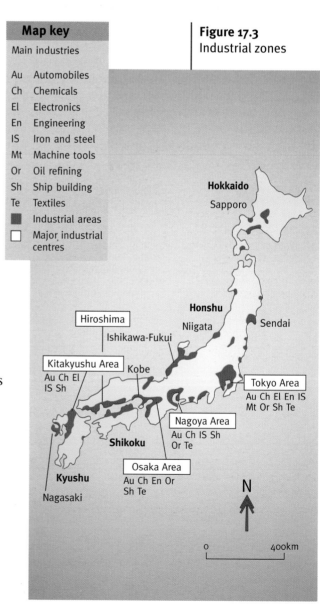

Map key

Main industries

Au	Automobiles
Ch	Chemicals
El	Electronics
En	Engineering
IS	Iron and steel
Mt	Machine tools
Or	Oil refining
Sh	Ship building
Te	Textiles
■	Industrial areas
□	Major industrial centres

Figure 17.3
Industrial zones

Hokkaido
Sapporo

Honshu
Hiroshima
Ishikawa-Fukui
Niigata
Sendai

Kitakyushu Area
Au Ch El
IS Sh
Kobe

Tokyo Area
Au Ch El En IS
Mt Or Sh Te

Nagoya Area
Au Ch IS Sh
Or Te

Shikoku

Osaka Area
Au Ch En Or
Sh Te

Kyushu
Nagasaki

N

0   400km

Figure 17.4 Part of the industrial zone of Kobe-Osaka

Manufacturing industry has developed at ports; the reasons for this are given in the next section. The five industrial zones have large deep water ports which are sheltered from the strong Pacific waves and **typhoons**. The five main industrial centres are the **cores** of Japan. They provide a large local market and attract other industries and services such as banking, insurance and government offices, a process known as **cumulative causation**. As levels of capital, technology and skilled labour increase, the region becomes more wealthy. More jobs are provided in schools, hospitals, shopping centres and transport which encourages more people to migrate from the rest of Japan.

The shortage of raw materials

Countries with modern developed economies, such as Japan, need many different **raw materials**. Japan has few of them. Farmers produce few industrial crops such as cotton, because the scarcity of land means that most of it is used to grow food crops. National Park status protects many of the forests, and the inaccessibility of the mountains makes transport costs high, so the timber industry is not large. 95 per cent of Japan's needs for timber are met by importing it from tropical forests.

The small mineral deposits within Japan, such as iron ore, have now been exhausted, so Japan produces very few of its mineral needs. Much ore is imported from abroad, such as iron ore from Australia and copper from Chile and Zambia. The small coalfields on the islands of Hokkaido and Kyushu have now been exhausted, and the mines are closed. A small gas field near Tokyo and an oil deposit on the west coast of Honshu are still in production, but 99.8 per cent of the oil needed is imported from the Middle East, Indonesia and Alaska, whilst 99.5 per cent of gas is also imported from Indonesia and Brunei. Almost all Japan's coal is imported from Australia and China.

Japan has many mountains and lakes, but most of the rivers and drainage basins are too small to be of much use for **HEP**, which provides less than 2 per cent of Japan's energy. Electricity generated using **geothermal heat** from the ground exists, but is of little importance. In order to reduce the dependence on imported fuels, especially oil, Japan has developed nuclear power, which now provides 10 per cent of its energy from 50 power stations. It is planned to increase it to 25 per cent.

An **import** is something which is brought in from another country. The cheapest way to import large amounts of raw materials and fuels is in very large ships called **bulk carriers**. They are used for dry goods such as coal and mineral ores, and **supertankers** are used for oil and liquid natural gas. These ships need deep-water ports and sheltered harbours where they can unload. The best of these are on the south coast of Honshu, and this is where the five industrial zones of Japan have grown, at Tokyo, Nagoya, Kobe-Osaka, Hiroshima and Kitakyushu. There, large ships such as 100 000 tonne bulk carriers bringing iron ore from Australia can be unloaded and the ore can go straight into steel works with no extra transport costs. All the **heavy industries** in Japan are next to ports in the industrial zones. Because there is a shortage of flat land for building new factories, areas of shallow sea have been reclaimed to make new land (**Figure 17.4**).

Factories which use metal and other products of heavy industry also locate in the industrial zones so that they are near their suppliers and because, in Japan, there are so few possible sites for building. Such companies are attracted by the high population densities and demand for their products in the industrial zones. They are also attracted by the large pools of skilled labour and the low transport costs if they are near their suppliers and their customers. These benefits from locating factories near each other are called **agglomeration economies**. Many jobs are created, not only in the manufacturing industries in the industrial zones, but also in the service industries which are linked to them. They include transport, advertising, and financial institutions. Service industries grow to meet the needs of the workers, and provide employment in education, health, local government, etc. The growth of cities is called **urbanisation**, and this takes place as the industry grows.

The shortage of raw materials has meant that most have to be imported. Industry and cities have grown at the ports to use the raw materials. The manufactured good are exported. The work available at ports has led to these being the areas with highest population densities.

The nature of Japanese industry

In the last 50 years Japan has developed into the world's second great industrial superpower. It has been successful because of:

- The high quality of manufactured products such as cars and televisions. Customers know they get value for their money, and a good reputation encourages more sales.

- The low prices of the products in comparison with similar goods from other countries.

The high quality of manufactured products
Goods are of high quality because of highly developed production methods in which workers are organized into teams. They can check on the quality of each other's work and have regular meetings to discuss problems and ways of improving methods.

The Japanese education system is one of the best in the world, with much emphasis on numeracy, science and technology. Workers have many skills and can

Figure 17.5 Automation

adapt quickly to changes in jobs. The training provided by companies is also highly developed. The Japanese spend large amounts on research and development to improve the quality of goods and to develop new ones.

The low prices of manufactured products
The system of '**lifelong employment**' means that most workers have only one employer during their working lives. They know they will not be made unemployed. They have the confidence to suggest improvements to production systems to keep prices low. In other countries, such improvements often involve laying people off.

Factories are organized using assembly lines, with teams responsible for a number of jobs. Japanese people work long hours, and even though they might have four weeks of paid holiday per year, they often do not take it all because they do not want to let down the other members of their production team.

Goods are produced in large volumes (**mass production**) so the cost of producing each item is low. As firms get bigger they gain the benefits of spreading costs even more; this is called gaining **economies of scale**. Another way to keep costs low is the **just-in-time** system of production. Components such as those for vehicles are transported from other factories to the assembly line in a continuous flow and arrive just before they are put on to the assembly line. In older systems of production, parts were brought to the factory, stored, and then taken to the assembly line. This involved higher costs such as building and heating the warehouse and employing people in it. In the just-in-time system costs are lower, but there is a greater reliance on fast and reliable transport systems as any interruption stops the flow of parts and hence the assembly line. In Japan factories are often grouped together in the industrial zones so distances are small, which means there is less chance of transport being disrupted.

Costs of production are increasingly being reduced by **automation**, which means that the machines or processes are controlled by computers. Robots (**Figure 17.5**) are often used in automated factories.

Robots can work faster and more accurately than people and they can work for 24 hours each day. However, they are expensive to buy and set up so they are mainly used in the high volume, mass production of goods. Japanese industry therefore uses much **capital investment** which means that money is used to buy machines rather than to pay many workers.

Factors influencing the distribution of the motor vehicle industry

Assembly plants are factories which put together the **components** or parts to make the final product. Assembly plants for motor vehicles are mostly grouped in the four industrial zones on the southern coast of Honshu at Tokyo (Honda), Nagoya (Toyota), Kobe-Osaka and Hiroshima (Mazda) (**Figure 17.6**).

The important locational factors for the car industry in Japan are shown in **Figure 17.7**.

Assembly plants need large areas of flat land for the long assembly lines. With only 17 per cent of Japan being lowland they have located on some of the larger plains. Mazda has two large component and assembly works in Hiroshima covering 2.3 km². Another making engines 70 km to the north at Miyoshi is 1.7 km², and two more built to assemble cars in the 1980s and 1990s at Hofu, 130 km to the west, cover 1.3 km².

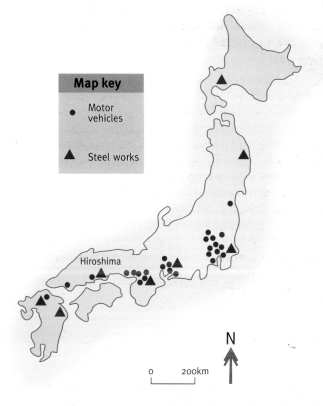

Map key

• Motor vehicles

▲ Steel works

Hiroshima

N

0   200km

Figure 17.6 The distribution of motor vehicle plants and steelworks

Figure 17.7 Location factors for a car assembly plant

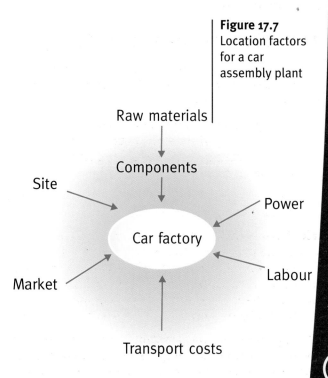

Raw materials

Components

Site

Power

Car factory

Market

Labour

Transport costs

Vehicles need much steel for the bodies. Steelworks have been built at Hiroshima (**Figure 17.6**) because it has a deepwater port. It is on the coast of the sheltered Inland Sea (**Figure 17.1**), where bulk carriers can unload iron ore from Australia and coal from China straight into the blast furnaces. The vehicle factory is built next to the steelworks to reduce transport costs as steel is heavy and bulky so it is expensive to transport.

Hundreds of small companies in Hiroshima supply Mazda with small components. The strictness of the just-in-time process forces Mazda to work closely with these small supply companies to ensure total quality management, no faulty parts, and yet to keep costs low. The firms are nearby, which keeps transport costs low and allows Mazda and the firms to meet frequently.

Electricity is available anywhere in Japan from the National Grid, so it has not affected the locations of car plants.

Hiroshima has 1.1 million people so there is a large and highly skilled workforce, a very important factor. There is a large local market, and as more than 60 per cent of the cars are exported, the location next to the deep-water port is another means of keeping costs low.

Increasingly, large Japanese companies such as Mazda are having components built in **newly industrialising countries (NICs)** in south east Asia where labour is much cheaper than in Japan. The new assembly plants at Hofu are next to a port and are able to import these parts whilst being near the headquarters in Hiroshima for other parts and management purposes.

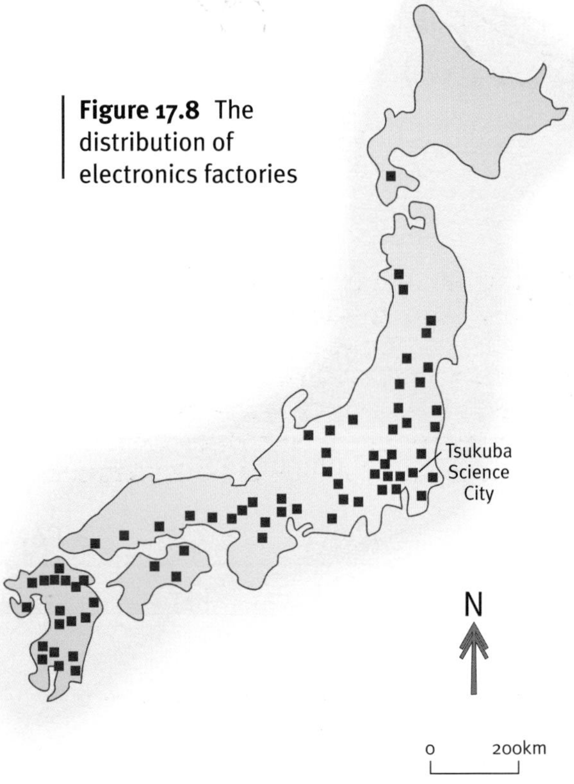

Factors influencing the distribution of the electronics industry

The distribution of electronics factories (**Figure 17.8**) is very different from the distribution of motor vehicle plants (**Figure 17.6**). Whilst motor vehicles are constructed in four small areas in Honshu, electronics works are scattered all over the country except in northern Honshu and Hokkaido.

The factors affecting the distribution of electronics plants are seen in the example of Tsukuba Science City (**Figure 17.9**).

Electronics factories need only small areas for their sites and are not limited by the small area of lowland in Japan. They use electricity which is available everywhere through the National Grid so they are not limited to locations near ports where oil and coal can be imported.

In the same way, they are not limited by the need to import minerals in bulk. Electronics products such as computers have little weight of raw materials in them. They have many different metals and plastics, which are made in many places. The electronics factory is not pulled towards any particular supplier of components or raw materials.

Because they are not limited to where they have to locate, they can be built on cheap **greenfield** sites well away from towns. Tsukuba Science City is 60 km from Tokyo, and is connected by railway and a fast motorway. The many components can be transported quickly and reliably for the just-in-time manufacturing methods.

The most important factors concern the workers. They are very highly skilled and want to live and work in areas with beautiful scenery and a nice climate. Tsukuba Science City is next to the Tsukuba National Park and Lake Kasumigaura (**Figure 17.9**). There are many electronics factories on the southern island of Kyushu where the climate is subtropical, with summer temperatures of 30°C and winter temperatures of 10°C.

Figure 17.8 The distribution of electronics factories

Tsukuba Science City

N

0   200km

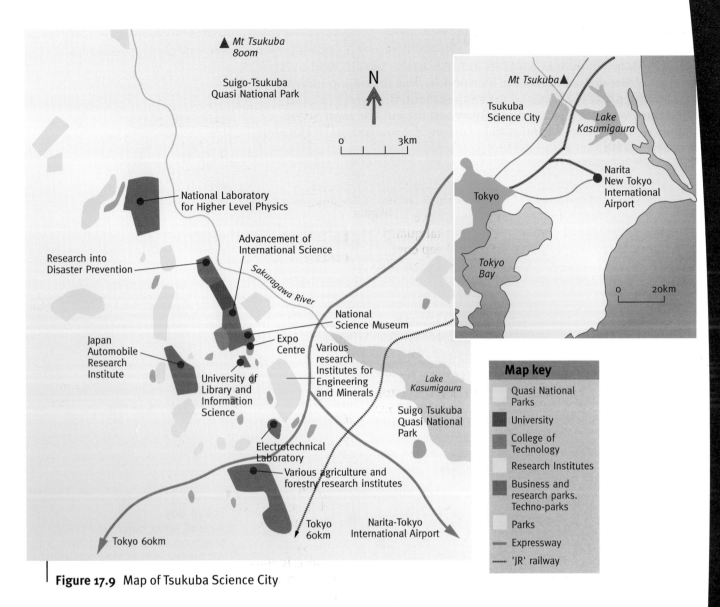

Figure 17.9 Map of Tsukuba Science City

The workers are often trained in universities; Tsukuba Science City has a university and a college of technology so a pool of highly skilled labour has built up. Research and development are very important to electronics firms so they can keep ahead of the competition. Universities are where much basic research is done, so the firms locate near them to keep in close contact. Tsukuba Science City has seven research institutes as well as the university.

Although they are evenly distributed over much of Japan, electronics firms tend to locate on science parks. There they can exchange ideas with nearby companies who supply them with components. They also share the pool of highly skilled labour. Tsukuba Science City has 18 science and business parks. In order to keep the attractive working environment, about 70 per cent of each park is grass, trees and lakes rather than buildings.

The advanced technology used in electronics involves experts from all over the world. Much of the production also goes abroad so there are frequent visits to and from other countries. Nearness to an airport, therefore, is very important. Tsukuba Science City is only 30 km from the new Tokyo International Airport at Narita (**Figure 17.9**).

EXAM TIP

Make a list of the differences between the factors affecting the locations of the motor vehicle and electronics industries. This will help in your revision.

Industrial pollution in Japan

After the destruction of much of its industry in the Second World War, Japan was determined to recover. The priority was to develop industry and less attention was given to the environment. Between 1950 and 1970 there was much pollution of rivers and the air. The most severe pollution occurred in the industrial zones on the south coast of Honshu (**Figure 17.10**).

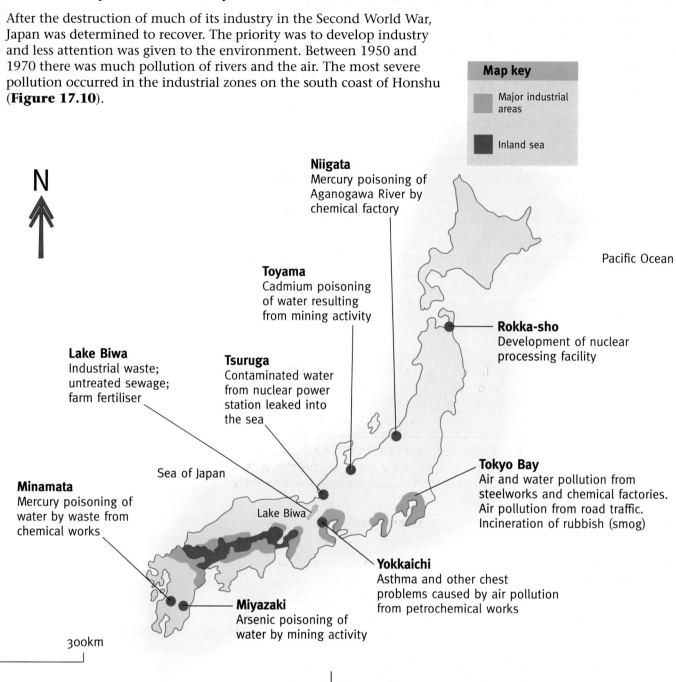

Map key

Major industrial areas

Inland sea

N

Niigata
Mercury poisoning of Aganogawa River by chemical factory

Pacific Ocean

Toyama
Cadmium poisoning of water resulting from mining activity

Rokka-sho
Development of nuclear processing facility

Lake Biwa
Industrial waste; untreated sewage; farm fertiliser

Tsuruga
Contaminated water from nuclear power station leaked into the sea

Sea of Japan

Tokyo Bay
Air and water pollution from steelworks and chemical factories. Air pollution from road traffic. Incineration of rubbish (smog)

Minamata
Mercury poisoning of water by waste from chemical works

Lake Biwa

Yokkaichi
Asthma and other chest problems caused by air pollution from petrochemical works

Miyazaki
Arsenic poisoning of water by mining activity

0   300km

Figure 17.10 Pollution in Japan

Water pollution

The Inland Sea (**Figure 17.1**) was polluted because waste materials from oil refineries, chemical and steel works and engineering plants in the Kobe-Osaka and Hiroshima industrial zones and elsewhere were allowed to enter it. They did not then flow into the Sea of Japan or the Pacific Ocean because the Inland Sea has only three narrow entrances and has weak currents in it. The results were that the **marine ecosystem** was badly damaged and many fish died. The fishing industry was severely affected by reduced catches.

Another example of water pollution occurred in Minamata Bay on the western coast of Kyushu. In 1956 the release of organic mercury (methylmercury) in waste from the Chasso Company chemical plant at **Minamata** killed many fish and sea birds. By 1997 the fish and shellfish eaten by people had affected 3000 people with blindness, deformed limbs and loss of co-ordination. The cause was only discovered in 1970. The solutions to the problem have been very expensive:

- In 1970 the Water Pollution Control Law was passed to stop the discharge of mercury, cadmium and other poisonous wastes into rivers and the sea.

- 1.5 million cubic metres of contaminated sediment have been dredged from the bed of Minamata Bay to stop it recycling into the water and fish.

- The victims have each been given £155 000 compensation by the Chasso Company.

- The government gives people in the area financial and medical help to remove their worries about living there.

- An institute has been set up to conduct more research into the disease.

Air pollution

Between 1950 and 1980 air pollution was severe in the industrial zones such as Tokyo. The high levels of sulphur dioxide, particulates and other gases increased the number of people with asthma and other breathing problems. In central Tokyo there were even vending machines every few hundred metres where people could buy breaths of oxygen! The causes of pollution included exhaust emissions from the large number of cars, the burning of household rubbish, and industry. Heavy industries such as steelworks were the main polluters of the atmosphere in the following ways:

- The factory chimneys were short so dust and waste gas fell on to the surrounding city.

- The burning of coal released much sulphur dioxide which caused **acid rain**.

- The wind blew much coal and iron ore dust from the large piles next to the steelworks. It spread over the surrounding areas of the city.

These problems have been combated in the following ways:

- The chimneys were built taller so that the pollution would enter stronger winds and be carried further and be diluted before settling.

- Chemical and sprinkler systems have been installed on the tops of chimneys to remove the sulphur dioxide.

- Water sprinklers keep the coal/iron ore piles wet so dust cannot form. Green 'corridors' of trees have also been planted around factories to trap any dust and to reduce visual and noise pollution.

1 *Page 167*

a   Using Figure 17.11 name: islands A, B and C; cities D, E and F; seas G and H; mountain I; lake J.

b   Why is there a low population density in the mountainous interior?

2 *Pages 167–170*

a   Using Figure 17.12 and your own knowledge, give two reasons why there are no industrial areas in area X.

b   Give two detailed reasons why the city of Kobe-Osaka extends for a long distance along the coast.

c   Area Z on Figure 17.4 was reclaimed from the sea.
   • Name the sea.
   • Suggest why area Z has been reclaimed.

d   Describe the changing use of energy sources in Japan as shown in Figure 17.13.

3 *Pages 170–172*

a   How have automation and mass production helped to make car assembly an important industry in Japan?

b   Describe the location of the car factory in Figure 17.14.

c   Give reasons why it was built there.

d   Study Figure 17.4. Using the photograph and your own knowledge, suggest reasons why a car assembly plant has been built in Kobe-Osaka.

4 *Pages 172–73*

Use the ideas you have learned on pages 172–173 to explain the location of an electrical goods factory on the outskirts of Kobe-Osaka.

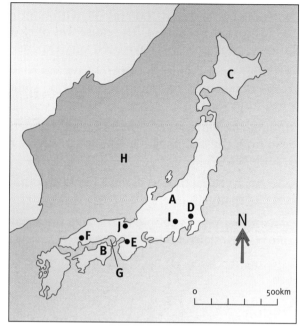

Figure 17.11 Some locations in Japan

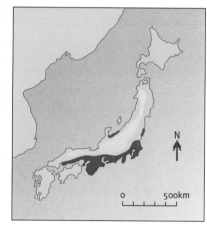

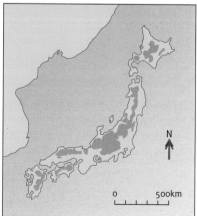

Figure 17.12 Industrial areas (a) and highland areas (b) in Japan

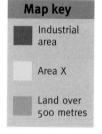

Map key	
	Industrial area
	Area X
	Land over 500 metres

Questions

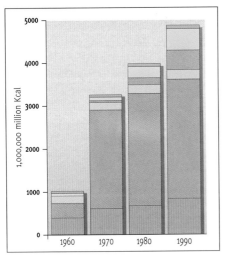

Figure 17.13 Sources of energy supplies in Japan, 1960–1990

Key
- Others
- Natural gas
- Nuclear
- HEP
- Petroleum
- Coal

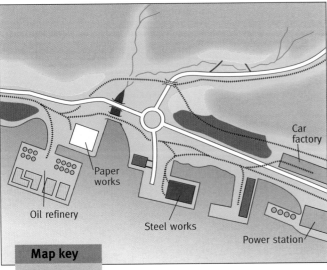

Map key
- Over 400 metres
- Residential areas
- Industry & commerce
- ...... Railway
- Major highway
- Sea area

Figure 17.14 An industrial zone

5 *Pages 174–175*

a Using Figure 17.15:
- Describe the distribution of victims of Minamata disease.
- Suggest how and why the disease spread so far from the factory.

b
- Describe and explain the environmental damage and pollution suffered by some parts of Japan.
- How have the Japanese authorities tried to solve problems of pollution and environmental destruction?
- Assess how effective the solutions have been.
- Suggest why it will take a long time to clean up the environment.

c When you describe somebody's attitude, you need to say exactly who the person is and their attitudes for and against. An example is: 'As a Japanese mum I am very unhappy about living next to the steel works because the coal dust blows onto my washing when it is drying, but I do not want the company to close, because of the cost of stopping the pollution, as my son has a good job there.'

Describe the attitudes to pollution of:

a a factory manager

b a factory worker.

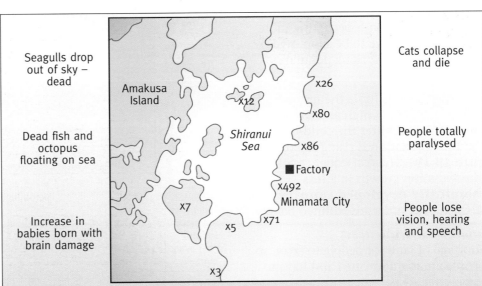

Figure 17.15 The effects of Minamata disease

Seagulls drop out of sky – dead

Cats collapse and die

Dead fish and octopus floating on sea

People totally paralysed

Increase in babies born with brain damage

People lose vision, hearing and speech

Amakusa Island

Shiranui Sea

x26
x12
x80
x86
■ Factory
x492
Minamata City
x7
x71
x5
x3

Population structure

Population structure is the composition of the population of a country according to age and sex. This pattern is shown in the form of a **population pyramid** and the various parts of the pyramid demonstrate different features of the population structure (**Figure 18.1**). You can refer back to Chapter 16 page 161 for an explanation of the differences in **birth rate, death rate, infant mortality** and **life expectancy**.

The **dependency ratio** is linked to the age structure of a population and is a measure of the ratio between those in a country who need to be supported and those who are economically active and are therefore supporting the remainder. It is calculated as follows:

$$\frac{\text{Number of non-economically active}\ (0\text{–}14\ \text{years} + 65\ \text{years and over})}{\text{Number of economically active}\ (15\text{–}64\ \text{years})} \times 100$$

In a country such as the UK the number of 0–14 year olds is decreasing, but the number of over 65 year olds is increasing, so that the population is becoming more elderly and these have to be supported by fewer people in the working population (**Figure 18.1a**).

In a country such as India the number of 0–14 year olds is very high and these children will soon enter the child-bearing age, so the population is rising rapidly (**Figure 18.1b**). The consequences of rapid population growth in a **less economically developed country (LEDC)** such as India are outlined below:

Economic consequences

* Shortage of land for people to farm, so people are malnourished and have to leave rural areas.

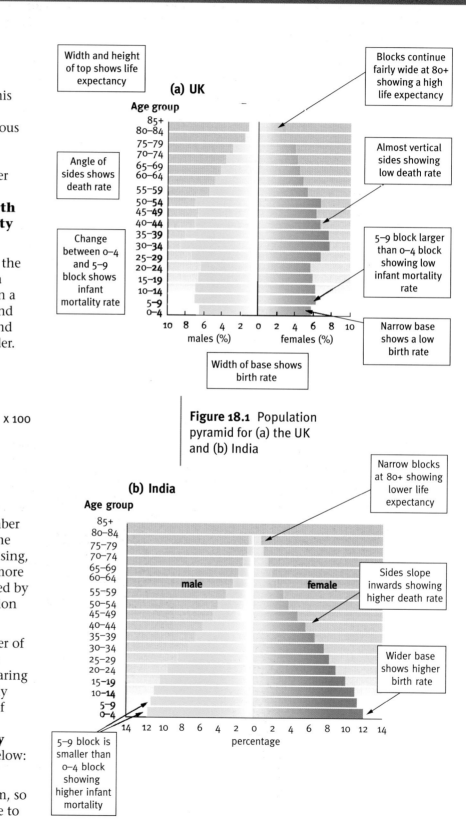

Figure 18.1 Population pyramid for (a) the UK and (b) India

- Shortage of paid employment so people have little money to spend and the government's tax revenue is low.

- The government does not have enough money to pay for services such as health and education for an increasing population.

Social consequences

- Insufficient housing so overcrowding occurs.

- Shortage of school places so illiteracy continues.

- Shortage of medical facilities such as doctors and hospital beds.

Environmental consequences

- Pressure on water supplies.

- **Deforestation** to create more farming land.

- **Desertification** as the water table falls and the removal of vegetation leads to soil erosion.

Urbanisation

The most urbanised areas in the world are:

- The **more economically developed countries (MEDCs)** e.g. USA, Britain and Australia.

- South American countries, e.g. Brazil. This is an anomaly since South America is not a highly developed continent, although its economy is expanding rapidly.

The least urbanised areas are:

- Less economically developed countries (LEDCs) e.g. Asian countries such as India and African countries such as Kenya.

Urbanisation occurs when an increasing proportion of a country's population live in the urban areas. It is caused by three main processes:

Figure 18.2 Global pattern of urbanisation

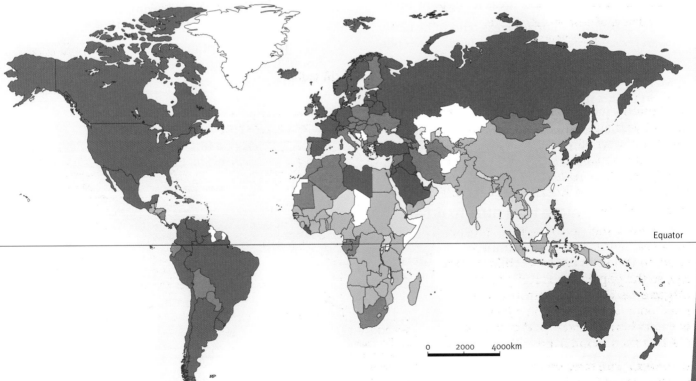

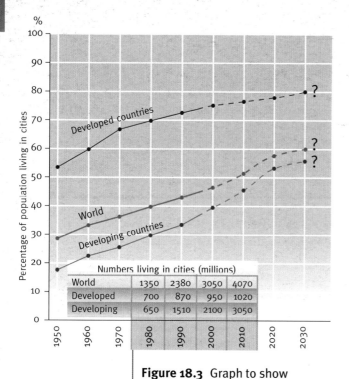

Numbers living in cities (millions)				
World	1350	2380	3050	4070
Developed	700	870	950	1020
Developing	650	1510	2100	3050

Figure 18.3 Graph to show rates of urbanisation

- The movement of people from rural to urban areas.

- Many of these migrants are in the 20–40 age group, i.e. they are in the child-bearing sector and so the birth rate in urban areas tends to be high.

- Medical facilities in urban areas tend to be better than those in rural areas, so the death rate tends to be falling rapidly.

In MEDCs, the rate of urbanisation is slowing down, while in LEDCs it is increasing rapidly (**Figure 18.3**). At the present growth rate Dhaka in Bangladesh will double its population in 12 years. Similarly, Delhi in India will double its population in 18 years, but London will take 1086 years to double its population at its present rate of growth.

Why do people move from rural to urban areas?

People move from rural areas due to **push factors** and they move to urban areas due to **pull factors**.

The push from rural areas is caused by:

- Lack of land to farm because the growing population leads to food shortages.

- Loss of farm labouring jobs due to mechanisation.

- Lack of other forms of employment.

- Shortage of housing due to the growing population.

- Shortage of school places.

- Lack of hospitals and doctors leading to increases in illness.

- Lack of social opportunities e.g. cinemas.

- Loss of food supply due to flooding, drought, etc.

The pull from urban areas is due to:

- Expectation of regular work which is physically easier and with higher pay.

- Expectation of the availability of a large number of varied job opportunities.

- Expectation of improved housing with piped drinking water, sanitation and electricity.

- Expectation of more schools with improved facilities and more highly qualified teachers.

- Expectation of more hospitals and doctors.

- Expectation of more leisure facilities e.g. cinemas.

- Freedom from traditional cultural restrictions.

Migration to Calcutta

Large numbers of migrants arriving in urban areas such as Calcutta have the following effects on the urban population structure (**Figure 18.4**):

- There is an excess of males in the 20–40 age group. This is the group which is migrating into Calcutta.

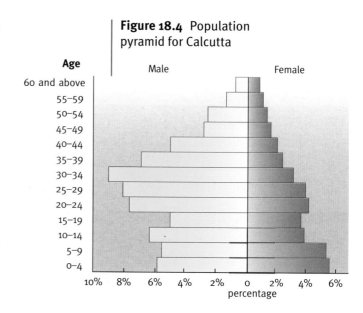

Figure 18.4 Population pyramid for Calcutta

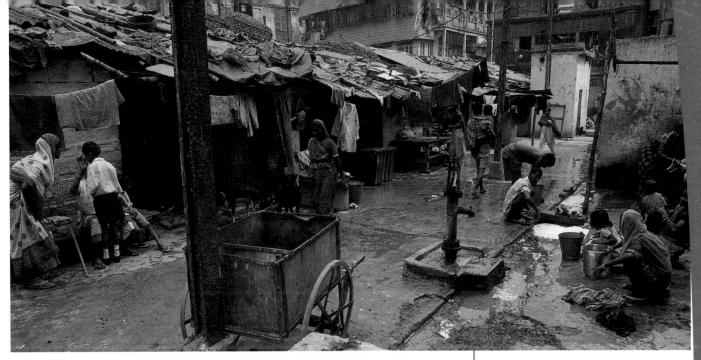

Figure 18.5 A squatter settlement in Calcutta

- There is a slight expansion in the number of females in the 20–40 age group. These are joining the males from the villages after the men have settled.

- There is a low percentage of 0–19 year olds. This is because the migrants do not bring young children with them.

- There is a low percentage of elderly people. This is because older people do not leave the villages to come to the town.

As the migrants settle in the urban area and marry, the percentage of children will increase. More recently, in some urban areas, the number of females migrating has been higher because they have been attracted to work in the factories being opened by the **transnational corporations (TNCs)**.

When migrants arrive in urban areas, they initially stay with relatives or sleep on the pavement, but soon many move to live in **squatter**

Figure 18.6 A land use map of Calcutta

Kamarhati

Dum Dum Airport

Dumjor

Bally

South Dum Dum

Howrah

Nanji

Behala

River Hooghly

Salt water lake

0   10km   N

Map key

- C B D
- Suburban business district
- Railway line
- Water
- Main roads
- Moderate quality housing
- Low quality housing
- Shanty town settlement
- Open space

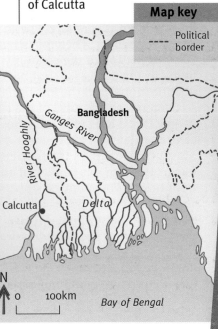

Map key

- Political border

India

Bangladesh

Ganges River

River Hooghly

Calcutta

Delta

Bay of Bengal

N   0   100km

settlements or shanty towns (Figure 18.5). These are usually found in two locations:

- At the edge of the urban area.

- On poor quality land, e.g. marsh close to the city centre.

In Calcutta 20 per cent of the population lives in squatter settlements which are known as **bustees** (**Figure 18.6**). These often occupy land illegally.

- Housing densities are extremely high, with over 150 000 people per km^2 in some areas. The lack of money means people cannot afford strong building materials so most houses are built of **wattle** (plastered wickerwork) with tiled roofs and mud floors. Inside, there is one room in which the whole family (often up to eight people) live, eat and sleep. There is usually no electricity as the authorities cannot keep pace with supplying a link to the expanding squatter settlements.

- Water is supplied by a single street tap for 35 to 45 families, and with an absence of sanitation, human effluent runs down the alleys between the houses often contaminating drinking water, especially after heavy rain.

- Health facilities are lacking because the city authorities do not have much money. With overcrowding and an absence of proper sanitary systems, diseases such as cholera, typhoid, dysentery, tetanus and measles occur.

- Educational facilities cannot cope with the large numbers of children so educational levels are low. Also many children cannot attend school full-time as they are needed to work to supplement the family income or to look after younger children whilst parents work.

- Employment is very rarely permanent or produces a regular income. There is a shortage of jobs in the **formal sector** of the economy. Many people living in the bustees do not have the necessary qualifications, and the location of the squatter settlements on the edge of the city means the people face a long expensive bus journey to the centre of Calcutta where most of the jobs are. Most people work in the **informal sector**. This means they are self-employed and often work from home. They may be street sellers or have small stalls selling goods they have made or bought from elsewhere (**Figure 18.7**). Some offer services such as shoe-shining, washing clothes or gardening. Very few people are totally unemployed, but often the work occupies only a few hours a week and provides a very low income.

EXAM TIP

In a question on push and pull factors, be careful

- not to give just opposites, e.g. PUSH – no jobs: PULL – some jobs

- not to use words like 'better' without some qualification
  i.e. not PUSH – poor education; PULL – better education
  but PUSH – schools with too few teachers; PULL – schools with well qualified teachers.

Figure 18.7 Work in the informal sector

What attempts are being made to improve conditions in the squatter settlements?

1 Often the local authorities try to improve conditions. For example The Calcutta Metropolitan Development Authority was established in 1970 to improve conditions and so far it has:

- Provided public toilets, which has helped reduce deaths from diseases such as cholera, typhoid and dysentery.

- Paved the alleys and dug drains so that contaminated water flows away from the houses.

- Improved drinking water supply by providing more taps.

- Installed street lights to make the settlements safer.

- Provided access to electricity for some homes so that people can operate small appliances e.g. sewing machines to help gain an income and children can study at home.

- Improved public transport so people can look for work in the city centre.

Most of the building work is done using manual labour rather than machines in order to provide employment.

2 Workshops are built so people living in the squatter settlements can rent them cheaply and make goods needed by the local population, e.g. furniture.

3 Self-help schemes are in place where the local authority provides a piece of land and the migrants provide the labour to make bricks and build houses. In this way the authorities save money which can be used to supply electricity, a clean water supply, a sewage system and surfaced roads. The advantages of a self-help scheme are:

- The houses can be extended in stages as the people can afford it.

- A community spirit is established.

- The cost of building is relatively cheap so more houses can be provided.

Attempts to improve conditions in Calcutta have been made easier as the rate of migration has slowed down due to:

- Industrial development in other nearby towns attracting migrants.

- Information about the lack of jobs in Calcutta is filtering back to the villages, discouraging migrants.

- The **Green Revolution** has improved rice yields, raising rural living standards.

1 *Pages 178–79*

Look at Figure 18.8.

a   In the pyramid for City B, what percentage of the population is made up of females aged 20–24?

b   In the pyramid for City A, what percentage of the population is made up of children under the age of 5?

c   Which pyramid shows the higher birth rate, and how can you tell?

d   Which pyramid shows the higher death rate, and how can you tell?

e   Which pyramid, A or B, is more likely to be the pyramid for a city in an LEDC? Explain your answer.

f   What is meant by a dependency ratio, and which two groups form the dependent population?

g   What are the problems of having a growing dependent population?

2 *Pages 178–79*

a   Draw a line graph to illustrate the population of India using the following figures:

Year	Population in millions
1901	241
1921	251
1941	320
1961	439
1981	684
2001	1000

b   Describe the population growth in India.

c   Describe some of the economic, social and environmental problems resulting from a population growth rate such as that experienced by India.

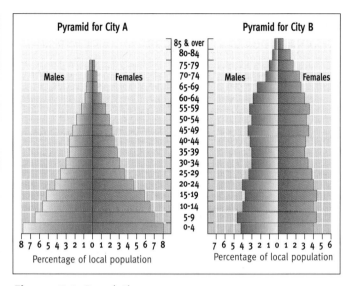

Figure 18.8 Population pyramids for two cities in different parts of the world

Figure 18.9 Graph of population change in Calcutta

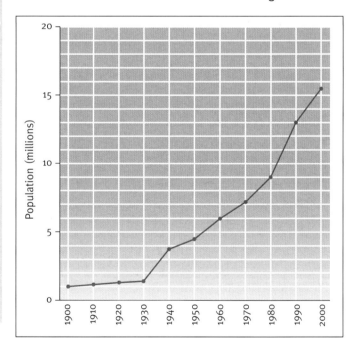

Questions

3 *Pages 179–181*

Look at Figures 18.9 and 18.10.

a   Describe what this graph shows about population change in Calcutta.

b   Give three reasons for this change.

c   State three different push factors which encourage people to leave their home region.

d   Choose one of the push factors and explain why it pushes people away from their home region.

e   State three different pull factors which encourage people to migrate to cities.

f   Choose one of the pull factors and explain why it pulls people towards the city.

g   What effect does the movement of people into cities have on the population structure of the areas which they have left?

4 *Pages 180–183*

Look at Figure 18.6:

a   Which river is the River Hooghly a distributary of?

b   What local name is given to the shanty town settlements shown on Figure 18.6?

c   State three facts about the location of these shanty town settlements.

d   Describe the housing and employment problems for people living in shanty towns.

e   Name the agency established in 1970 to improve conditions for shanty town dwellers and describe how it has improved health and employment conditions.

f   What is a 'self-help' scheme and why do local authorities in towns such as Calcutta encourage this approach?

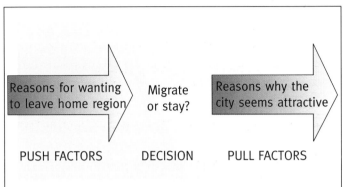

Figure 18.10 Rural to urban migration

19 Aid, investment and international development

What is meant by aid?

Aid is when a country or organization gives resources to another country. The resources can be in the form of money, goods, food, technology or people. Aid is provided to help Less Economically Developed Countries (LEDCs) improve their standard of living and quality of life by improving their economy and level of services.

A **donor** is a government, organisation or person providing the aid; a **recipient** is a government, organisation or person receiving the aid. There are four main types of aid:

1 **Official aid** is when the donor country uses money raised by taxes to give to the government of another country. The recipient government administers the aid.

2 **Bilateral aid** is when the donor country gives the aid to the recipient country with 'strings attached', e.g. the receiving country may have to buy goods and services from the country giving the money.

3 **Multilateral aid** is where richer governments give money to an international organization such as the World Bank, which then redistributes the money to LEDCs.

4 **Voluntary aid** is money raised from the general public in richer countries by voluntary organisations. Examples of such groups include Oxfam, Save the Children, Christian Aid and the Intermediate Technology Development Group. The money is given to LEDCs and is usually used for a specific project with no ties attached.

The problems with the first three types of aid are:

- Usually the money has to be repaid with interest, so often the recipient country builds up **debt**.

- The receiving governments do not like to be 'tied' economically to the donor government.

- The donor governments often will not lend to countries with whom they have political differences or whom they regard as undemocratic.

- Sometimes the money is withheld by corrupt officials, limiting the amount reaching the people who need it most.

Figure 19.1 Short term aid during a famine

Aid can be delivered over short or long timescales:

- **Short term aid** is relief for a limited period. It is usually given following natural disasters (floods, droughts, earthquakes) or human disasters (refugees from civil war). The aid can be both official and voluntary (**Figure 19.1**).

- **Long term aid** continues over a substantial period of time and is usually concerned with development programmes which aim to improve independence and self-sufficiency (**Figure 19.5**).

What is debt relief?

In 1999 there was a high-profile campaign to cancel Third World debt. The idea was that More Economically Developed Countries (MEDCs) and organisations like the World Bank would 'write off' the debts of LEDCs so that any money they earned could be used for development rather than returned to MEDCs in payment for loans received and the interest on them. Debt is a serious problem for the LEDCs. In 1998 the interest repayments for Africa were $10 billion, which was more than it spent on its health and education services. Britain is owed £10 billion worldwide, but to write off the debts of the poorest countries would cost £2.5 billion (less than is spent on trainers, cigarettes and concert tickets in a year).

Who are the main donors and recipients of aid?

In 1997 Japan and the USA were the largest aid donors, but the amount they gave as a proportion of their **GNP (Gross National Product)** was well below the 0.7 per cent figure recommended by the UN. In fact only four countries (Denmark, Norway, Netherlands and Sweden) exceeded the UN recommendation (**Figure 19.2**).

60 per cent of all aid went to some of the world's poorest countries which are located in sub-Saharan Africa (**Figure 19.3**). However, factors other than poverty also influence who receives aid, e.g.:

- Israel, with a strong Jewish lobby in the USA, receives large amounts of American aid.

- Kuwait, with large valuable oil reserves, receives aid from the richer countries who need the natural resource.

- Jamaica, a former British colony, receives British finance.

- The Philippines, which has a strategic military location in south east Asia, receives American aid.

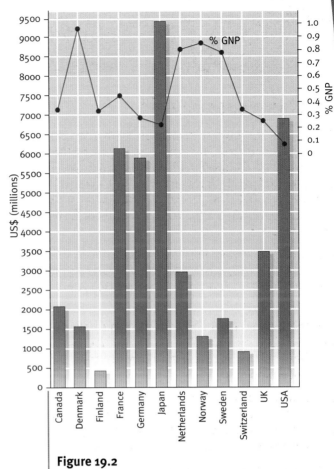

Figure 19.2
Major donor countries

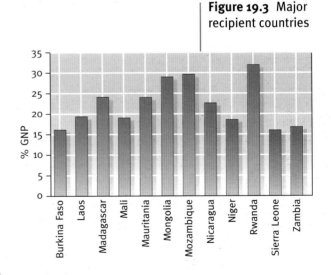

Figure 19.3 Major recipient countries

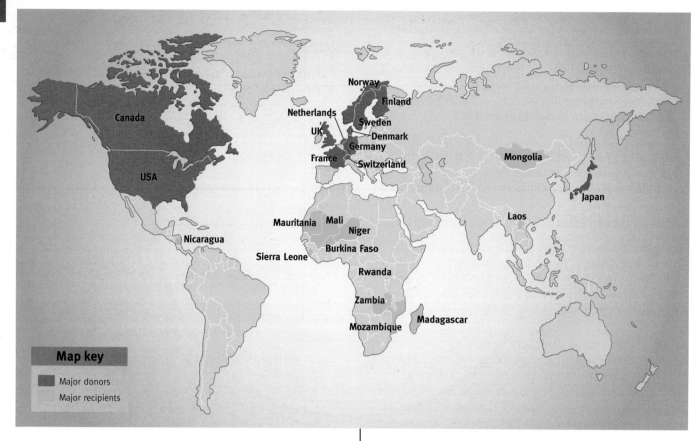

Map key

Major donors

Major recipients

Figure 19.4 World map showing major donor and major recipient countries

A development project in an LEDC – building a dyke in Vietnam

In Ky Anh Province, Vietnam, rice yields were low because farmland was often flooded by the sea, and became very **saline**. Using funds from the British Government's Department for International Development, Oxfam has worked with local government and local people to build a sea-dyke, 11 miles long, which stops the flooding (**Figure 19.5**). Roads have also been built to improve communications and trade.

This development project is:

- Financed by official aid money from the British Government and voluntary aid from Oxfam.

- Long term and will improve rice yields which will improve independence.

- **Sustainable** because it teaches local people how to dig and carry clay to build the sea dyke (**Figure 19.5**). It uses low cost technology such as hand tools. The local people will benefit as the rice yields will increase and any surplus can be taken to market along the new roads, so increasing the farmers' income.

Figure 19.5 Building a sea dyke in Vietnam

The role of international aid donors in encouraging sustainable development

The British Government office responsible for aid is the Department for International Development. It has three main objectives:

- To promote sustainable livelihoods.
- To provide better education, health and opportunities for poor people.
- To protect and improve management of the natural and physical environment.

In 1996, 50 per cent of official British aid was bilateral or 'tied', i.e. the countries receiving money had to agree to the purchase of goods and services from Britain. Since then the situation has improved in three ways:

- This type of aid has been reduced.
- All British Government supported aid programmes are 'checked' against the objectives listed above, including how sustainable they are.
- The British Government directs some aid through voluntary organizations where sustainability is a high priority, e.g. Oxfam receives approximately one third of its income from the British Government, the EU and the United Nations (UN).

What is the role of TNCs in international development?

A **transnational corporation (TNC)** is a firm which has branches **in at least two countries**, including the **home country**. The **home country** is where the firm was originally based and where the headquarters is normally located. A **host country** is where the branch factories are located.

A large number of TNCs originate in Japan, e.g. Sony, Toyota, and there are two main locations for the branch factories; within the EU and in the countries around the **Pacific Rim**.

Japanese TNC investment in the EU

The main type of investment is in manufacturing industry, particularly cars and electronic industries. The reasons for this investment in Europe are:

- To bypass the EU **tariffs**. Any manufactured goods made outside the EU but sold within it have to pay a tax. By manufacturing the bulk of the product within the EU the Japanese firms avoid having to pay this levy so the item is competitively priced.

Figure 19.6 The Nissan branch plant in Sunderland

- The transport costs, particularly for bulky items such as cars, are reduced so they can be marketed at a lower cost.

- EU labour charges are lower than those in Japan which reduces production costs.

- The EU provides a large market of 300 million people.

- In many parts of the EU **regional aid** is available which reduces the capital costs of building the factory.

- Many Japanese goods need adaptations to meet EU regulations or to suit the needs of the European market so it is easier to construct the product near to where it is to be sold.

The advantages to the EU of Japanese TNCs locating within its boundary are as follows:

- A large number of jobs are created. Employment is created directly in the factory. Local building firms gain work, component factories act as suppliers and the employees spend their wages in local shops etc. (This is known as the **multiplier effect**.)

- New working practices are introduced which make local firms more efficient.

- EU consumers have a greater choice of cars, washing machines etc.

There are also disadvantages to the EU of Japanese TNCs locating within its boundary:

- EU firms making similar products, e.g. cars, electronic goods, may not be able to compete successfully and may be forced to close.

- Research and design employment together with management jobs may be retained in Japan, restricting opportunities for EU residents to production work.

- In times of economic recession the Japanese firms may close their branch factories in the EU, retaining production in Japan and creating unemployment in countries such as the UK.

Figure 19.7 The Pacific Rim

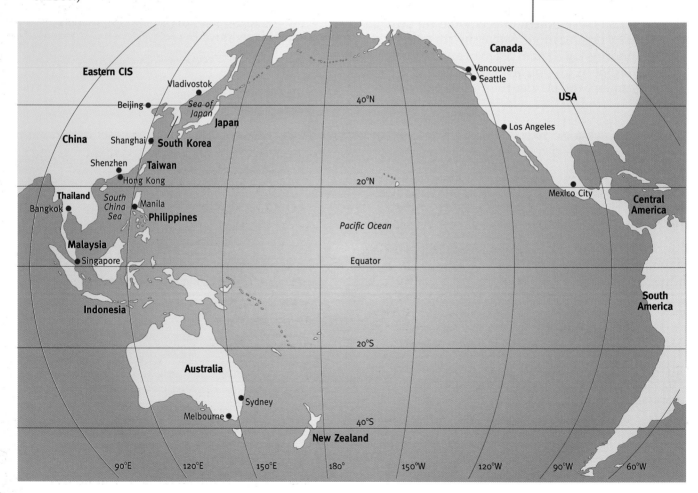

Figure 19.8 Seoul, South Korea

Japanese TNC investment in the Pacific Rim countries

The Pacific Rim countries are those that surround the Pacific Ocean (**Figure 19.7**). There are two types of investment in this area:

1 In MEDCs such as the USA and Canada, investment is similar to the EU, i.e. branch factories have been built to manufacture goods such as cars and electronic goods to supply the American market.

2 In the **newly industrialising countries (NICs)** of south east Asia the investment has been in two different areas: first, the opening of branch factories to supply components for factories in Japan and to make goods which involve a large labour investment, e.g. footwear; second, the development of subsidiaries to supply raw materials needed in Japan, e.g. timber.

Japanese TNCs have opened factories to make labour-intensive goods in south east Asian countries, e.g. China and Taiwan, for the following reasons:

- In the NICs the cost of labour is much lower than in Japan, so the product is made more cheaply.

- In most NICs the labour force is adaptable and educated to a sound basic level.

- Countries such as South Korea have low tax zones for firms making goods for overseas markets and this attracts Japanese companies manufacturing products to sell to Japan and elsewhere.

- As the economies of the NICs develop, the people become wealthier and this provides a large market for the Japanese TNCs to sell to.

- Often the labour and environmental laws are not as strict as in Japan so production costs are lower.

In South Korea the changes brought by Japanese TNC investment have been positive in the main:

- **Economically** there has been a large increase in GNP per capita and many people working in the Japanese TNCs have had a rise in income, enabling them to improve their houses and buy goods such as cars, washing machines and televisions.

- **Socially** the South Korean Government has received taxes to spend on public health, medical supplies and education. Most houses

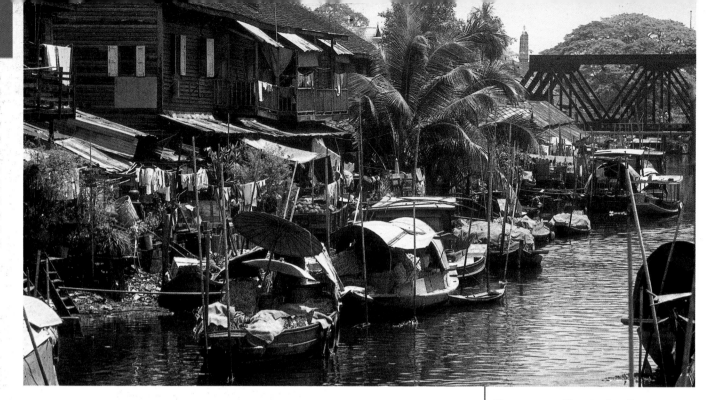

Figure 19.9 Shanty dwellers, Bangkok, Thailand

receive safe drinking water, the infant mortality rate has fallen by 75 per cent, and both primary and secondary education are available for most students. 30 years ago most men worked in farming and few females worked outside the home. Today both males and females have the opportunity to work in manufacturing or service industries. These jobs are in the urban areas such as Seoul (**Figure 19.8**) where there are high quality shops and entertainment such as cinemas.

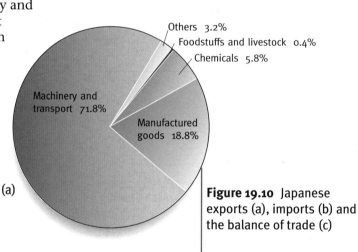

Others 3.2%
Foodstuffs and livestock 0.4%
Chemicals 5.8%
Machinery and transport 71.8%
Manufactured goods 18.8%

(a)

Figure 19.10 Japanese exports (a), imports (b) and the balance of trade (c)

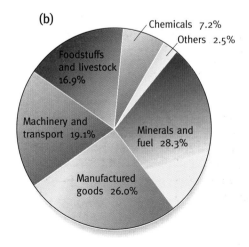

(b)
Chemicals 7.2%
Others 2.5%
Foodstuffs and livestock 16.9%
Machinery and transport 19.1%
Minerals and fuel 28.3%
Manufactured goods 26.0%

(c)

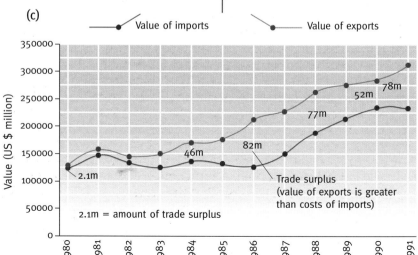

Value of imports   Value of exports

2.1m
46m
82m
77m
52m
78m

Trade surplus (value of exports is greater than costs of imports)

2.1m = amount of trade surplus

Value (US $ million)

1980 1981 1982 1983 1984 1985 1986 1987 1988 1989 1990 1991

In Thailand some of the changes brought about by Japanese TNCs have not been so positive. This is because the overseas firms have set up in Thailand in order to extract timber from the **tropical rainforest** to export to Japan. This has resulted in:

- The loss of rainforest, particularly large and valuable trees such as teak and mahogany.

- Soil erosion has increased.

- With potentially high profits, forest areas designated as reserves have been cut down and habitats are destroyed. As a direct result of this, there are no Siamese elephants left in the wild.

- The farmers living in the forest have been displaced and the highly mechanized timber industry creates few jobs. People from these rural areas have migrated to Bangkok and many are forced to live in **shanty areas**, particularly on boats in the harbour (**Figure 19.9**).

- The Thai Government does not receive a high tax revenue from the sale of the wood to Japan.

Does the Japanese trade pattern assist international development?

Trade is the flow of goods from one country to another. **Exports** are goods sent to other countries for which Japan receives money. **Imports** are goods sent to Japan for which Japan pays money. The **balance of trade** is the difference in value between imports and exports. A balance of trade surplus is when exports are greater than imports, whereas a balance of trade deficit is when imports are greater than exports. Japan's balance of trade is in surplus because it imports mainly cheap raw materials but exports expensive finished manufactured goods (**Figure 19.10**).

Many LEDCs have a trade deficit because they export low value raw materials (**primary products**) and import high value manufactured goods. For example, Thailand exports low value timber to Japan, but manufactured goods which the Thai people want to buy are imported at a high cost so the country has a balance of trade deficit. This means it is difficult for Thailand to develop economically without aid, while Japan becomes increasingly wealthy. However, some of the wealth obtained by Japan is returned abroad either as investment in overseas factories which provide jobs and income for the foreign country or as aid. This aid should help to improve educational standards and skills in LEDCs so that they can:

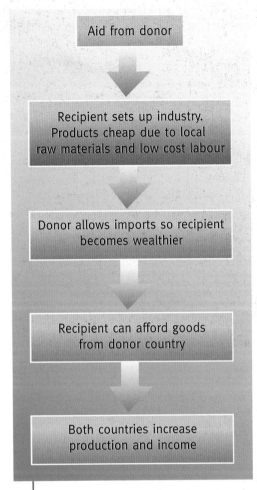

Figure 19.11 The recommended trade-aid pattern

- Improve crop production for their own consumption rather than for export.

- Develop sustainable industry so that expensive imports are not needed.

In addition, MEDCs need to buy products from LEDCs and not set up tariffs to protect their own industries. This will help the LEDCs to become wealthier and they will then be able to afford products from elsewhere so that all countries benefit (**Figure 19.11**).

Questions

1 Pages 186–188

Look at Figure 19.12.

a Is this a long-term or a short-term project? Explain your answer.

b Why can this development project be described as 'sustainable'?

c Look at Figure 19.13. Describe in your own words what is meant by the Poverty Cycle.

d Describe how the fish farming project shown in Figure 19.12 could help to break this cycle.

2 Pages 189–190

Look at Figure 19.14.

a In which country has most investment been made?

b How much money has been invested in the UK?

c Describe the main features of the global distribution of investment.

d Name the country in the European Union which has received the most investment.

e Why should Japanese companies wish to invest in the European Union?

Look at Figure 19.15.

f What name is given to companies like Sony which invest in more than one country?

g Give three reasons why Sony might choose to locate in South Wales.

h Describe and explain the possible attitudes of each of the following to the Sony investment:
  • An unemployed person living in Bridgend
  • A local builder
  • The local council
  • A local electronics manufacturer
  • The national government.

Figure 19.12 Fish farming for carp and shrimps in Bangladesh

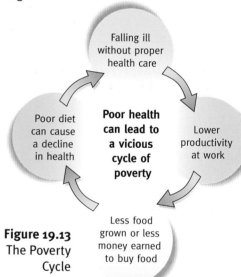

Falling ill without proper health care

Lower productivity at work

Less food grown or less money earned to buy food

Poor diet can cause a decline in health

Poor health can lead to a vicious cycle of poverty

Figure 19.13 The Poverty Cycle

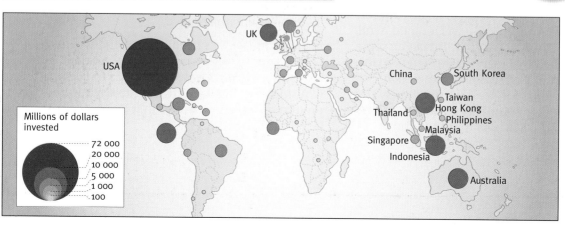

Millions of dollars invested

72 000
20 000
10 000
5 000
1 000
100

UK
USA
China
South Korea
Taiwan
Hong Kong
Thailand
Philippines
Malaysia
Singapore
Indonesia
Australia

Figure 19.14 Japanese overseas investment in the last 30 years

3 *Pages 190–192*

a   Look at Figure 19.14. Name the four countries on the Pacific Rim which have received the highest Japanese investment.

b   How is the investment in the USA and Indonesia likely to differ?

c   What is an NIC and why do Japanese companies choose to locate in such countries?

d   Name an NIC which has benefited from Japanese investment and describe what those benefits have been.

e   Name an NIC where Japanese investment has caused some damage and describe the negative effects.

4 *Pages 192–193*

a   Copy Figure 19.16. Give three examples of imports and three examples of exports for Japan.

b   Why is Japan described as having a 'balance of trade surplus'?

c   Why is the balance of trade in surplus?

d   Why do countries like Thailand have a 'balance of trade deficit'?

e   How can countries like Japan help countries like Thailand to develop and become wealthier?

Figure 19.15 Sony's CTV European Headquarters at Pencoed, Bridgend

Figure 19.16 Trade patterns

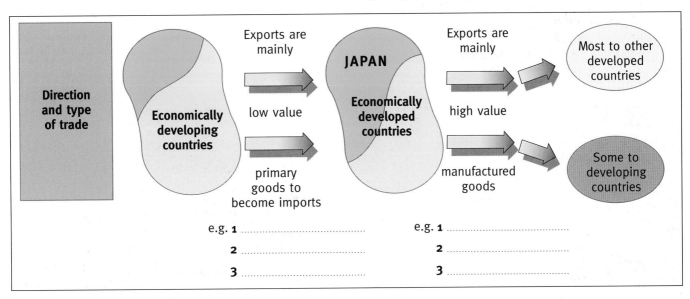

Direction and type of trade

Economically developing countries

Exports are mainly → low value → primary goods to become imports

JAPAN — Economically developed countries

Exports are mainly → high value → manufactured goods

Most to other developed countries

Some to developing countries

e.g. **1** ....
     2 ....
     3 ....

e.g. **1** ....
     2 ....
     3 ....

20 **Global warming – its causes and consequences**

Global warming and the greenhouse effect

Global warming is the worldwide increase in temperature and other changes in climate (**Figure 20.1**). **Figure 20.2** shows the latest predictions of change over the next century. It shows that the largest changes will be in the high latitude countries around the Arctic, which will become 6°C warmer. Smaller changes of 4 to 5.9°C of warming are predicted to occur in the Tropics, and the smallest amount of warming (less than 3°C) is predicted in mid latitudes, e.g. Britain and New Zealand. These figures might not seem to be very great, but it is only 5°C warmer now than at the end of the last ice age 10 000 years ago.

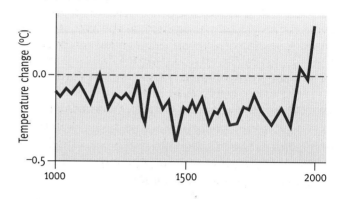

Figure 20.1 World temperature change, 1000–2000 AD

Figure 20.2 How countries will warm

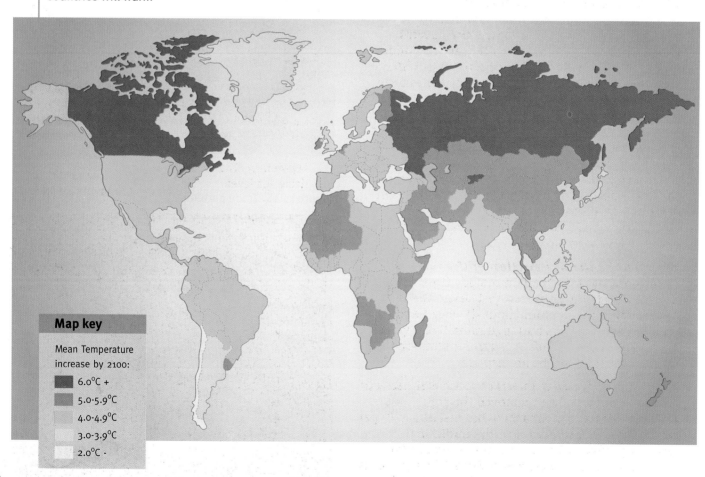

Map key

Mean Temperature increase by 2100:

- 6.0°C +
- 5.0-5.9°C
- 4.0-4.9°C
- 3.0-3.9°C
- 2.0°C -

The **greenhouse effect** is the process by which the Earth's atmosphere is warming. Energy from the sun reaches the earth as **short-wave radiation**. It is radiated back into space as **long-wave radiation**. Gases in the atmosphere allow the short-wave radiation to pass through to the Earth, but absorb much of the long-wave radiation before it can go into space. These gases are called **greenhouse gases** and include water vapour, carbon dioxide, methane, and nitrous oxides. These gases are constantly being cycled through the atmosphere; at the same time as a gas is added to the atmosphere, some is removed from the air by forests and **plankton** in the sea, so there is a natural balance. This keeps the Earth an amazing 33°C warmer than if there were no greenhouse gases. The reason global warming is occurring is that people are increasing the amount of greenhouse gases in the atmosphere in two ways:

- By increasing the amount of carbon dioxide through burning **fossil fuels**.

- By reducing the amount of carbon dioxide which forests take out of the air through destroying forests.

The effect of burning fossil fuels

When coal, oil and natural gas are burned, they produce carbon dioxide. Since the **Industrial Revolution** in the nineteenth century 850 billion tonnes of carbon dioxide have been put into the atmosphere. The amount of carbon dioxide in the atmosphere increased by 30 per cent since the start of the Industrial Revolution, and global temperatures have increased by 0.3 to 0.6°C. More carbon dioxide is produced in the MEDCs (75 per cent) than in the LEDCs (25 per cent). Burning coal and oil in power stations to make electricity is the main producer of the gas, followed by the use of petrol and diesel in vehicles. The USA is the biggest producer; it has 5 per cent of the world's population but makes over 20 per cent of the carbon dioxide.

The effect of the destruction of the rainforest

Plants grow by taking carbon dioxide from the air during the process of **photosynthesis**. The tropical rainforests can grow throughout the year because of the high temperatures and high rainfall (Chapter 15). They form one of the main routes for removing carbon dioxide from the atmosphere.

Nearly half of the great forests of south east Asia and central Africa have been removed through **deforestation**, and Amazonia has lost about 20 per cent. Chapter 15 showed how the traditional **shifting cultivation** of the Amazonian Indians does not affect the forest **ecosystem**. The main cause of deforestation is the clearance of larger areas by peasant farmers, ranchers, timber companies and the developers of mines, dams, etc. This in turn causes soil erosion and the climate becomes drier, so forests will not re-grow and less carbon dioxide is removed from the atmosphere.

Global warming and sea level rise

Sea level has risen 0.4 m in the last 140 years (**Figure 20.3**). It is estimated that it will rise another 60 cm by 2100 AD. The two reasons for this are:

- Temperatures are rising fastest near the poles, and this will speed up the melting of the great **ice sheets** in Greenland and Antarctica. There is so much ice in Antarctica that if the West Antarctic ice sheet were to slide off the continent and melt, sea levels would rise several metres throughout the world (**Figure 20.4**).

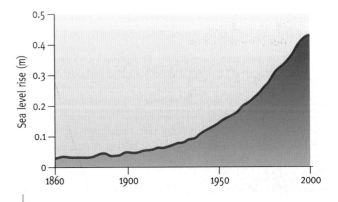

Figure 20.3 The rising sea level

Figure 20.4 The melting of the West Antarctic ice sheet

- As temperatures rise, warming spreads down into the depths of the oceans, making the water expand and sea levels rise. It will take 1000 years for warming to spread to the bottom of the sea, so sea levels will continue to rise. This is the more important of the two reasons.

There are many consequences of sea level rise. Very low lying countries such as Palau, a group of 200 islands in the Pacific, will be completely flooded. Ports such as Rotterdam (Chapter 10) will be flooded or will have to defend themselves.

The effects of rising sea levels on the Ganges Delta

The Ganges Delta is flat and most of it is at or just above sea level (Chapter 16). More than half of the 104 million people in Bangladesh live on the **delta** and are rice farmers. As sea level rises:

- The water in the ground becomes more **saline** and rice and other crops do not grow as well, leading to more hunger, especially as the population will continue to grow.

- Rivers have more difficulty flowing into the sea and flood the land more frequently and for longer as the water takes more time to drain away.

- **Storm surges** caused by **tropical cyclones** (see Chapter 16) can flood further inland.

- It is estimated that 30 million people might have to leave the delta as one third of Bangladesh is flooded by the rising sea level. The country is already three times more densely populated than Britain.

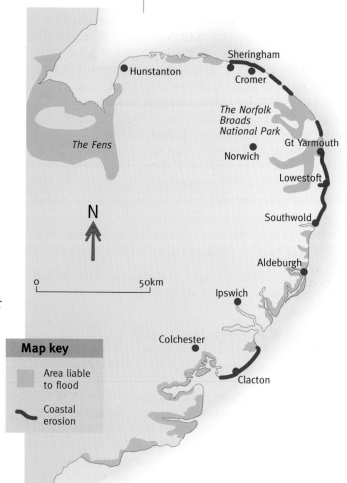

Figure 20.5 Threatened areas of eastern England

Map key

Area liable to flood

Coastal erosion

Figure 20.6 The Thames Barrier

The effects of rising sea levels on eastern England

Similar effects will occur in East Anglia (**Figure 20.5**):

- Much of the high quality **arable** land of the Fens is **reclaimed** marshland, and the peat soils have shrunk to below sea level. There is a great danger that they will be flooded by the higher sea level.

- The Norfolk Broads National Park is an area of freshwater lakes and marshes on the valley floors east of Norwich. They could be flooded by the sea.

- The clay cliffs on the East Anglian coast, e.g. near Cromer, are already being eroded quickly at over 1 m per year. With a higher sea level, the rate of erosion will increase.

- The southern North Sea has had disastrous floods caused by storm surges. The Thames Barrier was built to stop the City of London being flooded. The Barrier might have to be in place more frequently in future (**Figure 20.6**).

Climate change and extreme weather events

Out of the ten hottest years ever recorded in the world, four were in the 1980s and six were in the 1990s.

Britain

The climate of southern Britain with its previously warm, wet summers is becoming more like the climate of the Mediterranean area, with hot, dry summers and warm, wet winters (**Figure 20.7**). Extreme weather events are also occurring more frequently. The rising temperature of the Atlantic Ocean is causing more evaporation of water into the westerly winds which blow over Britain. This may be a reason for the record-breaking floods in Autumn 2000.

The climate is also becoming more unpredictable. **Figure 20.2** shows that the predicted temperature rise in Britain will be 2.5 to 3.5°C by 2080. This might have some good effects, such as hotter summers leading to a growth in the tourist industry. However, the prediction might be wrong. The melting of the Greenland ice sheet will stop the warm **North Atlantic Drift** from flowing so far northwards. Today, this ocean current heats up the sea and land adjacent to it in western Britain. If it is prevented from reaching Britain, the westerly winds approaching Britain will cross cold water and the temperature will fall by several degrees. Farming and other activities would suffer greatly as the climate becomes more like Iceland's.

The tropics

The extreme weather and a more unpredictable climate are also becoming more common in other parts of the world.

The spinning of the world on its axis makes currents in the tropical parts of the Pacific Ocean flow westwards helped by winds from the north east and south east (the **trade winds**) (**Figure 20.8a**). Warm water is moved to the west, and over time a higher sea level builds up there. The warm water warms the air above it producing **low pressure** and much rain is formed by **convection**. These heavy rains, together with high temperatures mean

Figure 20.7 Britain's climate by 2080? (a) change in average annual temperature, (b) change in average annual rainfall

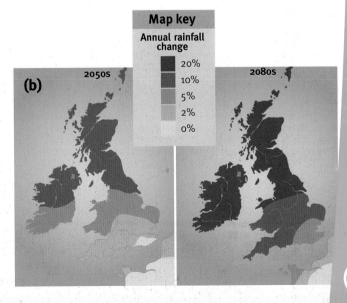

that Indonesia has a tropical rainforest vegetation. Meanwhile the east side of the Pacific, on the coast of Peru, is a desert because the cold water offshore makes air pressure high and rain cannot be formed by convection.

For reasons which are not yet known, in some years the westerly flowing warm water suddenly flows eastwards (**Figure 20.8b**) in what is known as an **El Niño** event. Colder water in the western Pacific creates **high pressure** there, which results in drought and famine. Meanwhile the warm water now off the Peruvian coast can lead to torrential rainstorms in the desert. The vast numbers of fish in the sea disappear (as the cold, nutrient-rich waters are no longer there) and the people who live on the coast and depend on the fishing industry are left with no work.

There is evidence to show that the warming of the world's climate is causing more El Niño events. They last for one to three years and return at irregular intervals of two to seven years.

The warming of the oceans and the air is allowing more evaporation of sea water to occur in the tropics. This is how tropical cyclones get their energy. There has been an increase in the number of them. More tropical cyclones in the Bay of Bengal will create more storm surges which could flood the Ganges Delta more frequently (Chapter 16 pages 156–157).

Figure 20.8 (a) Normal circulation of the Pacific Ocean, (b) El Niño phase

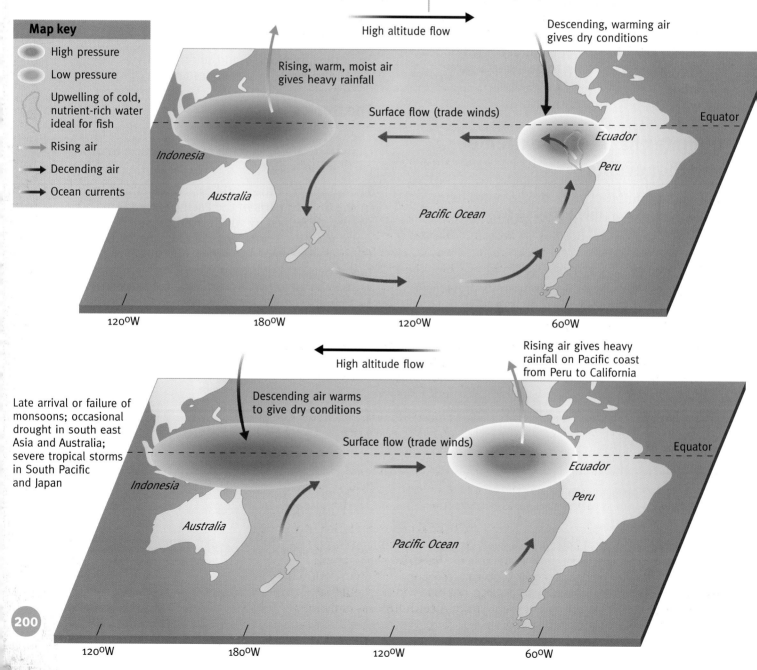

How can the burning of fossil fuels be reduced?

Global scale

In 1997 world leaders met at Kyoto to agree to 5.5 per cent cuts on 1990 levels of greenhouse gas emissions by 2010. Many scientists argued that the cuts should be more like 60 to 80 per cent. However, emissions have continued to grow by 1.3 per cent per year. In 2000, the leaders met again at The Hague to decide how to make these cuts. Two different methods were proposed:

1 The USA, Japan, Australia and Canada wish to continue to burn as much coal and oil as they want so that their industry will not be affected. They plan to soak up carbon dioxide from the atmosphere by planting forests and encouraging plankton in the oceans to grow more rapidly. These are called **carbon sinks**. Countries would be allowed to buy the right to pollute if they bought another country's unused pollution quota or planted a forest. Opponents argued that it is not easy to predict how much carbon dioxide would be removed from the atmosphere by planting a forest, and there is not enough unused land to grow such huge forests.

2 EU countries want to reduce global warming by reducing the amount of carbon dioxide emitted. Many techniques will have to be used, as shown by the example of the UK.

National scale

The British Government has adopted four main policies to reduce the burning of fossil fuels:

1 Britain has already cut its carbon dioxide emissions by 10 per cent by closing many coal fired power stations and switching to gas fired ones. It has been suggested that the expansion of nuclear power to make electricity would make further cuts in carbon dioxide emissions, but nuclear power poses other difficulties (see Chapter 4 page 59).

2 Renewable sources of energy generate 3 per cent of Britain's electricity at present. The plan is to increase this to 10 per cent by 2010 (**Figure 4.10**, page 61) through the following:

- **Wind farms** have been built in several places on land, and the first offshore wind farm was opened at Blyth in Northumberland in 2000. Two hundred more offshore wind farms and many more on land will be needed.

- 10 000 **wave-powered turbines** will be needed under the sea; 100 sites have been identified. Tidal power stations might also be required.

- **Solar panels** covering the roofs of 10 per cent of all buildings would generate all the power needed in Britain, but they are expensive to make until mass production brings costs down.

3 Through conservation, energy would be used much more efficiently. Only one third of a fuel's energy is converted into electrical power; the rest is lost into the atmosphere as heat. New **combined heat and power plants (CHP)** cut greenhouse gas emissions by 50 per cent. Loft insulation and the lagging of boilers and hot water tanks would also reduce energy loss. At present 47 per cent of greenhouse gas emissions come from the heating of buildings.

4 Carbon dioxide emissions from vehicles are rising. The British Government has been trying to reduce vehicle emissions by increasing taxes on fuel, with little success. Taxes have been lowered on small cars (smaller than 1500cc), which pollute less. Liquid Petroleum Gas (LPG) sells for only 30p per litre (petrol is 85p per litre) and emits only half the greenhouse gases, but few cars have so far been converted to use it, partly because it is not available at most filling stations. The government would like more people to travel on buses and trains as public transport emits much less greenhouse gas per person than cars.

Local scale

Local Agenda 21 is the programme in which local authorities in Britain are trying to reduce energy use and to encourage sustainability. An example is provided by Nottinghamshire County Council:

- Local sources of food and other goods have been listed on publicity leaflets to encourage people to buy locally. This cuts down on greenhouse gases emitted when goods are transported a long way to markets. Air travel is especially polluting because aeroplanes use so much fuel when taking off.

- Nottinghamshire County Council and other big employers such as Boots the Chemist are encouraging their workers to travel to work by public transport, cycling, walking, or by sharing lifts in cars.

- Like other local authorities, Nottinghamshire County Council is trying to reduce waste and to encourage people to recycle glass, metal and plastics which use a lot of energy during their manufacture.

- Education is an important part of Agenda 21 in order to show people how their individual decisions and actions can be important to the environment of the whole world. This is summarized in the phrase 'think global, act local'. It includes persuading people to switch off lights when rooms are empty, shut outside doors to keep heat in buildings, recycle paper, cans, etc. and use public transport rather than drive the car.

How can coasts be defended from rising sea levels?

Two types of coast are being affected by rising sea levels:

- Low-lying coasts, where the rising sea will flood the land.

- Coasts with clay cliffs, where the rate of erosion is increasing.

Low-lying coasts

In The Netherlands, in large cities such as Rotterdam/Europoort, most of the industries and the best farmland are between sea level and 8 m below sea level. The Dutch have no choice but to protect their coast from flooding, whatever the cost (pages 115–116). High flood banks (**dykes**) have been built, and dams block the sea inlets in the south west. Flood banks are called an **engineering** or 'hard' solution to the problem of rising sea levels. They are expensive to construct and maintain.

Bangladesh has similar problems. 80 per cent of the country is **floodplain** and **delta**, and the projected sea level rise of 60 cm by 2080 will flood 17.5 per cent of the land, and millions of people will be made homeless. Flooding by the sea is made worse by storm surges caused by tropical cyclones and by river floods during heavy rain. Bangladesh is one of the world's poorest countries. The World Bank solution (**Figure 20.9**) is a massive scheme to build flood

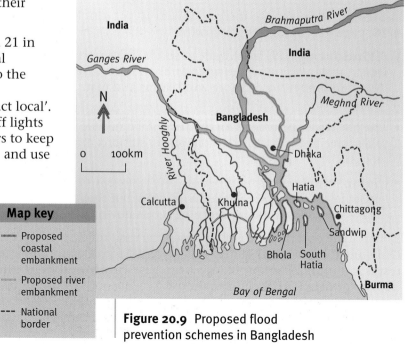

Map key

- ▭▭▭ Proposed coastal embankment
- ▭▭▭ Proposed river embankment
- --- National border

Figure 20.9 Proposed flood prevention schemes in Bangladesh

banks to protect the land from flooding by the sea and rivers. Concrete shelters set high on stilts will provide safe places if floods do occur, and there will be better early warning systems. However, it is not clear whether this will work because:

- The cost will be too great for the country to afford. If the floods cannot spread out over the land, the flood banks will have to be even bigger and more expensive to maintain.

- The farming and fishing industries need the floods to keep the soil and fish breeding areas fertile.

- Saline water will pollute the **groundwater** and reduce crop yields.

In Britain, the Fens in East Anglia are at or below sea level and are protected by flood banks. The country can afford to raise them above sea level, but would it be money well spent? Do we need the threatened land to grow food? Britain has food surpluses and the **set-aside** scheme is trying to reduce the area of arable land. Britain is also trying to increase its wildlife populations and diversity. Few people live on the Fens and there is little industry, so one proposal is to let areas like these flood so that they become natural marshland again and a suitable habitat for wildlife. The local people would be given compensation. Schemes like this are called **managed retreat** or 'soft' policies.

Coasts with clay cliffs – management of the coast of Holderness

7–10 m of land are eroded each year from Mappleton in Holderness (eastern England) and 5 km have gone since Roman times. This includes 29 villages in the last 1000 years and the rate of erosion is increasing as the sea level rises at 6 mm per year.

Erosion is rapid because:

- The boulder clay cliffs can easily be washed away by big waves, especially when they come from the north east, where there is a long stretch of open sea, i.e. a **long fetch**.

- Rain enters the clay and causes **slumps** which move large sections of the cliff on to the beach where there is much wave energy.

- The clay is broken into tiny particles which are suspended in the waves. There is little sand in the clay which could settle to form a beach. As the beach is low and narrow the waves lose little energy crossing it and hit the foot of the cliff with full force.

In 1990 a **coastal protection scheme** was constructed (**Figure 20.10**). It has two parts:

- Large blocks of granite were imported from Norway and were put at the foot of the cliff. They break up the waves as they hit the land so they lose their energy as friction, leaving little to erode the cliff behind. Over time the cliff will slump to become gentler and safer.

Figure 20.10 Mappleton and its sea defences

- Two rock **groynes** were constructed at right angles to the cliff. They stop the sand on the beach moving along the shore in the process of **longshore drift** (**Figure 20.11**). The beach builds up and becomes wider and higher. Waves lose energy crossing it and erosion of the cliff is reduced. However, places further south along the coast now receive less sand by longshore drift than before. Their beaches have shrunk and erosion of their cliffs has increased.

Figure 20.11 The process of longshore drift

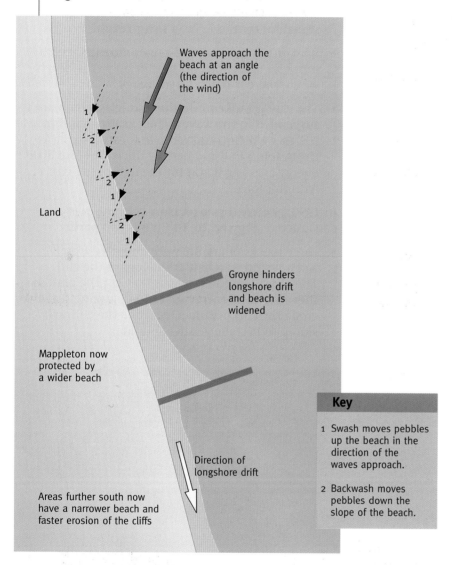

Waves approach the beach at an angle (the direction of the wind)

Land

Groyne hinders longshore drift and beach is widened

Mappleton now protected by a wider beach

Direction of longshore drift

Areas further south now have a narrower beach and faster erosion of the cliffs

Key

1 Swash moves pebbles up the beach in the direction of the waves approach.

2 Backwash moves pebbles down the slope of the beach.

Questions

1 *Page 196*

Use the Internet to carry out a research study of the most recent events related to global warming. List the events under the following headings and write brief notes to describe them:

- Temperature increase.
- Destruction of rainforest.
- Sea level rise and flooding by the sea.
- Extreme weather events in Britain.
- Extreme weather events in the rest of the world.

You could start by looking at the websites for the Meteorological office, the Environment Agency, Greenpeace and the BBC. You will also find useful sites at
www.heinemann.co.uk/hotlinks
www.greenpeace.org/-climate
www.bbc.co.uk/weather
www.environment-agency.gov.uk/flood
www.schools.detr.gov.uk/global/index.htm
www.environment.detr.gov.uk/climatechange/index.htm
www.foe.co.uk
www.tyndall.uea.ac.uk

2 *Pages 196–197*

a Describe how Figure 20.12 suggests that global warming is occurring.
- When did the present period of warming start?
- How much warming has occurred since the start of the present period of warming?

3 *Pages 196–197*

a Using Figure 20.13 find the correct figures for the following:
- Total world energy consumption in 1968.
- Total world energy consumption in 1993.
- Increase in total world energy consumption from 1968 to 1993.

b What did the three year-groups below have in common for total energy consumption?
- 1968–1973
- 1976–1979
- 1984–1990

c What does Figure 20.13 show you about the importance of fossil fuels in world energy consumption?

d Which is the most important source of power that is not a fossil fuel?

e What percentage of total world energy consumption is supplied from renewable sources?

f Explain how the burning of fossil fuels is thought to contribute to global warming.

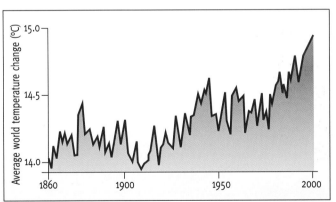

Figure 20.12
Average world temperatures since 1860

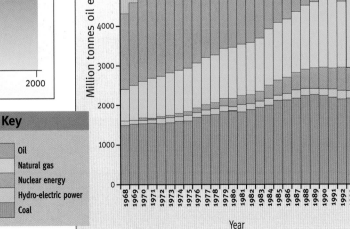

Figure 20.13 World energy consumption

4

Figure 20.14 shows the average amount of carbon emitted per person in various countries and areas.

a   Classify them according to how much carbon they emit. List the countries in each group and state the average for each group.

b   Describe the differences in emissions per person in Japan and India.

c   From your knowledge of these two countries, give reasons for the differences in carbon emissions.

5 *Page 197 and Chapter 15*

a   Give reasons for the destruction of the Amazonian rainforest.

b   Why is it difficult to reduce the rate of rainforest destruction?

c   What are the effects of deforestation on:
   • Carbon dioxide levels and global warming.
   • Total production of oxygen in the world.
   • Rainfall in Amazonia.

6 *Pages 197–198 and Chapter 16*

a   Describe the two ways in which global warming is causing a rise in world sea level.

b   In what ways will a rice farmer on the Ganges Delta be affected by the rise in world sea level?

c   Suggest what millions of people who live on the Ganges Delta might do when their region is permanently flooded by the sea.

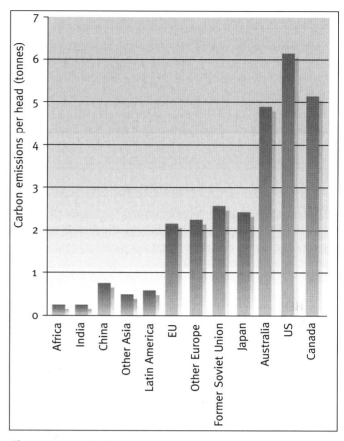

Figure 20.14 Carbon emissions per head

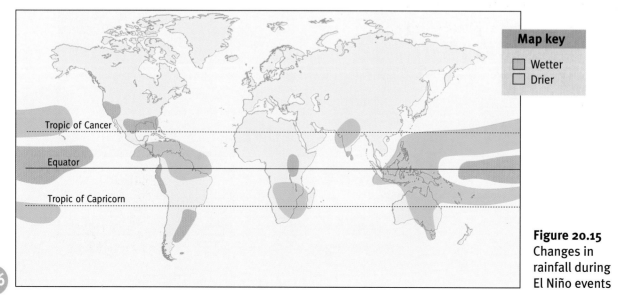

Figure 20.15 Changes in rainfall during El Niño events

7 *Pages 199–200*

Global warming is making El Niño events more frequent in the Pacific Ocean. El Niño affects the weather in parts of the rest of the world. Look at Figure 20.15.

a   Which parts of the world are affected by weather changes during El Niño phases?

b   Describe the distribution of these extreme weather events.

8 *Pages 201–202; Chapter 4; Page 169*

a   Suggest why the world continues to rely upon fossil fuels for so much of its energy consumption.

b   What has been the main reason for Britain's great reduction in carbon dioxide emissions during the 1990s?

c   HEP is renewable and does not contribute to global warming. Despite these advantages, only a small percentage of the energy used in Britain comes from HEP.
   •   What percentage of Britain's electrical power is generated by HEP?
   •   Give reasons why only a small percentage of the energy used in Britain comes from HEP.
   •   How has Japan reduced the percentage of its electricity generated by the burning of fossil fuels?

9 *Page 201*

Figure 20.16 is part of an advertisement placed in newspapers by British Nuclear Fuels.

a   Explain why the company believes that more electricity should be generated from nuclear power.

b   Many people disagree with the company. Explain why.

Figure 20.16 Advertisement by British Nuclear Fuels plc

21 Coursework

General points

- Coursework forms 25 per cent of the total marks available.

- It should be approximately 2000 to 2500 words. Remember that it is quality, not quantity, which is important.

- ICT must be used and you will gain marks for how well you employ it.

- Remember to check your spelling, punctuation and grammar. You can use ICT to help you.

- The mark scheme is out of 30; you should study it (**Table 21.1**). The points written in the Level 3 column will help you to decide how to collect, show, and analyse your data.

Structure of the coursework file

There is no recommended way to structure your file, but you might find the following useful:

1 Title page

- It helps you to focus on what you are doing if the title is written as a question.

- Write your name.

- You might wish to write the total number of words, which does not include those on diagrams and in any appendices.

2 Contents

- A list of headings and sub-headings with the pages they are on. Writing page numbers and then compiling the contents page is almost the last thing you do in your coursework.

3 List of photos, maps and diagrams

- Every photo, map and diagram must have a number and a title, e.g. 'Figure 10 A map to show the number of pedestrians'.

- Write the number, title and page number in this list.

4 Acknowledgements

- A list of everyone who has helped you and what they did. It is usual to leave out your teacher.

- If you collected information as part of a group, it is important to name the other members of the group.

- State which ICT software you used and whether you have used a spelling checker and grammar checker.

5 Aims and hypotheses

- The **aim** is often a development of the title of the coursework.

- Say where your study area is; a map is usually appropriate, but if it is just an outline of Britain with a dot to show a town, it will gain very little credit.

- **Hypotheses** are more detailed questions which break down the aim into parts that you can examine. They are easier to study if they are written as questions.

- An example of an aim and its hypotheses is:
  Aim: Why do pedestrian densities vary along the main street of Colne?
  Hypothesis 1: Does the type of land use affect the pedestrian density?
  Hypothesis 2: Does the location of car parking affect pedestrian density?

- You should not have many hypotheses; one to three is enough.

6 Methodology

Methodology concerns describing the methods used to collect **primary data** (data you have collected in the field). It does not include details about any **secondary data** (data you have collected from other sources). Secondary data should be only a small part of the coursework; many students use none. Methodology does not include details about how you drew particular maps and diagrams.

STRAND	LEVEL 1 – *MARKS 1-2*	LEVEL 2 – *MARKS 3-4*	LEVEL 3 – *MARKS 5-6*
Applied Understanding	The candidate locates the study area in a basic manner and through brief description, demonstrates some understanding of the ideas and concepts involved and can apply them in a simple manner to the geographical topic. Uses a limited range of geographical terminology.	The candidate locates the study area and, through description and explanation, using a range of geographical terms, demonstrates an understanding of the ideas and concepts involved, and can apply them to the geographical topic. Uses a range of geographical terminology.	The candidate locates the study area in detail and, through description and explanation, using a wide range of geographical terms, demonstrates a thorough understanding of the ideas, concepts and processes involved, and can apply them constructively to the geographical topic. Uses a wide range of geographical terminology.
Methodology	The candidate identifies a question or issue and lists the method used in obtaining the information. Selection, observation, collection and recording uses a limited range of basic techniques.	The candidate identifies a question or issue, the sequence of investigation and describes the methods used in obtaining the information. Selection, observation, collection and recording uses a range of appropriate techniques. The work is organised and planned and shows some evidence of the development of tasks.	The candidate identifies a question or issue, explains why that particular question or issue was chosen. The candidate describes the sequence of investigation, the methods used in obtaining the information and explains why the methods selected are relevant to their investigation. Selection, observation, collection and recording uses a comprehensive range of appropriate techniques. The work is well organised, planned and shows evidence of originality and initiative by the candidate.
Data Presentation	The candidate uses a limited range of basic techniques, some of which are ICT based, to present the information and expresses simple ideas with some degree of accuracy.	The candidate uses accurately a range of techniques, some of which are ICT based, to present and develop the information; and expresses ideas with considerable accuracy in the use of English.	The candidate uses accurately a range of more complex techniques, some of which are ICT based, to present and develop the information appropriate to their investigation; and expresses ideas in a clear, fluent and logical form using precise and accurate English.
Data Interpretation	The candidate gives a brief description of the results and/or suggests basic reasons for the results.	The candidate makes valid statements about the results. Attempts are made to analyse the results. Conclusions are drawn that relate to the original purpose of the enquiry.	The candidate demonstrates links through a detailed analysis of the material. In referring specifically to the data, valid conclusions are drawn that relate to the original purpose of the enquiry.
Evaluation	The candidate briefly describes how the enquiry process can be improved by questioning the reliability of the methods used to collect the data.	The candidate describes how the enquiry process can be improved by questioning the reliability of the methods used to collect the data and/or the accuracy of the results.	The candidate describes how the enquiry process can be improved by questioning how the reliability of the methods used to collect the data has affected the accuracy of results and the validity of conclusions.

Table 21.1 The coursework mark scheme

Questionnaires should be put to at least 30 interviewees.

You might find it helpful to bear the following questions in mind:

- What data are being collected?
- Why is the information being collected?
- Where were the data collected?
- When were the data collected?
- How were the data collected?

Say what you personally did, as it will help you to include details. If a group is collecting data, you should experience all the different tasks. Do not forget to include examples of questionnaire sheets or sheets with your writing on, as this is the 'recording' part of the mark scheme. You should comment on the reliability of, or problems with, your methods. This part should go in your evaluation section. There are two kinds of problems:

- **Difficulties** are problems which affect the amount or reliability of your data on the day, but might not occur on another day. An example would be few pedestrians in your survey because it rained all day. Do not spend long discussing this type of problem.

- **Limitations** are problems which are always in your method and will always affect the reliability of the data you collect. An example would be that your interviews of shoppers at 10 am on a Wednesday will always have few children and working people because they are at school or work. Spend some time writing about this type of problem. You will gain further marks by showing how it affects your data

In general, you should write in detail about your methodology. Two answers about mapping shops illustrate the point:

- An answer worth low marks might state that the type of shop was written on the map and that the reliability of the data was affected by the map being wrong in places.

- A higher level answer might include comments on:

  What were included in each shop type, e.g. did 'clothes shop' include men's, women's and children's clothing shops.

  The fact that only ground level land use was noted and how this might affect the reliability of the data.

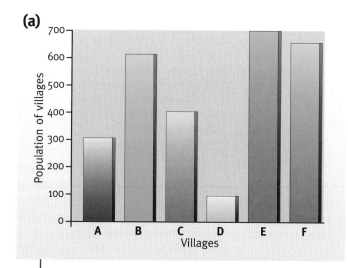

Figure 21.1 Presentation of place data (a) inappropriate diagram, (b) appropriate diagram

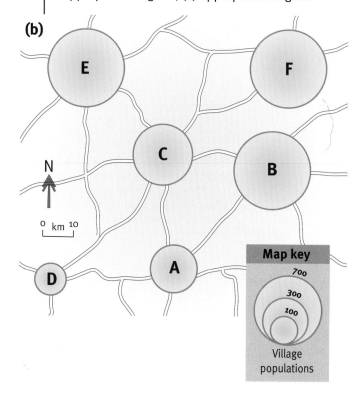

Whether judgements were made only from the shop window display and how this might be misleading.

The higher level answer would include actual examples of these problems.

You must show originality and initiative in your methods. For instance, draw a sketch or collect extra data without being told by your teacher to do so. When you write about your methods, say which parts were original and why you did them.

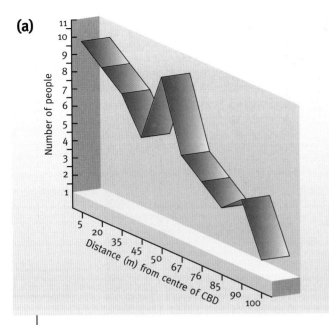

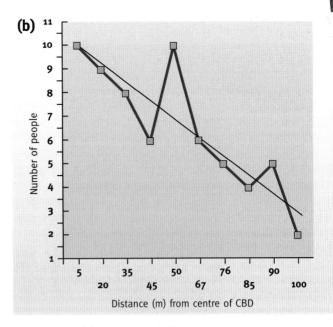

Figure 21.2 Presentation of graphical data (a) inappropriate diagram, (b) appropriate diagram

7 Data presentation

Your **data presentation** section will be marked according to whether you have used a variety of techniques, their complexity and, most importantly, how appropriate they are. The questions you should ask yourself when deciding which technique to use are:

- What do I want these data to show?

- What is the best way to show it?

Examples of inappropriate/appropriate techniques are:

- You want to show the variation in the population of several villages over an area. A bar graph would be inappropriate (**Figure 21.1a**). A map with circles whose centres are at the villages and whose sizes are proportional to the populations would be a more appropriate method (**Figure 21.1b**).

- You want to show the change in the number of people at 10 sites along a street. A three-dimensional line graph, which can be produced quickly on a computer, would be inappropriate, as it is too complicated (**Figure 21.2a**). A simple scatter graph with a best-fit line would be better (**Figure 21.2b**).

- **Classification** is a technique of presenting data either as a table of figures or as a map or diagram. If a land use map merely shows what was recorded in the field, it does not show classification. For instance, you should group shops into similar types. If you have more than about six categories, the map becomes too difficult to understand.

- Every map, graph, diagram and photo must have a number and title.

- Graphs must have labelled axes.

- Every map must have a key, scale and north arrow; they should be on the maps, not on separate pages.

- Photographs are often poorly annotated. The tip here is always to write a long phrase or sentence rather than one or two words. The annotation must be relevant to the aim of the coursework. **Figure 21.3** shows some examples of poor and good annotations on a photo which is part of a study of how environmental factors affect land use in a Lake District valley.

- At least two different ICT techniques must be used, e.g. word processing on at least one page, a photograph downloaded from the school's intranet or the use of a spreadsheet.

- The quality of your English will be included in this part of the mark scheme.

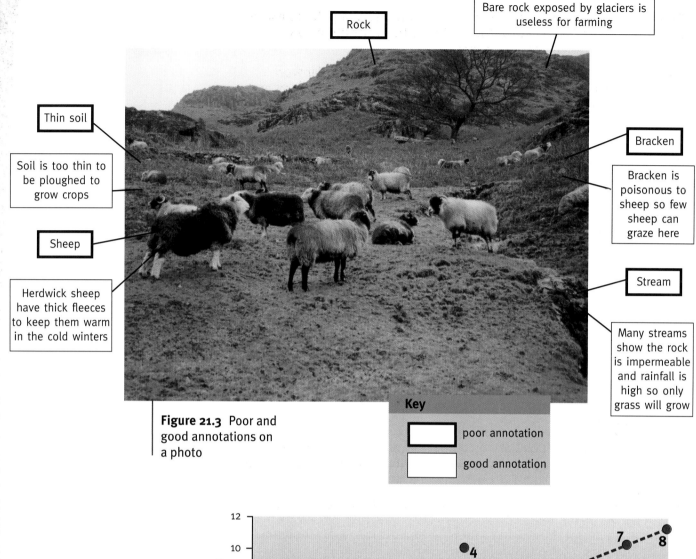

Rock

Bare rock exposed by glaciers is useless for farming

Thin soil

Soil is too thin to be ploughed to grow crops

Bracken

Bracken is poisonous to sheep so few sheep can graze here

Sheep

Herdwick sheep have thick fleeces to keep them warm in the cold winters

Stream

Many streams show the rock is impermeable and rainfall is high so only grass will grow

Figure 21.3 Poor and good annotations on a photo

Key

poor annotation

good annotation

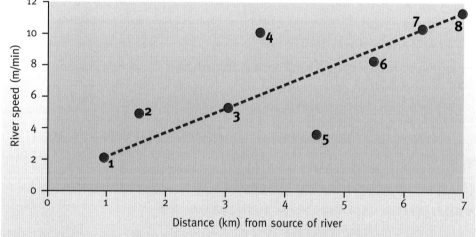

Figure 21.4 Changes in speed along the River Whitewell

8 Data interpretation, analysis and explanation

Description provides marks in both the 'understanding' and 'data interpretation' sections. When you describe, you should write about what you can see. You should not explain or try to give reasons. The main tips for description are:

- Describe patterns or trends rather than individual points.
- Describe using numbers as well as words, if appropriate.

Figure 21.4 is a graph of speed at 8 different places along the course of a river. **Table 21.2** shows how the quality of the description was improved from statement (a) to statement (f).

You can describe other sorts of maps and diagrams in a similar way. Many students find the easiest way to work is to draw graphs, maps and diagrams first and then to describe them in words. Remember to describe only what is relevant to the hypothesis you are investigating.

When you **analyse** information you have to give reasons for how the patterns you have described have been produced. This is probably the most difficult part of your enquiry. It varies enormously according to what your particular study is about. However, some guidelines are:

- Use general ideas you have learned in Geography. These ideas apply to many places as well as your own study area.

- Add details from your own study to your account of the general ideas.

- After you have explained the patterns in your data, explain the odd ones out. Students often find this part easier than explaining the overall pattern. However, the pattern should be explained first.

- It is always worthwhile thinking about how the methods you used may have produced inaccurate data and this may help with your explanation.

- Refer back to your original hypotheses or issues.

9 Conclusions

- This short section should summarize the main findings of your analysis and then use them to answer the question you wrote in your aim.

- It is an important section if you want to gain a high score in the marks for 'understanding'.

Table 21.2 Poor to good descriptions of Figure 21.4

Description	Comments
(a) Site 1 was slowest and Site 8 was the fastest.	No pattern; numbers not used
(b) Site 1 was slowest at 2 m per minute, and then speed increased to 5 m per minute at Site 2 and stayed the same at Site 3. At Site 4 it increased to 10 m per minute . . . etc.	A description of each point using numbers; no pattern identified; this is called 'data waffle'
(c) River speed increased from Site 1 to Site 8.	Pattern recognized; numbers not used
(d) River speed increased from 2 m per minute at Site 1 to 12 m per minute at Site 8.	Pattern recognized and numbers referred to
(e) River speed increased six times from 2 m per minute at Site 1 to 12 m per minute at Site 8.	The nature of the pattern is described using numbers
(f) River speed increased six times from 2 m per minute at Site 1 to 12 m per minute at Site 8. At Site 4 the speed was 4 m per minute faster than the best-fit line suggests it should be, and at Site 5 it was 5 m per minute slower.	The nature of the pattern is described using numbers; places which do not fit into the pattern are also identified and described; these are called **anomalies**

10 Evaluation

- However good the fieldwork methods were, all data collected are inaccurate in some ways. Try to show how these inaccurate data have led to inaccurate conclusions.

- Comment on how well your methods of presentation have worked in showing the reader what you intended.

- Suggest ways in which the coursework could have been improved, e.g.:
  Should different or extra methods have been used to collect data?
  Should it have been collected in more or different places?
  Should it have been collected at more or different times?
  Should different or extra hypotheses have been studied to understand the aim better?

11 Appendices

Appendices are pages of photos, information etc. which you do not want to include in your main study. They should be kept to a minimum. Some students include in an appendix the booklet which they used to record information when they were in the field. It might be torn, dirty or scruffy, but this does not matter. You must not copy out the information to make it look neat. It is better to include original fieldwork sheets in your methodology section.

1 River basins and their management

Abrasion (or corrasion)   When the load being transported by the river rubs against the river bed and banks like sandpaper and wears them away   6

Attrition   The erosion of the river's load. It is caused by the pebbles and sand in the load rubbing against each other   6

Bed load   The parts of a river's load which are transported by traction and saltation   6

Bouncing   The hopping motion of particles in a river's load when they are transported by saltation   6, 7

Condensation   When water vapour in the air changes into cloud droplets due to a drop in temperature   4

Confluence   The place where two rivers join   12

Deposition   The putting down of the load on to the river bed or sides. It occurs when the river's speed decreases and the river loses energy   7, 8, 9–11

Discharge   The volume of water passing a point on the river bank each second. It is measured in cubic metres per second or cumecs   6, 12–13

Dragging   The movement of particles along the river bed when they are part of the traction load   6, 7

Drainage basin   The area of land from which precipitation flows into a stream   4–6, 12

Erosion   The wearing away of rock by rivers, glaciers or waves   6, 8–9, 10–11, 36–41, 46–7

Estuary   A V-shaped arm of the sea extending into the land, where there is a river mouth   7, 8

Evaporation   Water is returned to the air by being changed into water vapour by the heat of the sun   4, 5, 13

Flood plain   A wide flat area on each side of a river where the river deposits its load when the river overtops its banks   9–10

Gorge   A narrow steep-sided valley formed by the retreat of a water   9

Groundwater   Water which has percolated down and saturated the rock, i.e. all the pore spaces and cracks are filled with water   5, 16

Groundwater flow   The movement of water sideways below the water table; it reappears on the surface at springs and in the sides of river channels   5, 12

Hydraulic erosion   When the pressure of water being forced into cracks in the river bed and banks makes the cracks wider, which forces rocks out   6

Impermeable   (impervious) Rock which water cannot pass through because it has no cracks, or because the pores are not connected   12, 16

Infiltration   Water soaking into the soil through holes, cracks, worm tunnels, etc.   4–5, 13

Interception   When precipitation is caught by vegetation before it reaches the ground   4, 5

Interlocking spurs   Fingers of higher land jutting out from one side of the valley into the other. They do this alternately   9, 40

Lateral erosion   Sideways erosion by a river which occurs on the outer bank of a meander and forms a river cliff   10–11

Levées   Raised embankments on each side of a river channel formed by deposition when the river floods   10

Load   The rock material produced by erosion which is being moved downstream by the river   6–7, 155

Meanders   Large bends in a river where it flows across its flood plain   10–11

Mouth   The mouth of a river is where it enters the sea   7, 8

Ox-bow lakes   Crescent-shaped lakes formed on flood plains   11

Percolation   Water flowing downwards through the pores and cracks in rock   5, 12

Permeable (pervious)   Rock through which water can pass along cracks in the rock and from pore to pore   15

Precipitation   Rain, snow or hail, formed when cloud droplets or ice crystals join together and become too heavy to remain in the cloud   4, 5, 21–3

Reservoir   A man-made lake formed by building a dam across a valley and blocking the river in it   15, 16–17

River cliff   A steep slope on the outer bank of a meander formed by undercutting by the fast flow of the river   10

Run off   Water flowing across the land surface, e.g. as a river   4, 25

Saltation   A hopping or bouncing motion of the river's load   6, 7

Slip-off slope   The gentle slope on the inner bank of a meander formed by deposition by the slow-moving river   10

Solution (or corrosion)   The dissolving of rock caused by acids in the river water   6–7

Source   Where a river starts, usually at a spring, bog or lake   7

Suspension   Particles in the river's load which are carried in the water without touching the river bed   6, 7

Temperature range   The difference in temperature between the warmest and coolest months   23, 35

Throughflow   Once it is in the soil, water flows downhill through the spaces such as natural pipes left by decayed roots   5, 12, 25

Traction   The rolling and dragging of the load along the river bed   6, 7

Transportation   The movement of the river's load downstream   5, 6–7

Tributaries   Small streams which join to form larger streams   7

V-shaped valley   A steep-sided narrow valley where the river channel fills the valley floor. It is usually found in the upland section of the river   8

Velocity   The speed of flow of a river   6

Vertical erosion   Downwards erosion where processes in the river channel rapidly lower its bed   8

Water table   The upper surface of the groundwater   5, 16, 25

Waterfall   Where a river drops from one level to a lower one, due to a band of resistant rock across the channel   7, 9

Watershed   The edge of a drainage basin which goes along the tops of ridges   12

Weathering   Rock forming the valley sides is broken up to form soil   8–9

2 Farming, food and the environment

Agribusiness   Farms which specialise in just a few crops using scientific advisers to produce the maximum yields and quality, and often have contracts with supermarkets and processors to buy the crops even before they are planted   31

Arable farms   Farms growing only crops   20, 28–33

Diversification   Making money in ways which are not to do with farming   27, 30, 43

Eutrophication   The removal of oxygen from river water which results in the death of plant and animal life in the water   32, 159

Extensive farming   Where low inputs to each hectare of land produce low outputs   25–7

3 Tourism in the Lake District National Park

4 Electricity generation for the future

Renewable energy   A fuel source which can be used over and over again, e.g. wind, water, geothermal, solar   57–8, 61–3

Thermal power station   Power stations which use heat to make steam which turns the turbines to produce electricity. This heat can be produced by burning coal, oil or gas or by using nuclear or geothermal sources   52–5, 59, 60

5 The changing location of manufacturing industry

Break-of-bulk   A place where raw material is imported in bulk and is then broken down into smaller units   68, 70, 113, 120

Brownfield site   A site which was previously built on, i.e. another factory or housing had been on the land and has since been demolished   71

Capital   The money needed to start up a firm   68, 72

Footloose industry   An industry which has a relatively free choice of location, since it is not tied to raw materials or fuel supplies   67–8, 71–3, 74, 122–3

Greenfield site   A site which was previously fields or similar and has not been built on before   71, 172

Heavy industry   One which uses bulky raw materials and usually manufactures a substantial volume of finished product   68–70, 119, 120, 170

Location   Where a factory is placed in relation to suppliers and markets   67–74

Raw material   An item needed to make a product   67, 68, 69

Secondary industry   Manufacturing industry, i.e. the making of a product   67

Site   The land on which a factory is built   67

6 Understanding the modern urban environment

Central Business District (CBD)   The area of public buildings, shops, offices and transport facilities which occupies the centre of a town   76, 79, 85, 87

Commuter   A person who lives in one settlement and travels every day to work in another   83–4, 129, 135

Commuter village   A village where a large number of the residents travel to work each day in another settlement and then back home each evening.   83–4

Comprehensive redevelopment   The rebuilding of housing and industry together with roads and environmental improvements   80

Counterurbanisation   The movement of people out of urban areas into a more rural environment   83–4

Gentrification   Where professional people and their families return to live close to the city centre. They buy older sub-standard housing which they improve so that it becomes worth more   84

Green Belt   The countryside around a town which is protected by law from development   89

Housing renovation   The improvement of homes e.g. installing bathrooms, inside toilets and hot water   81

Inner city   The area occupied by nineteenth century factories and terraced housing   76, 80–1, 84, 128, 129, 130

Migration   The movement of people from one settlement to live in another   98, 109, 135, 179–83

Out-of-town shopping centre   A retail park built in the countryside on the edge of a town   82, 85–6

Retail park   A group of large one-storey shops with car parks, usually built close to a major road, e.g. a ring road or motorway junction   82, 85–6

Rural-urban fringe   Where the edge of the built-up area of the town meets the surrounding countryside   82–4, 87

Shopping centre   A group of shops   85–7
Slum clearance   The removal of old and decayed housing   80
Suburb   An area of housing built in the outer part of a town but within the town boundary   77–8
Suburbanisation   The growth of housing and population in the outer areas of a town   83

Twilight zone   The area of decay between the CBD and the inner city   85

Urbanisation   When the percentage of the population living in towns within a country increases   170, 179–80
Urban morphology   The pattern of land use in a town   75–9

7 Rich and poor regions in the European Union

Core   A core area is the richest part of a country with the highest level of development   94

Gross national product (GNP)   The total income for an area for a year in $US (including income from overseas investment)   94
Gross national product (GNP) per capita (per person)   The gross national product divided by the number of people in a country   94

Level of development   How advanced an area is. It is reflected in the levels of income and services, e.g. schools, hospitals and transport provision   94–5

Periphery   The poorest region, with the lowest level of development   94, 95

8 Farming in southern Italy: problems on the periphery

Land reform   To change who owns the land   98–9, 100

'Push' factors   Those features which encourage people to leave an area   98
'Pull' factors   Those features which people expect to find in another area which they move to (these features can be real or imagined)   98

9 Tourism in Mediterranean Spain

Functions   The types of work done in a place   106–7, 109, 114

Situation   The position of a place in relation to the surrounding region   102, 103, 112, 118, 126, 133

15 Amazonia – development in the rainforest environment

Buttress root   Wood growing in the angle between the trunk and root of a tree which acts like a prop to secure the tree   145

Canopy   The continuous layer of crowns of trees which form most of the tropical rain forest   144, 145
Convection rainfall   Rain formed by the rising of warm, light air caused by the sun heating the ground. The air cools, which makes the water vapour condense to form cloud and then rain   22, 144

Deforestation   The removal or burning of trees   148, 150, 154, 179, 197
Drip tip   The point on a leaf, which speeds up the flow of rainwater from the surface   145

Eco-tourism   Travel to natural areas for holidays to understand the natural environment   151
Emergent   A tall tree which grows above the rainforest canopy   144–51

Leaching   Removal of nutrients from the soil by high rainfall   147

Rain forest   The natural vegetation of the Amazon region which is mainly trees because of the high rainfall   144–6, 193

Shifting cultivation   When a tribe leaves one clearing after three or four years of cultivation, clears another by the 'slash and burn' method, and then cultivates that area   147, 150, 153, 197

Sustainable development   Continued improvements for a population without causing any harm to the environment   160, 165, 189, 194

16 The Ganges Delta – dense population in a high-risk environment

Delta   A triangular, flat, low-lying marshy area at sea level found where some rivers enter the sea   155, 157, 158

Distributary   A river formed by a channel dividing into two channels on a delta   155

Eye   An area of calm in the centre of a tropical cyclone   156

High pressure air   Formed where land has cooled due to little heat from the sun, so the air becomes heavy and sinks   155–6

High yielding variety (HYV)   A strain of rice such as IR8 which gives an increased amount of grain   159

Hybrid seed   Created by crossing different varieties of rice   159

Low pressure air   Formed where land has been heated by the sun so the air is warmed, expands and rises   155, 156

Storm surge   A higher sea level than normal caused when strong winds push the sea inland   156, 157

Tropical cyclone   A deep low pressure system with winds up to 200 km/hr and an eye in the centre   156, 157, 164, 200

17 Japan – urbanisation and industrialisation

Assembly plant   A factory which puts together the parts to make a final product   170–2

Capital investment   Money used to buy machines, rather than to pay many workers in an industry   171

Component   A manufactured part which is put together with others to make a final product   171–2

Export   To send goods from one country to another   170, 172, 193

Import   To bring goods into one country from another   169, 193

Pollution   The release of waste into the environment from factories, houses, transport and agriculture   174–5

USA   The United States of America   187

18 Population growth and urbanisation

Formal sector of the economy   That part of the economy where employment is permanent and the workers receive a regular income   182

Informal sector of the economy   That part of the economy where workers are self-employed, often working from home. The work is usually erratic and the income is low   182

Squatter settlement   Where people build houses on land illegally   181–3, 192

19 Aid, investment and international development

Bilateral aid   The donor country gives aid directly to the receiving country, often with 'strings attached'   186

Debt relief   When money owed by poor countries does not have to be paid back to richer countries or the World Bank   187

Long-term aid   Aid which continues over a substantial period of time and is usually concerned with development programmes   187

Manufactured products   Goods made from raw materials or components   193

Multi-lateral aid Richer governments give money to an international organisation such as the World Bank, which then distributes the money to the LEDCs 186

Official aid The donor country uses money raised by taxes to give to the government of another country. The receiving government administers the aid 186

Primary product A raw material produced by mining, farming, fishing or forestry 193

Short-term aid Relief given for a limited period, such as after an earthquake 187

Trade The flow of goods between countries 193

Transnational corporation (TNC) A firm which has branches in at least two countries, including the home country 72, 109, 148, 181, 189–92

Voluntary aid Money raised from the general public in richer countries by voluntary organizations such as Oxfam and given to LEDCs 186

20 Global warming – its causes and consequences

Greenhouse Effect The process by which the earth's atmosphere is warming because some of the heat from the sun is trapped in the atmosphere by gases such as carbon dioxide 87, 197

INDEX

Index

Photograph acknowledgements

pp. 8, 27, 30, 38, 39, 40, 73 John Cleare/ *Mountain Camera Picture Library*; **pp. 14, 48, 49, 212** Arthur Robinson; **p. 28** NMU EMT/ Gareth Davis; *Environmental Images:* **p. 31** Graham Burns, **p. 32** Paul Glendell, **p. 33** Vanessa Miles, **p. 62** Martin Bond, **pp. 68, 70** Dave Ellison; **pp. 36, 71, 142** *Aerofilm;* **p. 52** Killingholme Power Station; **p. 55** BNFL Magnox Generation; **pp. 78, 80, 86, 88,** Janet Helm; **p. 73** UKAEA; **p. 74** *SMN Archive/* Chris James; **p. 77** BBC Hulton; **p. 82** Taylor Weaver; **p. 92** (both) Graham Pritchard; *Collections:* **p. 94** Robert Hallmann, **p. 198** Michael George; *Robert Harding Picture Library:* **p. 95, p. 105** Billy Stock, **p. 107** Phil Robinson, **p. 126** R Lundy, **p. 129** MPH, **p. 133**; *Travel Ink:* **p. 107** Ronald Badkin, **p. 109** Angela Hampton, **p. 113** David Toase; *Corbis:* **p. 107** Nik Wheeler, **p. 114** Paolo Ragazzini, **p. 117** David Cumming, **p. 117** Paul Almasy, **p. 125** Manfred Wollmer, **p. 170** Michael S Yamashita; *Eye Ubiquitous:* **p. 108** Julie Waterlow, **p. 108** David Cumming; **p. 109** James Davis Travel Photography; **p. 140** Eurotunnel; *Panos Pictures:* **p. 159** Heldur Netocny, **p. 160** Peter Barker, **pp. 181, 182** Jeremy Horner, **p. 186** Betty Press, **p. 191** Jean-Leo Dugast, **p. 192** Sean Sprague, **p. 194** Jim Holmes; **p. 169** Kansai International Airport Co Ltd; **p. 188** Oxfam; **p. 189** Nissan Motor Manufacturing (UK) Ltd; **p. 195** AIWA (UK) Ltd; **p. 197** Bryan and Cherry Alexander; **p. 203** APS (UK).
Cover photo by

Text acknowledgements

pp. 9, 63 Questions 6a & b, 3e from AQA GCSE Paper 1 (2000), **pp. 71, 96, 125, 176** Questions 4, 2a, Figures 11.10, 17.12 from AQA GCSE Paper 2 (2000), **p. 57** Figure 4.8 AQA Geography Advanced Module 2001, **p. 209** Table 21.1 AQA Specification B 2001; **pp. 18, 29, 111, 205** Figure 1.20, Questions 6a & b, Table 3.2, Figures 20.12, 20.13, Question 3a from NEAB GCSE Paper 1 (1997), **p. 19** Question 5b from NEAB GCSE Paper 1 (2000), **pp. 19, 28, 35, 50, 62, 63, 80, 110, 111** Figures 1, 24, Questions 2a-d, Figures 2.21, Questions 1a & b, 2c, 3, Figures 3.21, 9.12, 9.13, 9.17 from NEAB GCSE Paper 1 (1996), **pp. 34, 50** Figures 2.17, 3.21 from NEAB GCSE Paper 1 (1995), **pp. 34, 50, 51** Figures 2.19, 3.22, Question 6c from NEAB GCSE Paper 1 (1999), **pp. 96, 97, 177** Questions 2d, 5a, 5b, Figures 17.13, 17.14, 17.15 from NEAB GCSE Specimen Paper 2 (1998), **pp. 110, 111, 142** Figures 9.14, 9.15, 9.16, 14.7, Question 3b from NEAB GCSE Paper 1 (1998), **p. 139** Figure 14.2 from NEAB Syllabus B Paper 2 (1999); **pp. 13, 17, 18, 34, 103, 104, 118** Figures 1.13, 1.19, 1.21, 2.20, 9.2, 9.5, 11.1 from Waugh (1997) *UK & Europe* Nelson; **pp. 39, 173, 174, 202** Figures 3.5, 17.9, 17.10, 20.9 from Waugh (1994) *Key Geography 1* Stanley Thornes; **pp. 52, 56, 178, 200** Figures 4.1, 4.4, 18.1, 20.8 Waugh (2000) *Geography An Integrated Approach* Nelson; **p. 180** Figure 18.3 from Waugh (1998) *The New Wider World* Nelson; **p. 17** Figure 1.18 from Punnett & Webber (1985) *The British Isles* Blackwell; **p. 26** Table from NFU website; **p. 42** Table 3.1 from LDNPA pub. no. 88/97/914, **p. 42** Figure 3.9 LDNPA Tourism Fact Sheet (1997), **p. 43** Figures 3.10, 3.11 LDNPA Facts & Figures (1994), **p. 46** Figure 3.15 LDNPA Employment Fact Sheet, Figure 3.16 LDNPA Footpath erosion fact sheet (1997); **pp. 37, 54, 56, 91** Maps reproduced from Ordnance Survey maps with the permission of the Controller of Her Majesty's Stationary Office © Crown Copyright; License No; 10000230; **p. 56** Figure 4.7 Scottish Power; **p. 70** Figure 5.4 Johnson et al. (1994) *Spotlight Science 8* STP; **pp. 94, 100** Figures 7.1, 8.7 Nagle and Spencer (1996) *A Geography of the European Union* OUP; **p. 141** Figure 14.5 Port of Dover Business Performance Report; **p. 196** Figure 20.1 Hadley Centre Meteorological Office; Figure 20.2 *New Scientist* 11 November 2000; **p. 199** Figure 20.7 Climatic Research Unit, University of East Anglia.

The publishers have made every effort to trace the copyright holders, but if they have inadvertently overlooked any, they will be pleased to make the necessary arrangements at the first opportunity.